Getaway

21 years of African travel writing

Getaway

21 years of African travel writing

JACANA

First published by Jacana Media (Pty) Ltd
in association with Getaway Books
(a division of RamsayMedia (Pty) Ltd) in 2010

Jacana Media
10 Orange Street
Sunnyside
Auckland Park 2092
South Africa
+2711 628 3200
www.jacana.co.za

Getaway Books
3 Howard Drive
Pinelands 7405
South Africa

ISBN: 978-1-77009-886-2

Cover design by Maryanne Cruikshanks
Text design by Abdul Amien
Illustrations by Marisa Steyn
Set in Minion 10.3 on 13.5 pt
Printed by CTP Printers Cape Town
Job no. 001317

See a complete list of Jacana titles at
www.jacana.co.za

Contents

☞

5   East meets West
    Owen Coetzer – February 1990

'Oh, East is East and West is West, and never the twain shall meet.' Of course, Kipling wasn't
talking about Durban. And if he had been, he'd have been wrong ....

10 Rovos Rail
    Patrick Wagner – March 1993

Whether you're a lover of steam trains, a lover of wildlife or a lover of the usual kind, Rovos Rail
provides the perfect setting for a romantic interlude in the golden age of steam travel.

20 The spirit of the Great Karoo
    David Rogers – August 1994

What is it about the vast and arid Karoo that has freed the souls and inspired the
creativity of so many South Africans? David Rogers set off, with his camera, to capture the essence
of the land where Olive Schreiner and Chris Barnard have their roots.

32 Gone fishing at the Skeleton Coast
    David Bristow – January 1995

Adventurous types are drawn to the Namib, seeking solitude and grandeur. While the desert is
bleak and uncompromising, the Atlantic Ocean that washes its shores seems to overflow with pelagic
abundance. David Bristow discovered what it's like to hit pay dirt on the fabled Skeleton Coast.

37 Kudu Canyon
    Jackie Nel – May 1996

Only two and a half hours from Jo'burg awaits an utterly otherwise, very affordable game
experience. Jackie Nel went exploring by barge, zebra-striped Land Cruiser and Unimog.

43 Walking back through time
    Cathy Lanz – December 1996

There was a time in Africa when our forebears met the creatures of the wild nose to nose; when
lions were a threat to life; and death was a black-mamba bite away. Cathy Lanz rekindled these ancient
roots and sensations during a three-day wilderness trail through the Hluhluwe-Umfolozi Park.

49 Kaokoland – Lords of the Namibian desert
    David Rogers – October 1997

Along the dry rivers and dusty plains of Kaokoland, David Rogers went on a journey in
search of desert elephants. The dung which lay in the sand of the Ombonde River was the first real
clue that the desert elephants of Kaokoveld were near at hand.

Introduction

❧

Getaway is one of the longest-standing travel magazines in Africa, and it is hard
not to be overwhelmed by the variety of voices that have told their stories during
this time. And what a time it has been! As the saying goes, 'If you want to reach the
stars, you have to stand on the shoulders of giants'. Having immersed ourselves in
thousands of travel features during the selection process, spanning an incredible
21 years, this sentiment has proved itself true time and time again.

Getaway has lived through a tumultuous period in Southern Africa's history,
and has witnessed the rise to independence of both Namibia and South Africa.
It is worth noting that, in the 70s and 80s, travel into neighbouring countries by
South Africans was practically unheard of – people of colour were hindered by
the oppressive apartheid regime, while white South African passport holders were
considered *personae non gratae*. Following independence in the early 90s, however,
travel restrictions were lifted and South Africans began to explore further afield.

Getaway photographers and journalists led the way into Africa, guided first
by David Steele and then David Bristow and Don Pinnock – all of whom were
travellers first and editors second (as it should be). The stories in our pages
immediately reflected the inspiration and practical advice gained by our travelling
journalists, allowing readers to follow in our footsteps. In this way, *Getaway* has
played a crucial role in shaping the lives and travel habits of countless South
Africans.

Who among us has not stared in wonder at the pictures, devoured the stories
and put our own travel plans into action? And we're better for it. After all, when
our time comes after the great journey of life – it's not the half-year reviews or the
February tax return that we remember. It's those moments where we broke free of
the confines of our daily existence and travelled, discovered new destinations, and
spent time with family and friends. It's the times that we got stuck on the banks of
a flooding river, or spent the night on a mountain, having lost our way and been
caught by darkness, that fill our memories.

Travelling in search of these phenomenal stories has unfortunately not been
without incident. Patrick Wagner, one of our great friends and colleagues, and
arguably the best photojournalist ever to work on the magazine, died in an airplane
crash on assignment in Kenya. But his memory lives with us constantly, and the
walls of our office are still decorated with some of his finest images.

Elephants have walked through our journalists' tents at night, some have had broken ankles after following crazy climbers in Namibia, they've been lost at sea and fallen off horses, tripped up by hippos and had skirmishes with poachers. One even flashed her breasts on the top of Kilimanjaro (although the image was never published). In short, our journalists have been given the opportunity to live super-lives. Collectively they have seen some of the greatest sights in Africa: from the Masai Mara migrations to the wonderful stone churches of Lalibela in Ethiopia; from the wild seas that crash on the shores of Cape Agulhas to the tranquil dive sites of the Red Sea. And each time they have returned with 'the story'.

Although there have been many awards along the way, which is testament to the magazine's consistently high standard of writing, the certificates and statues just gather dust in a corner of our office. If you ask the journalists for their travel highlights, none of them mention these accolades, but rave instead about their experiences on the road. Awards are far from our minds when we find ourselves waiting in departure lounges or ensconced behind the wheel on a trans-African safari.

This book, then, is a thoughtfully selected collection of great African travel writing by *Getaway*'s journalists, and it is by no means complete. The selection covers the lifespan of *Getaway* magazine with a wide geographic footprint that is confined only by the boundaries of Africa. Other editors may have picked 20 or 30 different stories, and the resulting book would have enthralled readers just as much as this one will. The book is not intended to be read cover-to-cover, (although you'd be crazy not to!), but dipped into at leisure, uncovering the stories and destinations that intrigue you most. Be warned, however: serious wanderlust lies ahead! Don't fear though – you're never too old to break free and hit the road.

In John Steinbeck's words:

'When I was very young and the urge to be someplace was on me, I was assured by mature people that maturity would cure this itch. When years described me as mature, the remedy prescribed was middle age. In middle age I was assured that greater age would calm my fever and now that I am fifty-eight perhaps senility will do the job. Nothing has worked. In other words, I don't improve, in further words, once a bum always a bum. I fear the disease is incurable.'

These days we simply call this the *Getaway* Travel Bug. Enjoy the infection!

Cameron Ewart-Smith
Editor

Getaway

Acknowledgements

⁓

The acknowledgements for a book of this magnitude, spanning so many years and representing the output of so many different people, can never be appropriately inclusive. So, to start, a big thank you to everyone who has worked on *Getaway* magazine throughout its 21-year history. From the shortest editorial internships to the longest serving members of our adsales teams – this great magazine would not have been possible without *your* efforts.

A number of people had a hand in the creation of this collection. Justin Fox requires a special mention, for his assistance in the editing process and guidance in compiling the final list of stories. A huge thanks to the writers and editors who suggested, and provided, material for the book – David Bristow, in particular, was critical in the initial selection process. Thanks also to Don Pinnock, David Steele, David Rogers, Alison Westwood, Jazz Kuschke, Margy Beves-Gibson, Catherine Hofmeyer (née Lanz), Robyn Daly, Owen Coetzer, Patrick Wagner, Jackie Nel, Peter Frost and Narina Exelby for their invaluable contributions.

Sarah Isaacs and Keryn Rheeder were instrumental in finding and digitising the older *Getaway* stories. Maryanne Cruikshanks, Maggie Davey and Abdul Amien deserve special mention for investing so much time and energy in the final design of the book – it is truly magnificent. Marisa Steyn's illustrations open each story, and they have made a world of difference. Thanks to the entire production team at Jacana – especially Bridget Impey and Pete van der Woude who kept cracking the whip when our minds wandered back to the road – without your efforts this book would simply never have come to life.

A final word of thanks to Jacqueline Lahoud and Sue Walker who kept the production on schedule from the *Getaway Books* side.

East meets West
Owen Coetzer – February 1990

'Oh, East is East and West is West, and never the twain shall
meet.' Of course, Kipling wasn't talking about Durban.
And if he had been, he'd have been wrong ....

Grey Street, Durban. Step across the road and into another time ... almost another place. Most certainly another culture. For despite Kipling's famous words, East meets West right here!

This busy ribbon of road, just off Durban's central business district, marks the division as effectively as a border post. Cross Grey Street and you could be in Bombay or Calcutta or Madras, or even beautiful Delhi.

It is here that the fascinating, mysterious world of the East – as integral a part of Durban culture as Bay-of-Plenty surfies or punters at the 'July' – really begins, and the visitor is wafted headlong into a scented world as alien to him, more often than not, as Mars.

The Westerner is overwhelmed. High, nasal devotional and film music blasts the ears from just about every shop. Pungent spice odours tickle the nose. Agrabathi (incense) wafts from shops in waves of sandalwood and rose, and the language of bartering fills the languid air.

To the initiated, however, Grey Street is home to a culture that was highly civilised while people in the West were still daubing themselves with paint.

The traditional devotional blue figures of Lord Krsna (Krishna, if you put in the Sanskrit vowels), the multi-armed Siva and the beautiful Saraswati – serene with a vina, heavenly musical instrument of the gods – speak of a timeless land, an ancient religion. You can still buy the North Indian sitar with a single or a double gourd, impressively inlaid with bone or ivory. The rare South Indian vina (which is more mellow than the sitar and different in that its frets are fixed) is available, too. But a true exponent of this religious musical instrument would prefer it to be made for him in India, with his date of birth and the position of the planet at the time worked into its design.

Tabla (right and left, treble and bass hand-drums), mdringum (a single bass and treble drum), tanpura (a monochromatic twin-stringed instrument which provides the background sound to most classical Indian music), Indian violins (the western violin is derived from this ancient instrument) and harmoniums are also on sale.

But it is the gullible tourists that the curio shops draw like magnets. A Greek sea captain, nonchalant, hands in pockets, makes overtures to buy a pair of finely engraved elephant tusks. They are from India, not Africa – imported as are most of the other goods: inlaid sandalwood boxes, beautiful jugs, finely worked bronze representations of the dancing Siva Natraj with many arms. An Aladdin's cave.

After much bargaining the tusks go for R8000. The captain watches as they are carefully wrapped and placed in a huge wooden crate.

Pride of place in another shop is a metre-long silver chariot drawn by silver horses marking Krishna's victory over Arjuna (and death), the subject of the Second Discourse of the Hindu religious epic Bhavagad Gita. The chariot is made up of thousands of minuscule hand-cut silver pieces. It should be in a museum.

Nothing is too much trouble. Everything, initially, is just talk ….

'Good morning, kind sir. I see you are interested in this fine sandalwood representation of Siva. Excellent craftsmanship, kind sir. Directly from the holy city of Benares. For you, only R400.'

'Too much!'

'But, kind sir – the craftsmanship is excellent. Just look at the individual cuts. See how the nose is shaped, the hands. It was specially imported for us here, directly from the holy city of Delhi. It is a fine work of art!'

'R200.'

'An impossibility, eminence. Why the wood alone costs twice that! It comes from Madras, the holy city.'

'R100!'

'My lordship, an artist took six years, yes sir, six years to make this. His poor fingers think of them!'

'R70 – and that's final!'

'Sir, you joke!'

But of course, the punch line (for this exchange did in fact take place) was mine.

'No, I just lived here for 20 years,' I said. He smiled; the bartering stopped.

'For you, R65 in that case,' he laughed.

Naturally, it does not work like that all the time and you cannot expect an expensive piece to be knocked right down as a matter of course. But bargaining is part of the magic of the East. Without it, you are lost.

The biggest mosque in the southern hemisphere is in Grey Street, its golden domes reflecting the splendour of Islam. Attached to it is a madressa – a school where once the faithful were instructed.

Today, Madressa Arcade is one of the most colourful in Durban, with hawkers plying their wares in the narrow lane, and bargains at each shop.

Here a watch for R7, guaranteed for a year. There a pair of flashy sunglasses – 'Cheap for you, sir. R1.'

You can also buy fabric and have a suit tailor-made almost while you wait. The going rate is about R70, and you can watch the tailor at work as he sits in his window facing the arcade crowds.

Shoes – R90 anywhere else – will cost you half the price here. But you have to be discerning and examine each one. You could land up with two left feet.

Grey Street is the real heart of Durban, and its people the lifeblood.

'For you, sir, this jewellery. Only R700. All genuine hand-picked diamonds from our very own mine in the heart of India. Genuine gold, made by hand, covers genuine silver made by our very own workmen in the holy city ....'

The temporal, however, gives way to the ethereal along Chatsworth's Higginson Highway. The high lingam towers and golden roof of the Hare Krishna temple – Durban head-quarters of the International Krishna Consciousness Movement – stand out among the lush green of the surrounding area.

Visitors are welcome (shoes are taken off at the entrance) and often stand, staring in awe at the splendour of the golden interior, reflected in huge roof mirrors. Scenes from the life of Sri Krishna are also depicted.

Try to get there for midday prayers (12h30) when the altar is revealed and bareheaded devotees, many of them white, supplicate themselves.

And, moving away from the scents and the spirituality of the East, you encounter the Durban of the West, fresh as paint after a thorough beauty treatment.

It was Durban city councillor Don Smith who said it: 'Durban is blazing the way'.

While other major cities in South Africa are suffering the effects of a dying central business district, Durban has had the foresight to take steps to remedy the situation in time.

And the result is the totally revamped beachfront with its wide promenades, pink and turquoise railings, walkways and kiosks (it sounds terrible, but looks marvellous!). There have, of course, been some problems recently, but one hopes they will be sorted out before too long.

There is now talk of digging up the bay-side Esplanade, diverting the double roadway somewhere else, and revamping the area with new hotels and low-slung condominiums, each with its own square of water-front.

But pride of place goes to The Workshop, a R44-million shopping complex in Commercial Road, which stands where once the deafening clamour of steam hammers forged Victorian locomotives for the Natal Government and the Cape Railways.

The Workshop opened in 1986 with a celebration that would probably have left even Queen Victoria mildly amused, with the pealing of the bells of nearby St Paul's church and a 21-gun salute fired from miniature cannons.

The man who dreamt up The Workshop, architect Len Bendel, says it is one of the world's most exciting 'theme' centres, and it has added a new dimension to the central city area.

Many of the 126 shops are 19th-century British colonial-style reproductions, some with fanlight doors and large windows, others small-paned village-store style; some in wood, others brass trimmed, painted in gleaming red, dark green, and black and white.

There are speciality shops – one sells Colony of Natal flags and other 'Last Outpost of the British Empire' memorabilia – as well as branches of major chain stores. Many assistants are dressed in period costume.

There are several Victorian features – the old Port Natal stationmaster's house, for instance, has been rebuilt on the site as a restaurant, with a 19th-century railway pub.

The Workshop's original Victorian beams and girders, vaulted roof and high-arched windows have been retained and restored.

The hub of the complex is the central ground floor, Victoria Main Street, which has been planted with fully grown trees .... The olde-worlde atmosphere is heightened by the use of Victorian barrows, hired out for the day at R15, plus a stool. There is a daily licence fee of R2.75.

Restoring the building took special skills, and care. In certain areas, part of the old brickwork had to be replaced with individually made bricks, no two being exactly the same size.

The original steel structure, made in Bristol and shipped to Durban by sea, was in remarkably good condition, with wrought-iron bolts and rivets.

The Workshop certainly lives again – it's open seven days a week – and around it you will find flea markets which rival even those of Cape Town.

New Indian Market opens in March

When fire destroyed Durban's historical Indian market in March 1973, the army and police had to be called out to control a crowd of some 15 000 people, many of whose livelihoods had just gone up in smoke.

The 63-year-old market in Queen Street was one of the city's most famous tourist attractions, providing a living for about 10 000 families. Indeed, many stalls had been passed down from one generation to the next.

What was going to happen? Why, build a new market, of course. But this was easier said than done – and a 15-year wrangle between stall holders and Durban City Council began.

In the interim, the market was moved to a non-descript building in Warwick Avenue which, inside, was a sprawling riot of stalls selling everything from fresh produce, and exotic herbs and spices, to jewellery, clothing and curios.

But now a new, R20-million market, with 11 domes – each one modelled on a public building in India – is nearing completion, and should be ready to open in March this year. Hopes are that it will become a major commercial and tourist attraction in Durban. It is bounded by Victoria Street, Cemetery Lane, and Russell and Queen streets.

The market comprises a parking basement for 180 cars and a ground floor where 80 stall holders will display their exotic curries and other goods. The curries have always been a speciality of the Indian market, ranging from mild in strength to positively volcanic, with names to match – 'Hellfire' and 'Mother-in-law Masala' are typical examples.

Many stall holders have the basic spices – such as ground chilli, turmeric, ginger, dhania and jeera (ground cumin) – which they will blend to order, enthusiastically mixing giant tubs of the stuff in response to a tentative query. Many is the shopper who, originally only wanting a small bag of curry, has felt obliged to buy a lot more, not being aware that the traders know exactly what they are doing and that nothing goes to waste – the rest of the bag has probably already been ordered by one of the surrounding stores.

In the new market there will also be a first-floor trading area with 50 shops and several restaurants, and a separate fish and meat market. This market is linked to the main market by a first-floor pedestrian walkway. Architect Cassim Kadwa, who worked in association with Mr JD Marech, said research had taken more than two years. Dominant colours that he has selected combine to provide a beautiful clash of green, purple, cream and pink.

It is hoped that this new market will successfully recapture the marvellous colour and life of the original undertaking, which was probably as Indian as you could get without actually going to Bombay.

Footnote: The fire that destroyed the original market was lit by an Indian tailor to warm him. He set fire to newspapers in a gutter but a wind swept them up into the market, causing all the damage. The tailor was arrested and appeared in court on a charge of arson. This was later amended to one of contravening Durban City bylaws by lighting a fire without the permission of the mayor. He pleaded guilty but was cautioned and discharged.

Rovos Rail
Patrick Wagner – March 1993

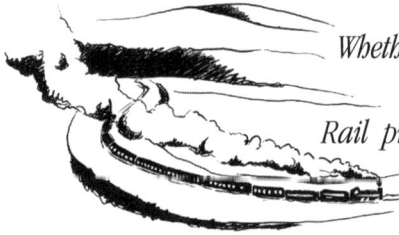

Whether you're a lover of steam trains, a lover of wildlife or a lover of the usual kind, Rovos Rail provides the perfect setting for a romantic interlude in the golden age of steam travel.

Clickety-clack, clickety-clack.

'So where're we goin' tomorrow?' enquired Sara Powell as she stared over the rim of her freshly charged glass of Buitenverwachting Buiten Blanc.

'Nowhere in a hurry, ma'am,' replied train manager Walter Watzinger, waiting patiently as we pondered over the delicious-sounding lunch menu.

'But we're goin' to Londip ... or Londo ... how'd you say it?' she drawled in her southern accent.

'Londolozi, ma'am ... we're going to Londolozi,' answered Walter. 'It's an exclusive private game reserve adjoining the Kruger National Park.'

'Sounds good,' she said with a grin, and delicately sipped her wine.

Clickety-clack, clickety-clack.

The dining coach rocked gently, swaying in time to the monotonous sound of steel wheels running over steel rails. Gusts of fresh air flowed fiercely from humming ceiling fans.

Sara decided on Canadian smoked salmon with onions and capers as her choice of hors d'oeuvre, and Indonesian chicken salad as the main course.

I settled for the other starter and main course on the menu, avocado pear with a water-chestnut mayonnaise, and beef fillet with horseradish and mild mustard sauce.

An arm appeared next to my right shoulder and smooth red liquid tumbled from the dark-green bottle into the tall crystal glass. Another generous portion of Meerlust Rubicon.

Clickety-clack, clickety-clack.

A magnificent monster of an old steam locomotive huffed and puffed only a few coaches from the plush dining carriage in which we were seated.

The whistle shrieked and the throb of puffing steam reached a thunderous crescendo, and then slowly faded into its regular huff and puff.

The sound produced wide smiles from all the guests as well as from the numerous spectators we sped past, who stopped in their tracks to marvel at this blast from the past.

Clickety-clack, clickety-clack.

'What happens if this old train breaks down?' I asked Walter.

'Then we have more time for wining, dining and relaxing,' he answered with a broad smile, and moved off to take care of our order.

Welcome to the relaxed atmosphere of Rovos Rail and the golden age of steam-train travel.

Sara and I were seated in Rovos Rail's beautifully restored Shangani dining car. A 75-year-old architect from Florida in the United States, she was a fascinating old lady who radiated charm and experience, and even kept us up at the bar on some nights! She had just spent Christmas with friends in Dubai in the Middle East and was on the last leg of her month-long tour of Southern Africa.

This involved stepping into the green-and-cream-coloured coaches of Rovos Rail and stepping back in time to the pre-war age of steam travel.

I was on assignment to research and photograph this beautifully restored 1930s train for this month's cover story. And to think the trip was classed as work!

The train accommodates 46 people in four royal suites and 19 de luxe suites attended by 16 professional staff members. On this trip it was about 80 per cent full and most of the other guests were foreign. I had already met Mel and Margaret McGrath from Yorkshire and had briefly chatted to a young family from Germany.

Then, of course, I had met and spent some time with the entrepreneurial owner and brains behind the train.

Rovos Rail is the brainchild of self-made millionaire Rohan Vos who, strangely, had initially established himself as a businessman in the motor-spare industry.

The concept of a private and exclusive steam-hauled hotel and touring train was born in 1986 when Rohan was introduced to the world of steam strains at his Witbank-based business.

At first he planned to have a few private coaches as a holiday train for the family. But when he discovered the magnitude of the maintenance and running costs, he realised he would have to derive some sort of income from the train if he planned to keep it in operation.

After much negotiation, Spoornet eventually gave Rohan the go-ahead to use its lines in the Eastern Transvaal, on condition that he used Spoornet drivers and conductors and that Rovos Rail be charged on a per-kilometre basis.

This eventually blossomed into Rovos Rail, which is now marketed as 'the most luxurious train in the world' and 'the Pride of Africa'. It is also believed to be the first train in South African history to be owned by a private individual.

Over the past six years Rohan has lavishly and lovingly restored 12 abandoned coaches and four magnificent steam locomotives (collected from all over the country) to their original pre-war state, and established regular trips between Pretoria and Hazyview, as well as a longer journey between Pretoria and Cape Town.

And Rohan wasn't shy to set an example by mucking in and doing most of the basic work himself. In fact he supervised every detail, from the overall bottle-green tone of the train to the make of crystal glasses used in the dining car.

My steam-train experience with Rovos Rail started at the Victoria Hotel, which is just opposite Pretoria Station. I had been promptly collected from Jan Smuts Airport and dropped off mere metres from the reception desk of the hotel.

Headquarters of Rovos Rail, the Victoria Hotel dates back to 1892 when it was known as the Station Hotel. By 1896 it had been renamed the Hollandia Hotel, and in 1900 it was renamed the Victoria Hotel by Lord Robert's British troops who occupied Pretoria at the time.

Rohan initially intended setting up office in the station, but soon noticed the potential of the nearby hotel, which was in the process of being converted into shops.

He has since restored the run-down building into a graceful Victorian hotel which, apart from housing his offices, also has 11 spacious suites, and a cosy fireside reception area that allows passengers to relax before departing on the train. In fact the atmosphere of the hotel sets the tone for the grandeur awaiting them.

I spent a night in the Kruger Suite and one in the Anthea Suite, and was most impressed with their spaciousness.

The Kruger Suite consists of three inter-leading rooms comprising a private lounge, a large bedroom and a bathroom.

The Anthea Suite was even bigger. Complete with a broad balcony boasting a view of the station, it also had a private lounge, a bedroom, a dressing room and a huge bathroom.

The only negative feedback I encountered with regard to the hotel is that it is situated in a less than salubrious area of Pretoria, which means security can be a problem. However, I was pleased to see that the management is well aware of the problem and has taken precautions. For example, the front entrance area is constantly under guard, and guests wishing to take short walks to the nearby bank or café are escorted by hotel staff.

When it comes to boarding the train it's literally red-carpet treatment all the way, and the build-up to boarding creates an almost theatrical atmosphere.

Some guests arrive a day before departure and overnight at the hotel, while others (especially the very punctual Germans) arrive some hours before departure and wait patiently in the reception area, sipping tea or coffee.

When the clock strikes the departure hour, the guests waltz enthusiastically over to the station (it's a two-minute walk) where the reception is marvellous.

You stroll onto the broad platform to be met by the train manager and his band of attentive and attractive hostesses, who hand out glasses of chilled sparkling wine and lead you aboard along a red carpet!

I was assigned to compartment 1830 Timbavati, and Ilse Louw was my hostess. The thick, yet light, wooden sliding door opened smoothly and I entered a room small by hotel standards, but huge by train standards.

The top end of the compartment was dedicated to a sprawling double bed, while the remaining space was designed around a small private lounge with two graceful chairs separated by a polished table.

Neatly arranged on this were a sparkling silver ice bucket with a bottle of Pierre Jourdan Cuvee Brut on ice; a chrome flask of chilled water; a bowl of fresh fruit; a packet of biltong; and a folder with a welcoming note from Rohan, Rovos Rail postcards, writing paper and envelopes, and a comment card.

The compartment was finished in wood panelling and illuminated by original SAR ceiling lights, which created a comfortable atmosphere of woody warmth. And this was just the standard de luxe suite. The train's four royal suites are even more spacious (the standard suits are 12 square metres and the royal, 16 square metres).

Ilse soon appeared in the doorway and showed me round the compartment, indicating where the light switches were and pointing out the mosquito repellent and pair of goggles on the shelf. She said the goggles were used when you hang out of the window to admire the view.

'Soot in your eyes is the unromantic aspect of steam travel!' she laughed.

She turned round and clicked open the door to the en suite bathroom. It had very striking décor, the floor covered in elegant black and white tiles and the walls and ceiling finished in complementary panels of white and brown.

But what surprised me was the size of the bathroom. I was expecting something similar to the rather cramped compartments you find in large caravans. But this was a whole room.

Plated glass fronted the large gas-heated shower, a glimmering silver washbasin with highly polished taps and pipes occupied one corner (in some compartments the basins are the original SAR tip-up type) with an electric hair dryer nearby, and a floor-to-ceiling cupboard provided generous hanging space.

'If you need anything, just leave the door half open,' said Ilse, and left with a friendly smile.

The steam engine soon coughed into life and at about 13h00 on a rainy Saturday afternoon we left Pretoria bound for Hazyview in the Eastern Transvaal. For me it was a moment that evoked mixed feelings. The last time I had left on a long train trip I was bound for Potchefstroom and two years in the army!

But that afternoon saw me sitting opposite Sara Powell, wining and dining to the harmonious huffs and puffs of steam travel.

Clickety-clack, clickety-clack.

The Shangani dining car, coach 195, is arguably the most impressive of the train.

As you enter, the visual effect is quite startling. Seven pairs of beautifully carved wooden pillars and arches flow down the length of the coach, with Art Nouveau light fittings, ceiling fans, draped curtains and colourful flower arrangements combining to create a vibrant atmosphere.

Built by the SAR in 1924 at its Pretoria works, the coach was purchased from an Alberton owner in 1986, in a severely dilapidated condition. According to Rohan, it took 18 months of painstaking restoration work to convert it to its present condition.

Two of the pillars had to be replaced and the missing cut-glass lamp fixtures had to be individually built, since they were no longer obtainable.

Forty-six guests can be comfortably seated at tables for two or four. The cutlery and crockery are top class, the wine and food excellent, and the service professional, attentive and always friendly.

Very attentive I thought as, yet again, the arm appeared next to my right shoulder and smooth Rubicon tumbled into my glass (barman Hennie Loubser had gone to the trouble of chilling the red wine very slightly).

Clickety-clack, clickety-clack.

Dessert was a choice between meringues with fresh fruit and youngberry mousse, so I tucked into the meringues.

We finished off with a cup of good coffee, after which I headed to my compartment for a nap.

But my rest didn't last long. I had just finished unpacking and got settled when I noticed that the train was battling a rather steep incline. We were doing no more than walking speed and the train was gradually slowing to a halt.

This is usually no cause for concern, since the train makes frequent brief stops to slot in with Spoornet's schedule. However, leaning out of the window I noticed much activity in and around the billowing plumes of steam engulfing the labouring locomotive. So I picked up my camera bag and strolled through the train to the guard's van, stepped onto the rusty gravel, and walked to the front of the train.

Here I found Rohan, still in dinner dress (although he had discarded the jacket and tie), walking in front of the train in the pouring rain, packing pieces of gravel onto the lines!

This struck me as a rather odd pastime, until he explained that the gravel gave the locomotive a better grip. The rainy conditions that afternoon together with the incline meant that the wheels were slipping. He said the locomotive (named Shaun after his son, and rescued from a scrap-metal dealer in Witbank in 1986) had built-in sand boxes to deal with the problem, but the stock of sand had been exhausted during the afternoon. So we spent the next hour walking next to the train, packing gravel onto the lines.

This is a leader genuinely not afraid of getting his hands dirty. In fact, train manager Walter told me that on one occasion, after some confusion with Spoornet, he and Rohan ended up shoveling coal in their dinner suits!

The labouring train eventually rolled into Witbank and I noticed Rohan beginning to relax. This is where the steam locomotives are swapped for a modern electric engine for the leg to Nelspruit.

Said Rohan, 'The running of 1930s locomotives on modern lines is so complicated and expensive, I'd actually prefer to use diesel or electric all the way. But this would obviously detract from the steam-driven atmosphere.'

He pointed out that one steam locomotive used more than 300 litres of water and up to 75 kilograms of coal per kilometre!

After a half-hour stop in Witbank I returned to my compartment to clean up for dinner.

In keeping with the elegant atmosphere of the train, guests are required to dress for dinner, which meant having to don a jacket and tie.

For someone accustomed to trips such as white-water rafting on the Zambezi and wall diving in the Comoros, I initially felt a bit awkward. But with the warm ambience of the train and the friendly chatter of the staff, I was soon swallowed up in elegance, joining Rohan for dinner in the Shangani dining car.

Once again the menu was a delight. Hors d'oeuvres were a choice of escargots in puff pastry or turbans of sole with smoked-salmon mousse on a lemon beurre blanc. The main course offered either Cape rock lobster on rice pilaf with drawn butter, or lamb noisettes with waterblommetjie puree in phyllo pastry.

Dessert was a choice of kiwi crepe with a sabayon sauce or hazelnut parfait with chocolate ganache.

After dinner we all moved down the length of the train for a nightcap in the lounge area, or observation car. The dining car and its adjoining kitchen car are towed directly behind the locomotive and guard's van, while the observation car is fixed to the tail end of the train. This makes for an interesting late-night stroll, especially after a huge meal and a generous dose of white wines such as Boschendal Grand Vin Blanc and Simonsig Chardonnay, and red wines such as Hamilton Russell Pinot Noir and the Meerlust Rubicon.

The observation car is another impressive coach. It dates back to 1936 when it was built by the SAR, also at its Pretoria works. In 1987 it was purchased from a club in Sandton and a great deal of meticulous restoration work and modification led to its being such a special feature of the train.

For example, all the windows have been enlarged to ensure unobstructed views, and the back end has been completely glassed, a feature that Rohan says exists on no other train in the world.

Barman Hennie dished out generous glasses of Cape Velvet Cream, port and sherry, and we all relaxed and chatted in the peaceful atmosphere. (Another pleasing aspect of this trip is that the fare includes all drinks and meals.)

The coach couldn't have provided a better setting for that night. A full moon had climbed through the tall trees above the high koppies and illuminated the startling landscape through which we were cruising.

Because the train is designed to travel at only 40km/h and Rohan insists that the trip be unhurried and relaxed, the observation car enables you to sit back in a tall armchair, gaze at the lovely view, absorb the romantic atmosphere and not have a moment's worry about spilling your glass of port or sherry.

But it's the romantic spirit of the train that makes the trip so alluring. Although Rovos Rail should appeal to lovers of steam, wildlife and travel, Rohan says it's become very popular with pure romantics. And whatever kind of lover you are, you certainly don't do this memorable trip on your own.

During the night we passed through Middelburg, Belfast and Waterval Boven, stopping at Nelspruit early in the morning to hook up with the steam locomotive Brenda (named after one of Rohan's three daughters). A strikingly beautiful steam engine, Brenda is a Class 19D locomotive purchased from a scrap-metal dealer and restored at Rohan's Witbank workshop.

We left Nelspruit at about 06h30 and travelled through what must be the most spectacular scenery of the Eastern Transvaal leg. The line follows a beautiful 30-kilometre gorge lined with a tumbled array of pink and brown granite boulders.

This is definitely the moment to open the windows of your compartment, drink in the savage scenery of Southern Africa and have coffee brought to you in bed!

On the other side of the gorge we stopped at Kaapmuiden for the locomotive to take on water, and then steamed up a branch line to Hazyview. And this was my view while I wolfed down a tasty breakfast of assorted fruit juices, melon balls in Calvados, yoghurt, croissants, and French toast with bacon and maple syrup, all washed down with a few cups of rich coffee.

We even managed to take in some game viewing, and had distant sightings of baboon, kudu, zebra, warthog and impala, as well as three white rhino wallowing in the muddy water hole.

The drought currently ravaging the subcontinent had obviously been broken in this area and the bush was a striking mix of green-toned woodland interrupted by odd patches of lush savanna.

Later that morning Brenda rolled to a noisy halt at Hazyview Station where the passengers disembarked for the eagerly awaited trip to Londolozi in the Sabi Sand Game Reserve.

Because there is such a wide variety of excellent private game lodges and country retreats scattered throughout this region of the Eastern Transvaal, many of the passengers arrange their own itineraries from Hazyview, using the trip between Pretoria and Hazyview merely as a romantic interlude. After all, if you have the time it's much more exciting than flying or driving.

Rovos Rail is more than happy to tailor-make any itinerary to suit your requirements.

Getting to Londolozi involved a 30-minute bus ride to the Sabi Sand gate followed by a further 30-minute trip in an open Land Rover.

Last year Londolozi was rated as South Africa's top game lodge, and Rohan says that in three and a half years of running trips into the area he tried all the big names of the Sabi Sand Reserve and was eventually satisfied that this highly rated lodge was indeed the best.

Although things got off to a shaky start (we had to wait around for about half an hour at the gate before being collected, and a welcoming letter in my room was addressed to Mr and Mrs McGrath) the one-night game-viewing sojourn added a spirited African flavour to the trip. It was thoroughly enjoyed by all – especially the foreigners on board my Land Rover, who happened to be Sara Powell and Mel and Margaret McGrath.

It was very pleasing to see that ranger Bruce Simpson and tracker Kruger Mhlaba didn't rush round the property trying to find the big five as quickly as possible. They also spent time looking at the 'little' things of the bush, for example dung beetles, fireflies, terrapins, a large-spotted genet, trees and birds. And we still saw the big five!

One of the most rewarding aspects of the visit was seeing how beautifully the bush had recovered from the drought.

The Sand River was flowing more strongly than it had in the past five years, and the shallow dry riverbeds showed signs of water having flowed almost waist-deep!

We encountered an impressive variety of general game including zebra, warthog, hippo, giraffe, blue wildebeest, grey duiker, steenbok, impala, kudu, nyala, bushbuck and waterbuck.

On the big-game side we came across a small group of buffalo, two lone male elephant, an elusive female leopard, 25 lion and one white rhino.

One of the elephants provided the highlight of the trip by inspecting the back of the Land Rover when we were boxed into a thick chunk of woodland next to the Sand River (the McGraths were in the back and will never forget him).

The leopard had downed an impala but she was rather shy and moved into impenetrable bush; the 25 lions were seen in three sightings of three different prides; and the white rhino was a solitary male found strolling quite nonchalantly through an open area.

Because of the excellent game viewing the trip to Londolozi ended on a high note and, after a late breakfast in the bush, we were quickly transferred back to Hazyview and the train for our return to Pretoria.

At Hazyview some of the guests were complaining about the lack of air conditioning. We were travelling during the heat wave that blasted through the country in early January and many of the foreigners, especially those from Europe, were suffering in the heat. But air conditioning the train would involve sealing the carriages and coaches, and much of the traditional noise of steam-train travel would be lost. In addition, passengers would not be able to open the windows. But Rohan says he is experimenting with various systems although the heat is not usually a problem; he believes the cold Karoo and Highveld winters are more of an issue.

The return trip to Pretoria was just as enjoyable as the first leg, but this fortunately didn't mark the end of my steam safari. I also joined the 48-hour trip from Pretoria to Cape Town.

We left Pretoria on a Wednesday afternoon and (using an old Spoornet locomotive) steamed through Johannesburg to Klerksdorp where we changed to modern power. Once again it was a night of dining, wining and relaxing in elegance until we reached Kimberley the next morning.

Freelance tour guide Jean Bothomley was at the station to meet us, and conducted a comprehensive tour of this old diamond-mining city. The tour included a trip in a 1930s tram through the city to De Beers' reconstructed diamond-mining village at the Big Hole.

We left Kimberley on a hot afternoon and rolled through the arid flatness of the Karoo, where dramatic thunderclouds scattered the purple light of the setting sun all over the western horizon.

The morning of the second day saw us arriving for breakfast at the Lord Milner Hotel in Matjiesfontein, where the hotel manager, Mervyn Turner, took us on an amusing tour of the tiny town in a reconditioned 1950s double-decker London bus.

It was still complete with signs such as 'Do not spit … £5 fine.'

Later that afternoon we stopped at Daljosafat to connect with another old Spoornet steam locomotive for the final leg of the trip, which involved cruising through the winelands and orchards of the Cape en route to the Mother City.

Arriving in Cape Town in the shadow of Table Mountain provided a memorable ending to the delectable life on board 'the most luxurious train in the world'. But remember, if you travel on board this train, don't go alone.

Clickety-clack, clickety-clack.

The spirit of the Great Karoo
David Rogers – August 1994

What is it about the vast and arid Karoo that has freed the souls and inspired the creativity of so many South Africans? David Rogers set off, with his camera, to capture the essence of the land where Olive Schreiner and Chris Barnard have their roots.

Rosalie Willis, Beaufort West's publicity lady, chuckled softly as she recalled an incident during the build-up to the historic 1994 election. An American observer had left her office, bound for a hamlet 200 kilometres west of the town. After travelling for 50 kilometres and seeing nothing, he turned back.

'There's nothing there,' he told Rose when he arrived back in her office.

'That's the Karoo, son,' Rose had explained patiently. 'You just have to keep on driving.'

Colleague Cathy Lanz and I also dropped in as observers but, unlike the American, our task was to seek out the spirit of the Great Karoo.

Beaufort West seemed the perfect place to start. Not only is it central but we knew that this was where we would find Rosalie Willis. Her claim to fame is *Rose's Roundup*, a one-page newsletter which she crams with Karoo news and sends off to *Getaway*, town clerks and even a reader in Russia.

'Do you know,' one issue reads, 'in addition to having the highest winds measured in South Africa at its airport, Beaufort West also at one time had the highest death rate in the country? This was in the last century when chest sufferers flocked to the region hoping for a cure. Some had waited too long.'

Considering such gems of information, we decided that Rose Willis and *Rose's Roundup* were as central to finding the spirit of the Karoo as Pam Preller and the *Sunday Times* were to playing Finders Keepers.

Although not a Karoo meisie by birth, Rose beams with the radiance of a city PR-person who has opted for the relaxed lifestyle of Beaufort West.

Chris Barnard is a true Beaufort Wester and Rose recalls meeting him and his youthful wife Karen at several town promotions. 'People say Chris turned his back on the Karoo, but he still has his heart here,' she confided. 'In fact, he told me that when he dies he's going to have, "You see I came back!" written on his gravestone.'

Rose has an enormous area to promote – even in Karoo terms. It covers 5500 square kilometres and an entire wall of her office is obscured with a montage of 1:250 000 maps covered with pins. One marks a spot between Richmond and De Aar called Deelfontein.

'It was a British Boer War hospital,' said Rose wistfully. 'Now it's being used by a local farmer to pen cattle.' Rose hopes it will be proclaimed a national monument and suggested we include it on our visit.

'It's a bit out of our way,' I replied meekly, realising as I said it that in the Karoo people are prepared to travel 300 kilometres just for lunch and that unless I was careful, I, like the American, could become a victim of the Karoo.

We said farewell to Beaufort West and to Rose, happy with the weighty stack of brochures she had given us. As we studied the things to do, places to go and people to visit, we realised we were nibbling at the edges of the Karoo; the hotel at Melton Wold, the Nevada-like scenery of Fraserberg and the homestead at La-de-da farm would have to wait for another visit.

We chose the nearby Karoo National Park to stay the night. It's an excellent destination with superb facilities and serves the important function of restoring badly overgrazed sheep ranges back to pristine Karoo veld.

Springbok were bountiful in the arid Karoo and Kalahari at the turn of the century and trekbokke migrated across the countryside in herds a million strong.

In *Karoo*, author Lawrence Green recalls the experience of an old dorsland trekker named Albert Jackson who slept on the veld during the 1896 migration. 'Often I put my ear to the ground, and even at night, when the buck were resting, it felt like an earth tremor,' he wrote.

Although springbok have never been anywhere near extinction, it was encouraging to see lambs tottering about the Karoo National Park on their fragile, new legs. We also saw an aardwolf during a night drive which was quite pleasing as these nocturnal animals, although fairly common, are extremely shy.

Karoo National Park's Fanie van Tonder confirmed that three black rhino had recently been re-introduced to the area and that the next big game earmarked for the park were lion and cheetah. Not all the neighbouring sheep-farmers, who have a long tradition of eradicating 'vermin', will welcome the news. The farmers in the Karoo have had a difficult time of late. Let alone leopard and jackal, they have had to contend with a five-year drought and poor lamb prices. They survive through harsh experience and by starting new business ventures. The economic slump has had an upside for tourists – many farms have opened their doors to guests.

The accommodation businesses we visited were ably run by farmers' wives who treated us like their own family.

'How can you be working over a weekend?' Lynne Minnaar said with concern when she heard of our Friday night visit. 'You must rest on weekends.'

The Minnaar farm, Groenvlei, is in the Sneeuberg between Beaufort West and Colesberg and, given Lynne's almost maternal warmth, we were sorry to be late, but we had been held up on the way by two fascinating experiences.

Making our way towards the Sneeuberg in warm sunset light we came across a group of karretjiemense. In roughly fashioned wooden mule-drawn carts, these colourful family groups can be found in the most isolated regions of the Karoo. Where do they come from and how do they fit into the fabric of this harsh land?

We stopped and found out.

Piet de Villiers and his family were preparing supper and looked surprised when we dropped in on their makeshift camp. 'Ons soek werk met die skape by Murraysburg, baas,' Piet told me. Some say these diminutive gypsies are the last vestiges of the Bushmen and I took photographs as he told me how they move from farm to farm shearing sheep and doing odd jobs in the area.

Unemployment is rife, particularly in Karoo towns, and we were to come across many who had far less than the de Villiers family. Nevertheless we were happy to pay them R10 for a memorable photographic session and with calls of 'totsiens' resumed our journey. As we drove towards Murraysburg, we couldn't help wondering what the future holds for the karretjiemense of the Karoo.

We entered Murraysburg at dusk and could just make out election posters which revealed that all sides of the political spectrum were well represented in the little Karoo town. Black and white mingled freely in the little hotel pub and as we washed the dust from our throats we noticed a sign, 'NO POLITICS IN THIS PUB', in bold letters beside bottles of Klipdrift and Oude Meester brandy. I decided that I would have done just about anything not to tangle with these folk having their Friday evening drinks. Instead, we watched the final one-day test between South Africa and Australia on a small television set.

As I cheered for the fortunes of the heroes in green and gold, I realised that cricket is not particularly strongly supported in Murraysburg and we departed before I made a complete spectacle of myself.

The road winds from Murraysburg into the Sneeuberg and about one hour later we arrived at Groenvlei. The Minnaars were watching the last few overs in their study and we settled down with them to watch our team's ultimate demise. They are typically friendly Karoo people and we were shown the family album.

'You know this person,' Johann announced. Amazingly I did. The sheepish-looking adolescent dressed up for a dance in a leather jacket, brown shirt and brown polka-dot tie was none other than Stirling Kotze, *Getaway*'s advertising manager. It transpired that he and Johann had shared a room at school – the first of many occasions where we met people whose lives had crossed paths with ours. We decided that the Karoo is central to South Africa in more than purely geographical terms.

Dinner was delicious: roast lamb, sweet potatoes, pumpkin fritters, peas and mint sauce. There is something spectacular about the taste of Karoo lamb; most ascribe it to the skill of the cooks and the spekboom and herbs on which the sheep dine. Be warned, health fanatics, that your resolve is likely to be severely tested by the delicious Karoo fare. Colesberg, like all Karoo towns, is centred around an imposing church which serves as a visual reminder to the far-flung congregation that Sunday mornings are not a time for lounging around at home, but for being in kerk and meeting old friends. Church has been a social highlight of the Karoo for centuries, since the pioneers met in make-shift buildings for their quarterly nagmaal.

On Sunday morning we stationed ourselves outside the Dutch Reformed Church in the main street and watched the parade. First to arrive was the organist, whose smart Mercedes Benz sported mayoral number plates. She was followed by the usher dressed in a white suit with matching shoes, then by the rest of the congregation. We were fascinated by this 'who's who' of Colesberg. They were turned out in their Sunday best: bright red dresses, polka-dot jackets, maroon trousers, velvet suits, blue-rinsed hair and fruit-filled hats. Down the road at the brownstone dopper church the conservative congregation restricts their outfits to more muted colours and, in some cases, kappies.

Jackie Twigg, who edits the *Towerkop Indaba*, has been a friend of mine for many years and I prevailed upon her to guide us round the town. She is an arty sort of city person; not quite what you'd expect to find in Colesberg, but as I discovered, the Karoo specialises in the unexpected.

We wandered – three city slickers – through the old part of the town past a hotch-potch of buildings. While some are made of ugly concrete and glass, others show more graceful Cape architecture with 'broekie lace' balconies and meticulously maintained gardens. Many buildings are painted shocking pink and blue.

There are charming guesthouses in Colesberg. Karoo Huise is an entire street of restored dorpshuisies, but Cathy and I decided to experience a typical dorp hotel. Just about every Karoo town has one – a concrete slab on main street, with small windows, off-sales, cool interiors, plush red carpets and wooden bannisters.

The Central Hotel in Colesberg is such a place and for years it has been a superb stopover. Unfortunately, we visited the hotel during a change of ownership and the service was shocking. Half the staff deserted their posts for an ANC march in the high street, and the rest went to a dinner-dance in Philippolis. The wine we had ordered with dinner never materialised, and we waited for one hour to discover that all the food had run out. The hotel has now been bought by the owner of the Merino Inn (Zola Budd's uncle) and hopefully he will restore it to the high standard it previously enjoyed. 'It was the highlight of our trip through the Karoo for over 30 years,' one couple from Johannesburg sighed wistfully.

We did eventually have a drink in Colesberg that Saturday night amid all the excitement of the ANC march. We found a pub and joined a cosmopolitan collection of Irish, French and Scottish UN observers for drinks, darts and gesels. One wall depicted a Merino ram which was pock-marked by bullet holes left by a previous group. The thought of lead ricocheting round that small pub made our skin crawl. Searching for all that is interesting in the Karoo, we were delighted to happen upon the Tuishuise in Cradock. In what was previously the poor section of the town, you can now have a fully-restored furnished cottage to yourself for R80 per night on a self-catering basis.

The Tuishuise were originally bought in poor condition for just a few thousand rand each by owners Sandra Antrobus and Letitia Moolman. They have subsequently restored them with great sensitivity and furnished them with interesting Cape antiques and memorabilia such as old spectacles, pipes and brass cooking pots. Several Satour awards, and a Simon van der Stel gold medal for restoration, are testimony to their skill.

The delightful Victorian dining room was formal without being stuffy and we enjoyed dry sherry followed by dinner with Sandra, Letitia and the rest of the Antrobus family. The polished wood, copper, silver and fine, brightly coloured fabrics made a lavish yet comfortable setting.

The calm was broken by Letitia's husband, Adel Moolman, who arrived after supper and stood at the head of the table for more than an hour telling us stories of his native Karoo. Clutching a half-litre mug of 'pale Coke' the tall, tanned and fit Adel recalled how his ou swaar used to poach gemsbok until a farmer caught him with one in the back of his bakkie.

'I found it in the sloot,' he had explained, quick as a flash. 'The poor bok broke his neck.' Flushed with his own brilliance the swaar used it again the following week with the same farmer, who was less light on him the second time.

A short hop from the Tuishuise takes you to the centre of Cradock where a wide main street is flanked by 100 metres of low, white municipal buildings on one side and an imposing church on the other. The church is a replica of St Martin-in-the-Fields and was inspired by Scottish parson Andrew Murray, whose preoccupation with ordered English architectural styles influenced not only Cradock's place of worship but Graaff-Reinet's as well. There, the church is a copy of Salisbury Cathedral. Cradock's municipal buildings are a national monument but over-restoration has rendered them quite lifeless. Tiled floors, glass doors and new window frames all detract from what must once have been a beautiful building.

Olive Schreiner grew up in Cradock and her family home in Cross Street is now an interesting museum. According to her husband, Samuel Cronwright, her famous book *The Story of an African Farm* had its beginnings in a room at nearby Klein Gannahoek farmhouse where she worked as a governess for the Fouche family. It was a 'sordid primitive shelter with no ceiling, a leaking roof and a mud floor,' writes one biographer. 'When it rained hard, Olive would sit under an umbrella and make a small furrow in the floor to lead the water out of the room.' It is equally likely, however, that she did much of the work at the larger Gannahoek which belonged to her friends the Cawoods.

Olive Schreiner was also a leader in the women's suffragette movement and her rejection of the tight shackles of chauvinistic Victorian society must have had deep roots in the freedom offered by the Karoo environment. Energetic followers of this feminist writer can climb to the top of Buffelskop where Olive is buried together with the bodies of her child and their much-loved dog Nita. Rainstorms pound the Karoo from time to time, turning the dry sandstone soil to a fine clay mud – with so little vegetation and such fine soil particles very little moisture sinks into the ground. Instead it spills off the hills in sheets, collecting in streams and running off into the sea. It takes just a few hours for a flash flood to turn a dry river bed into a raging, dangerous river.

During such a storm some 20 years ago visitors and staff at Mountain Zebra National Park heard what they thought was a far off explosion or an earthquake. The following morning they went to investigate.

A rock the size of a house was at the bottom of the mountain. Loosened by rain, it had carved a 100-metre gash in the scree slope. Standing on the rock you can look up and trace its path which, once a raw patch of soil, is now a deep, tree-lined gully.

The park is some 30 kilometres outside Cradock – close enough in Karoo terms to be considered very much part of the town – and is near to Gannahoek where Olive Schreiner sought inspiration.

Park warden Etienne Fourie and camp manager Louis Viviers were unlike other National Parks Board staff I have encountered. Their professional but easy-going management style suggested that the Karoo affects even the bonds imposed by government institutions.

The 6500-hectare park, which was proclaimed in 1937, has been successful in saving the small, stocky mountain zebra from extinction. The national park has for a number of years now reached its carrying capacity and its excess breeding herds have been translocated to other Cape reserves.

There are 48 kilometres of game-viewing roads and we were rewarded with sightings of many mountain zebra and red hartebeest which, judging by their glossy coats, were in fine condition. On our short walk we saw eland, grey rhebuck and many bird species and I made a silent note to return here one day to do the three-day Mountain Zebra Trail. While the Karoo has created big-hearted game wardens, pioneering heart surgeons and authors of note, it has also given root to less orthodox, but no less brilliant, talent. Until her death nearly 20 years ago, the reclusive and inspired Helen Martin lived in the little town of Nieu-Bethesda where she created a world of concrete statues and glass mosaics which is called the Owl House. It inspired the writings of Athol Fugard in *The Road to Mecca* and is the subject of Anne Emslie's coffee-table book called *The Owl House*.

The Owl House is an unimposing building in one of the most beautiful little towns in the Karoo. Looking down on the valley you feel as though you've arrived in Mini-town. Set deep in the Sneeuberg – with the pyramid-shaped Kompasberg as a backdrop – the neat squared-off fields, poplar rows, church spires and low white houses could as easily be in Switzerland as in South Africa.

Koos Malgas is the caretaker of the museum and is eminently qualified for the task. He was Helen's assistant and much of what you see at the Owl House was made by him under her direction.

Helen Martin had a tyrannical, Bible-thumping father and one of the weirdly decorated rooms in the house – the lion's den – is a dark reminder of this domineering influence.

Elsewhere glass fragments are stuck like wallpaper to the floor, walls, cupboards, suitcases and other flat surfaces. Apparently she would spend hours watching the moon and candles reflect off the shiny coloured surfaces, bringing light into her world of darkness.

The Owl House is incredibly cluttered inside and out and in the 'Camel Yard' you have to weave your way through statues of owls, camels, mermaids, people and other shapes.

Was Helen Martin mad? It's hard to say, but her determination to create a world of light and beauty must have much to do with the barren, wide open spaces of the Karoo.

We exchanged R60 for three Koos Malgas 'originals' and set off for The Village Inn.

Egbert Gerryts runs the Village Inn and we found him baking scones, surrounded by postcards, owls, memorabilia and books. Over tea, he explained how he had given up lecturing in Pretoria for the small community of intellectuals, artists and Buddhists who live in the quaint town.

'The average age of the town is quite old,' said Egbert, 'mainly because young people cannot find employment.'

The ANC Youth League were putting up election posters in the town and certainly none seemed older than 10. Nelson Mandela didn't seem to mind appearing upside down and soon he was smiling from every lamppost.

The Owl House is an incidental attraction of Nieu-Bethesda – it's a scenic town with superb facilities. Egbert showed us self-catering dorpshuisies called Huis Nommer Een and Lonsdale, which are both tastefully restored. We tried to see another called Stokkiesdraai, which offers dinner, bed and breakfast, but they were moving to new premises.

As with the Tuishuise in Cradock, these little guesthouses are homely. There was superb attention to detail with antiques and fine fabrics, fresh flowers, milk and rusks on the table.

We chose to stay overnight at Weltevreden Farm just outside Nieu-Bethesda because it offered full board and although Egbert's directions were not the best (he told us to turn right, not left, after 12 kilometres) we arrived in time to settle into 'The Prison'.

Apparently the guesthouse was originally used by an early owner to keep convicts locked up, but the story goes that they would escape through the chimney each night and return the following morning in time for breakfast! You can still see shotgun barrels which served as burglar bars in the small windows.

'The Prison' is now equipped for self-catering and there is an upstairs and a downstairs double bedroom.

Judi and Howard Sheard run the farm and we had dinner with them and their parents, Clare and Trevor. They treated us to another wonderful Karoo meal and, as coincidence would have it, their photograph album included a picture of Shalto Kroon who was goalkeeper in my high school water-polo team.

Giving lie to the impression that the Karoo is a hot, flat dust bowl we saw photographs of their beautiful mountainside farm taken just after heavy snowfalls.

'We often phone our friends to come and have a look,' said Judi, 'but by the time they arrive the snow has usually melted.'

The Sneeuberg mountains are more than three kilometres above sea level in parts and in the cold grip of winter temperatures can fall to minus 10°C. According to a visiting professor from Stellenbosch this area is suitable for trout; although I did not meet anyone who had actually stocked their waters, I had the impression that as soon as one farmer does so the rest will quickly follow suit.

Howard is typical of new-age Karoo farmers who monitor rainfall, study stock levels and ensure they nurture the fragile soil in the area. Although the grass was growing high, he remains cautious about the future and meets with Shalto Kroon, and other farmers, regularly to study trends and prospects. Driving up the winding road towards the viewpoint overlooking the Valley of Desolation, I narrowly missed being hit by a speeding vehicle coming in the opposite direction and I could not help but notice a klipspringer on the side of the road that had been less fortunate. According to officer-in-charge of the Karoo Nature Reserve, Pieter Burbett, 70 000 people visit this popular tourist attraction each year. Judging by the speed of that vehicle, however, I suspect that many spend only a few minutes at the top and certainly don't absorb the spirit of the place.

The Valley of Desolation has been declared a national monument on account of its fragile beauty and I savoured many hours sitting alone at the top. Looking down between my velskoene at the Plains of Camdeboo, I thought about the people who live in the Karoo in tin-roofed farmhouses in intense heat and icy cold and decided that this really was 'the land of the brave'. I recalled Lawrence Green's observations in *Karoo*.

'Weaklings did not survive in the Karoo', he writes, 'and those that grew up in the germ-free atmosphere were among the healthiest people on the earth.'

Perhaps it is for this reason that many of the children of the Karoo have been so successful. For out of hardship comes fierce independence and creativity, but as I was to discover wherever I went in the Karoo, so does warmth and hospitality.

The Valley of Desolation is situated in the northern section of the Karoo Nature Reserve which lies a few kilometres outside Graaff-Reinet, and is not to be confused with the similarly named Karoo National Park at Beaufort West. While Cathy Lanz researched her features on the town, I explored the awe-inspiring valley.

The first lookout lets you gaze down on the town and towards the distinctive conical koppie known as Spandau Kop. A little further up the road is the second parking lot, which leads to the valley itself. You can walk to the three main lookout points and back in about 15 minutes or, if you have the time, you can do a one-hour round trip which brings you back to the car park.

There is more to the reserve than simply the valley. A 1500-hectare area on the banks of the Van Ryneveld Dam has been set aside for buffalo, kudu and the third largest population of mountain zebra in South Africa. Growing in the reserve are gifbol (*Bophane disticha*) geophytes, an onion-like bulb used, amongst other things, to bandage the circumcision wounds of young tribal initiates. Although we knew the Karoo was once a great cycad-fringed lake roamed by prehistoric amphibians and reptiles, we did not expect to meet any on our trip. As luck would have it we met a *Dinogorgon rubideia*, a ferocious beast, with teeth as long as my feet, that patrolled the area more than 200 million years ago.

This pre-Jurassic mammal-like reptile has pride of place in the private fossil collection at Wellwood Farm. The hall in which it is housed contains hundreds of other treasures collected over several decades by Sidney Rubidge – perhaps the most prolific amateur palaeontologist of all time. It is one of the largest private collections in the world and includes 118 type specimens. These are important to science because they were the first of their type to be discovered, and the ones by which new species are described. Current owner Richard Rubidge stressed that Wellwood is a private working farm, not a tourist attraction and anyone who wants to see the collection must apply in writing.

Sitting in the mellow surroundings on a large, flat lawn in front of their stately home, Richard bounced his grandson on his lap and told me that his son Robert is the fifth generation stud master. The farm, which dates back to 1838, is apparently the oldest merino stud in South Africa. The eldest son has followed in his grandfather's footsteps and is currently the resident palaeontologist at the University of the Witwatersrand. Wellwood also has a well-appointed guesthouse far removed from the main homestead.

Prehistoric treasures are to be found throughout the Karoo. Sidney Rubidge discovered his first fossil in 1934 while he was having a picnic and realised he was using it as a seat! The van Rensburgs, at nearby Rietvlei farm, recently had a similar experience. While walking in the veld past some flat rocks they saw scratches they had never seen before. Only when they took a closer look and saw the shape of antelope and human figures did they realise they had stumbled across Bushman petroglyphs. In contrast to the more colourful Drakensberg rock paintings, the Bushmen who lived in the interior plains of Southern Africa did not paint but engraved their art onto flat surfaces.

Lyell van Rensburg maintains a rustic guest camp called Kiepersol and takes tours to the nearby engravings. The Great and the Little Karoo are firmly divided by a spectacular ridge of Cape Fold Mountains called the Swartberg. We hugged the northern ridges of this range from the bright blue Beervlei Dam, near Willowmore, to Klaarstroom at the foot of Meiringspoort, and then to Prince Albert.

Looking at these deeply folded mountains, which almost resemble strips of hand-shaped plasticine, it is hard to imagine the power of the two colliding continental plates that created them.

Olive trees, orchards and pastures run strip-like through the austere mountain valleys and many people find solace in weekend retreats round here. One such place is Prince Albert at the base of the Swartberg Pass.

We made a beeline for the Fransie Pienaar Cultural History Museum where we met Ronél van der Spuy. She runs a small weaving business but is also responsible for publicity.

There are many interesting places to visit in the area and we had a tough time choosing between The Hell (Gamkaskloof), dinosaur footprints, a private mineral collection and a historical tour of the town.

We chose the last and visited the water-mill, a national monument, and also the houses which feature the characteristic Prince Albert gables. These are distinguished by the holbol shape which is a concave dent followed by a convex bulge. Our last stop on our journey back to Cape Town was The Lord Milner Hotel at Matjiesfontein and we included this oasis-hotel-town as the final high note to our Karoo odyssey. The brain child of a rags-to-riches 19th-century tycoon called James Logan, Matjiesfontein was established as a refreshment station for well-to-do railway travellers in the 1880s and later became a popular health resort. Logan spared no expense in introducing innovative features. The village was said to be the first in South Africa to have waterborne sewerage and electric lighting and even the lamp posts were imported from England.

'He would insist on his village being as clean as the deck of a ship,' wrote an early visitor. 'It has the appearance of a smart London suburb, and close by are the golf links, cricket ground, tennis and croquet courts, and swimming bath fed by a sulphur spring.'

Logan had marketing flair and when the illustrious Major General Andrew Wauchope was killed at Magersfontein in the Northern Cape he fudged the truth and arranged for him to be interned and buried in a small graveyard 10 kilometres outside the town towards Cape Town.

Visiting the hotel today it's not hard to imagine mining magnate Cecil John Rhodes, the illustrious Sultan of Zanzibar and Olive Schreiner walking down the street in deep conversation.

For nine days I had been carrying round a suit and tie and a clean white shirt in preparation for Matjiesfontein and it was with great ceremony that I extracted them from my suitcase and ironed out their creases. The night begins with a 'booooooop' from a lone bugler and then it's downstairs for the guided tour of the town in an old-fashioned London bus. When it had shuddered to a halt, driver-cum-commentator Mervyn Turner had us seated in an old railway dining car for wine-tasting.

Dinner was formal and delicious and there was lots of it, and we rounded it off with a night cap at the Laird's Arms. I was disappointed to discover that Muriel, the accountant and resident pianist at Matjiesfontein, had died and the traditional hat party sing-alongs which were something of an institution were now a thing of the past. You can visit Muriel in the graveyard behind the hotel where she is buried with the hotel parrot and 'a much-loved alsation'. Mervyn – who turned out to be a childhood friend of my editor – reassured me that they were on the lookout for a replacement.

Even today, Matjiesfontein remains something of a novelty stop-over and weekend resort and continues to attract visiting statesmen, local politicians and tourists.

Did I find that elusive spirit of the Great Karoo? I cannot say. I certainly saw its symbols – windmills, candy-floss clouds, black children on the roadside selling ingenious wire toys, karretjiemense, gnarled farmers, sheep, vast open vlakte and flat-topped koppies. Perhaps you have to be born, or live, there to catch a glimpse of its soul. I suspect that Voortrekker leaders like Andries Pretorius and Gerrit Maritz must have known it. So too would Chris Barnard, Guy Butler, Anton Rupert and Olive Schreiner.

What I did sense was the exuberance that Olive Schreiner must have felt when she wrote: 'Now I am going to put my hat on and walk into the Karoo. Such a wild sense of exhilaration comes to me when I walk over the Karoo.'

Gone fishing at the Skeleton Coast
David Bristow – January 1995

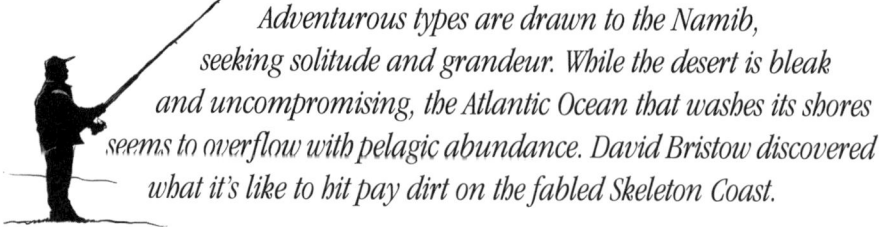

*Adventurous types are drawn to the Namib,
seeking solitude and grandeur. While the desert is bleak
and uncompromising, the Atlantic Ocean that washes its shores
seems to overflow with pelagic abundance. David Bristow discovered
what it's like to hit pay dirt on the fabled Skeleton Coast.*

❦

'Hell man, I just don't like to see a woman fishing. It's like seeing an oke working in the kitchen,' bemoaned the bear-like Paul as we drove past a couple pulling out kabeljou on the long stretch of beach near Mile 100.

The men who fish these frigid waters are real men and you can bet they don't let the fish get away if they can possibly help it. When they descend in droves, in 4x4s, buggies and trucks to cast about for their supper, you just know the fish are in for a hiding. This is man's work and their women and children must sommer entertain themselves on the barren stretch of sand between the Orange River Mouth and the Kunene. One thing there's no shortage of here is sand. Or fish.

Most of the women busy themselves in their makeshift kitchens preparing food, bait and, even more important to the hard-working manne, the drinks.

While the land is unfertile, the cold sea yields overwhelming quantities of piscatorial delights – steenbras and kabeljou, galjoen, blacktail, sharks, cat-fish …. In just two days of intense fishing (for me it was intense, for the rest of the guys it was all in a day's good fun, umm, work) I landed about 70 good-size kabeljou, a couple of steenbras and a catfish. Others caught galjoen and sharks, but we were going strictly for that was biting.

The seasoned local fishermen know what biting is. They see the mysterious 'holes' in the surging swell as if by a sixth sense, driving two or three hundred kilos in a day if necessary to find them. If after two, or at the most three, casts they don't pull in a few fish, it's off to the next spot. When you hit a hole, you know.

Cast, nibble, strike, reel in – often one fish on each of your two hooks. Bait up with sardine fillets, cast again, wait a few seconds while you feel the nibbling, then strike, reel in and play, land it, or them, again and again. Ten in an hour; 70 a day; no sweat. A brandy or seven, Coke, lots of ice. One thing you don't go into the desert without is ice. Water is strictly for girls. If you want to clean your fish or yourself there's the entire Atlantic Ocean at your toes.

'YOU WANNA GO FISHING, ON THE SKELETON COAST?' someone had boomed down the phone at me a few months previously.

'Well, um, yes, I suppose so,' I replied, realising that it is Mecca to local surf fishermen. 'When?'

'NOW, YOU READY? HAHA.'

'Ahh, well not right now,' I stammered, 'but how about, umm, September. I'll be going to Swakopmund at the beginning of the month ….'

'SEPTEMBER, THAT'S GREAT, SEE YOU THEN.'

The voice belonged to Paul Greef, pedal steel-guitar virtuoso, raconteur, adventurer and no mean fisherman.

Paul has set up Dik Dik Adventures, a unique concept based round his converted Daimler bus. The problem on the Skeleton Coast is that, apart from Henties and Terrace bays and two other forlorn, wind-blasted camp sites, there's nowhere to stay when the fish are biting – and they could be biting anywhere.

Now fishermen are something of an extremist sub-culture and when it's summertime, and the fish are jumpin', they want a place to lay their heads right there on the beach where they can hear the fish calling their names even as they sleep.

With the bus you can drive to Jakkalsputz or Mile 108 (they measure everything in miles north of Swakopmund), park next to the beach, fish all day, have a lekker braai and then retire to your neat bunk for the night. The bus is fitted with a caravan-type washroom with shower and toilet, and designer sleeping bunks complete with shelves and packing space.

'The guys I bring out here', Paul informs me, 'don't want to bait their own hooks or clean their own fish, or have to cook for themselves after a hard day's fishing. They just wanna relax and have a good time.'

The 'guys' are mostly professionals and businessmen who want to get away into the desert, do a spot of fishing (with fish guaranteed), chill out with a frosty or three, eat some good Namibian beef, and maybe do a little team building so the company picks up the tab. Sometimes it's a group of buddies out on their annual jol, sometimes even a family group.

The bus sleeps up to 10 people, but there is camping space available for larger groups. At the back is a fully fitted kitchen capable of handling just about any number of people – together with the crucial fridge and freezing units. This is backed by a Bedford truck and a Land Rover for shipping in supplies and taking guests for trips into the surrounding desert – from day trips to full safaris depending on the group's itinerary.

Since our arrangements had been less than synchronised I was surprised when Paul pitched up at my hotel in Swakopmund only one day late (not bad for Namibia, which had recently reverted from daylight-saving time), with his buddy Marcel in tow. It took me a further three days to work out exactly how Marcel fitted into the Dik Dik adventure. It turned out he didn't; he's just an agreeable guy who came along for the fishing – and the fun.

Paul, Marcel and I, along with the other boys who made a draai by our camp at Jakkalsputz, shot the breeze, chewed the fat, and the biltong, and over the next few days knocked a big hole into a case of Klipdrift (they thought I was a bit of a sissy because I preferred rum).

I heard stories short and tall: Nick and Pat told us of their early ventures into the Kaokoveld; Herman and Wolfie argued about the virtues of galjoen versus kabeljou – galjoen was either 'too rich' or 'too sweet' while kabeljou were 'hamburgers'. Herman was young and cocksure and didn't realise he was arguing with a pro; but then Wolfie fell for his bait. Everyone laughed. Kraai ordered himself another brandy and Coke. Everyone followed suit.

People reminisced about the bush war. Nick told us about the time there were so many harder jumping in the mouth of the Kunene that people (including some very senior conservation officials) jumped in with their shoes on to catch them in their hands or hats if they had them. Everyone laughed some more. Kraai ordered another brandy and Coke. Once again everyone concurred as more fishing tales were proffered, parried and bettered.

When it comes to tall fishing stores, flyweight Wolfie Langenstrassen is a man you don't mess around with. For those Dik Dik adventurers who are really serious about their fishing, Paul has teamed up with West Coast Angling and Tours, run by ace anglers Wolfie, and Henry Loubser. They are the kingpins of Swakopmund's Penguin Angling Club, virtually a shadow national angling squad.

When Paul stands next to Wolfie they look like a veritable David and Goliath, but in this case they're allies and you can only feel sorry for the fish.

Now Wolfie (or Wolfgang if you want to show him the respect he so easily commands) is, like Henry, a born Swakopmunder – a confident, mercurial man who prefers to speak with actions rather than words. When it comes to action, Wolfie is a marlin among mullet: he casts further than any fisherman around, catches more fish (he's the only person I know who guarantees his clients will go home laden with fillets – prepared and packaged), and when it comes to baiting and getting out hooks, he's the fastest rod in the west.

Leather-skinned, salt-dogged fishermen up and down the coast watch him with envious eyes. They use the same bait, try to cast where he casts and reel in their empty hooks while Wolfie hits the jackpot with just about every throw. Being his client, I was happy to stand in his shadow and reel them in too. The secret, he told me, is to be able to cast further than anyone else.

On day one of a four-day fishing safari we made our first stop at Mile 68: two casts each, one fish. We pushed on to Mile 72: same story. Pushed on to Mile 108. There Wolfie saw his friends Chris and Lesley so he made a quick turn in (the guys from the Penguin Club don't stick around if there's no action).

Wolfie, Paul, Marcel and I threw in our lines and within seconds one, two, three of us had tight lines. I had a washing line: that's one fish on each hook. During the course of my trip a lot of laundry was done.

Around midday we joined Chris and Lesley, who were braaing an average size galjoen over cool coals for lunch (their ingenious braai fire was made inside the drum of a stainless steel washing machine). We ate the incredibly oil-rich meat with bread, each of us having his fill.

'When Jesus fed all those people with just two fish and five bread loaves,' quipped Lesley with a slight *bry*, 'the fish must have been galjoen'.

For dinner that night Marcel excelled himself, pulling out a bag full of Kalahari truffles, or !Nxabas as the Bushmen call them. I first read about them in a cookery book by Sir Laurens van der Post and for years had been dying to try them.

Marcel peeled the tough, black skins off the golf-ball size fungi, boiled them and then baked the spongy, grey inner flesh with garlic butter. We also had fresh oysters, baked in their shells on the braai with garlic butter and black pepper – another gastronomic revelation.

On the third day Paul, Marcel and I took a trip to the Skeleton Coast National Park, staying the night at Terrace Bay. We saw gemsbok along the Uinab River and springbok there and elsewhere on the gravel plains. There is a small canyon on the river valley, not easily accessible, and here we saw the fresh spoor of lion that had recently been introduced to the park.

We were lucky to stay in the VIP house at Terrace Bay and Paul, who doubles as a professional photographer, was as keen as me to photograph the colourful beach pebbles, dead seals, cormorants, ship wrecks, bleached whale bones and the skeletons of various failed human endeavours on this treacherous coastline.

Conservationists Koos and Kobus told us they'd been up to Möwe Bay, but that the fishing was unusually poor: they'd caught only 13 fish that day (maybe it was the actual number that bothered them). Someone blamed the poor fishing on vibrations from an oil rig working off shore. Another suggested the anti-aircraft batteries and armoured cars used to guard 'Sampie' (President Sam Nujoma) when he comes fishing here might have frightened off the fish.

Others said it was the seals – possibly even more so than the fishermen.

'You just have to know how to fish properly,' he mocked the others.

On our way back to Hentiesbaai we stopped in to see the famous seal colony at Cape Cross, where Marcel's view seemed to be vindicated.

One of the largest breeding colonies of Cape fur seals appeared to be decimated by an unknown cause – some people said it was overfishing (by the fishermen or the seals? I wondered); others blamed it on the seals having been protected for too long and that last year's massive die-offs were just a natural process. More likely – although as yet unproven – is that the widespread red tide around that time had something to do with it.

Next to the seal colony is an oily, smokey factory belching greasy orange fumes, the floor an ooze of glutinous black sludge. This is where seals are 'harvested' and processed for meat, pet food, fertiliser, skins, whatever. If ever there was a seal Auschwitz, this is it.

Tied to the roll bar of Chris's spanking new red bakkie was a bottle of Klipdrift with a ready-fitted optic for quick, one-handed pouring between taking a fish off his line and fixing the next bait. He and Lesley are also members of the envied Penguins. They seem to have salt water in their veins and the intense gaze of gamblers, or gold prospectors. The Atlantic Ocean is their El Dorado, there to plunder. There is always another fish, always a bigger one out there, and when you hit pay dirt you harvest.

Towards evening on my last day, when our group had landed some 200 fish, I turned to Lesley and asked him: how many fish are enough for one day? He stared at me blankly, not knowing how to answer, as if I'd asked how much sand is enough for a dune, or how much Klipdrift is too much.

Wolfie's enthusiasm for fishing I could understand: he and Henry gave up corporate jobs at Rossing Mine to become professional anglers and they supply most of Swakopmund with fresh seafood. For me 'enough' has always been how much you can reasonably eat. For an enthusiast I would imagine enough to be a decent stock in one's freezer. But what do you do with 40 five-kilogram fish in just one day? And the same again the next!

By this stage I'd had enough. I put down my rod, poured myself another drink and put up a mental note – 'gone fishing'.

Kudu Canyon
Jackie Nel – May 1996

Only two and a half hours from Jo'burg awaits an utterly otherwise, very affordable game experience. Jackie Nel went exploring by barge, zebra-striped Land Cruiser and Unimog.

I was glad she'd dropped off the bontebok head before meeting me. 'I took the head into the taxidermist to mount,' said Theresa.

I was amazed, appalled: 'You drove here with a dead bontebok in your car?'

'Oh no, just the head. We put it in a coolbox.'

'Did you cut it off yourself?'

'No, the boys did that. Now they're planning a feast,' she said as we turned out of Wonderboom Airport – the vehicle chock-full with two Staffordshire-cross pit bulls, a microwave oven, a coolbox and cardboard trays of mangoes – and headed for Kudu Canyon.

Set midway between Vaalwater and Ellisras in the Waterberg region of the Northern Province, Kudu Canyon is the place where Trevor and Theresa Wright have created their own unconventional chunk of Africa.

'I've always loved the bush,' explained Theresa. 'One time we were driving at Ngala and saw all these vultures circling overhead. We followed them to an impala carcass; then Trevor said, 'You know, I think I'm going to buy a game farm.'

'I told Phillip, the estate agent, that I wanted four things,' Trevor took up the story later, 'mountains, canyons, rivers and baobabs.'

He got three out of four with Kudu Canyon (no baobabs). There weren't too many animals initially, since it used to be a hunting farm, but visits to various game auctions have resulted in the introduction of all manner of animals, from the only herd of bontebok in the Transvaal (because Theresa likes bontebok) to some fine examples of white rhino.

'Well, okay, I'd like lion too; I like their roaring at night. But lions just sleep all day, they don't do anything. Maybe elephants ….'

The latest acquisition was buffalo.

And that's not all. Two secluded self-catering lodges, fully serviced and equipped, and each sleeping six, means that the 2200-hectare game farm is accessible to visitors. Both Lourie and Kingfisher lodges have three bedrooms (with overhead fans) and bathrooms, a sitting area, kitchen, veranda, boma, braai and swimming pool.

Alternatively, guests can stay in one of the downstairs rooms in the main house. There are three bedrooms and a spacious lounge decorated with artificial flowers and the mounted heads of buffalo, eland and wildebeest. A stuffed lilac-breasted roller in flight is affixed to the wall; in the dining room a pair of kudu heads presides over the table.

The upstairs houses Trevor and Theresa and their noisy aviary with its collection of parrots, toucans and even a (live) lilac-breasted roller saved by Trevor; it was knocked down by a truck and has a broken wing.

Other pet animals include a lemur, kept in a cage with a leather jacket of Trevor's for its nest, and a much-loved billy goat with water on the brain, which kept falling over because its head was too heavy. He would then bleat in distress until Theresa ran out to pick him up.

What got me – more than the unsteady goat, more than the wide steps in the swimming pool so the rhino could get out if they fell in, more than the complicated system of farm gates which separated the livestock from the game, more than Trevor's habit of feeding all his animals, including the rhino – what really got me was the sheer enormous size of everything. From the huge songololos to the lumbering, 14-seater, diesel-fuelled Unimog, everything was larger than life, including, and especially, Trevor himself and his eagerness to show guests round his piece of paradise.

It was the hottest time of day, no good for game viewing, so Trevor took me – in the Unimog – to see the crocodiles in the Mokolo Dam, formerly the Hans Strijdom Dam. It was even too hot for the crocs, but that didn't deter Trevor.

'See their tracks,' he said, parked at the dam while the nearby fishermen watched in amazement. He jumped from the vehicle – tall as a tree – and pointed. 'Here's the tail, see the tracks on either side, there are crocodiles here, know what I mean? And these are my tracks, I was here yesterday.' He pointed to a spot under the Unimog, just behind the cab, 'see the tracks?'

It was the most inaccessible spot in the entire nature reserve, but I obligingly craned my head to look. When I reappeared Trevor was off in the distance, finger outstretched. 'He went here, see the tracks, see, see, see.'

I ran after him. 'Yes, yes, yes.'

Trevor was also very keen to point out the litter. 'This is run by Nature Conservation but no one looks after it, know what I mean? See this,' he scuffed with the toe of his boot at a cigarette butt; 'see here' scuff-scuff at the ring-top of a cool drink can; 'see' kick at the label from a brandy bottle. 'That's the problem here, know what I mean?'

'And drink and guns didn't go together, know what I mean? There are kudu here and these people shoot them, see the kudu tracks.' Trevor trotted off after the spoor.

Shooting of animals is clearly a pet hate of Trevor's, and on the drive back he voiced his opinions. 'People shouldn't interfere with nature; I don't know how they can shoot a kudu.'

I leapt from the Unimog to open a farm gate; clambered back on.

'Lions especially.'

I leapt to open another gate, damaged by rhino so I had to ruk it a bit, and then regained my perch on the Unimog. 'Even elephant, they shoot elephant, know what I mean?'

In that heat the only game we came across was ostrich. 'Watch this,' Trevor revved the engine and charged the bird, which ran behind a gate. 'I thought he'd put on a display,' Trevor frowned at the ostrich.

Back at the house I sank into the swimming pool, built to resemble a rock pool – but not before Trevor had fished out the longest, thickest, songololos I've ever seen and pointed out the view. 'You see the dam,' he pointed from the braai area. 'That's where we've just been; sometimes if the wind is blowing it'll carry the noise here and those people can be pretty rough. It disturbs the peace, you with me?'

I dived underwater, enjoying the silence, and surfaced to an insistent 'hello, hello!' I braced myself for another onslaught of hospitality, but it was just one of the parrots.

'Blehhhh, blehhhh,' the goat had fallen over again.

An evening game drive and sundowners at The Viewpoint held much promise. There are three vehicles – one painted to resemble giraffe hide, one zebra-striped and the other in rhino grey (the Unimog is in the colours of a green mamba). 'We wanted them to blend in,' explained Theresa.

The game drive didn't yield much game, to Trevor's deep disappointment, but we did see two blesbok. 'See the blesbok! Shame, we used to have 20, but the leopard loves them.'

He kept up a running commentary. 'Look-look-look, what's that? Leopard spoor. You see there? What did I tell you, what do you see? Leopard spoor!'

We also saw three rhino, munching the lucerne Trevor puts out for them. 'I can't help it, I'm a feeder, know what I mean? I like to feed my animals.' We made our way to the viewpoint where, over sundowners, Trevor pointed out the view of the dam. A field mouse appeared to see what all the noise was about and Trevor began throwing handfuls of trail mix at it.

'But one mouse can't eat all that,' I protested.

'That's enough now, Trevor. Stop it,' said Theresa as Trevor took another hand-ful of trail mix from the bag.

'But this is for me,' said Trevor cunningly, eating some of it but surreptitiously throwing a little more at the mouse.

On the return drive he was determined to find kudu. 'You can't come to Kudu Canyon and not see kudu, this is kudu country, know what I mean? If there's no kudu round the next corner,' he warned, 'I'm going to scream.'

'No, please don't do that,' I begged.

We rounded the corner; no kudu. I held my breath; watched Trevor.

'If there's no kudu round the next corner,' he warned, 'I'm going to scream.'

We rounded the corner: there in the headlights, mercifully, were kudu.

'Kudu, kudu, kudu!' screamed Trevor, roaring up to the startled antelope. 'See the kudu.'

Back at the house was Hugh and Sue, long-time friends of the Wrights and regular visitors, and Trevor shepherded us upstairs to watch him feeding the lilac-breasted roller.

Downstairs in the kitchen we poured drinks and started preparing supper while Trevor chased insects around the table; putting them in a bucket to feed to the roller on the morrow (we wouldn't let him feed the bird any more that night).

'Look at the size of the praying mantis. And watch out for our spiders. You saw the songololos; watch out for our spiders, know what I mean?'

A late supper was enjoyed around the fire: mealies, pap en sous, pork ribs and potato salad; pasta for the vegetarians and chicken for Hugh and Sue, who'd bought their own food.

If you don't want to cater for yourself you can be catered for, but notify Theresa beforehand and be prepared to pay a bit more. Maybe you'll be lucky to try ostrich egg for breakfast. 'We've got one in the fridge now, but we'll have to wait because Philemon's on leave; he gets them open with a bolt.'

07h00 Saturday morning: I stepped outside. 'Did you hear the rhino last night? They were in the garden when I went to feed the lemur; I could see their tracks. See there, what do you see? Rhino spoor! See? See there. What's this? Rhino spoor!'

Trevor disappeared down the gravel drive pointing at prints; I had no option but to follow. 'I'm with you Trevor, I see.'

A cruise was the morning's activity, and fellow passengers were William and Dalita Ramwell of Jo'burg, who were staying in Kingfisher Lodge. The equipment for the excursion comprised the Unimog, to negotiate the bumpy hour-and-a-bit drive to the dam and push the barge into the water; the barge itself, a huge craft mounted on pontoons with a canvas awning for shade; an assortment of pets, towels, cameras, suntan lotions, bird books and binoculars; and a lavish brunch which appeared from a series of cool boxes and was prepared over Cadac skottels in a suitable scenic spot.

From the barge we admired the sheer cliff faces, the riverine vegetation, a green-backed heron, a fish eagle nest, a pair of fish eagles ….

Theresa steered the barge towards a solitary gnarled tree sticking from the water in the middle of the dam, and Trevor grabbed it to use as a mooring.

'See the tree spider?'

'No, where?' I leant over the side.

'Here, on the tree. See the tree.'

'No.'

'Here, in the water,' said Hugh, catching on. 'See the water?'

'No, what water?'

But Trevor wasn't going to be beaten so easily. He looked around. 'Maybe we'll see the osberry.'

'The … the what?' 'The osberry, like a fish eagle. (I gathered he meant osprey.) He flies here every year from Britain, but then he goes back again. Maybe he's gone back already.'

'Must be a subspecies of the raspberry,' said Hugh.

On the cruise and the return drive we saw several species of antelope, Vicky the rhino and many a bird.

'Martial eagle, martial eagle,' shouted Trevor.

'Actually, I think that's um …' William consulted his Roberts, 'a Black-breasted snake eagle.'

'Black-breasted snake eagle!' shouted Trevor. 'See the Black-breasted snake eagle.'

But even the occasional raptor sighting wasn't good enough; and in his boundless enthusiasm he condensed, time and again, three years of game viewing into one glorious game drive which had, from every bush and round every corner, kudu and sable leaping, fish eagles and giant eagle owls flying, African goshawks soaring, pythons slithering, leopards stalking ….

'We used to see hippo, we used to see klipspringer, and we used to see mountain reedbuck here all the time.'

'Trevor takes it as personal insult if you don't see all his game,' explained Hugh.

'Blehhhhh.' Back at the house the goat had fallen over again; Theresa picked it up and Trevor fed it some foliage. 'Blehhhhh.'

Although the cruise had allegedly been a breakfast one, the shadows were already lengthening and the light was turning the rosy golden colour of late afternoon, such had been Trevor's enthusiasm in showing us round.

We all trooped pool-wards to cool off as the day cooled down, looking forward to the next two excursions: an evening game drive and, the next day, an early-morning walk into the canyon to see the porcupine cave, the black eagle nest, the Bushman paintings and possible even the osberry.

'Yes, you need stamina for one of Trevor's game drives,' said Hugh with a chuckle. 'But it's all included; you can never say you don't get your money's worth here.'

Even Trevor, basking on the wide steps, had to laugh 'People come here for two days then they go home for a holiday,' he said.

I knew what he meant.

Walking back through time
Cathy Lanz – December 1996

There was a time in Africa when our forebears met the creatures of the wild nose to nose; when lions were a threat to life; and death was a black-mamba bite away. Cathy Lanz rekindled these ancient roots and sensations during a three-day wilderness trail through the Hluhluwe-Umfolozi Park.

'There are eyes,' whispered Cathy as she returned to the fire after a teeth-brushing expedition on the outskirts of the camp. Fear lent an edge to her soft Canadian accent.

Dozens of pairs of glinting orbs flashed in our torch-light and confirmed that the camp was under close surveillance from an inquisitive herd of impala.

Then the noise began. A hyena's chilling howl cracked the river-mud darkness of the night. The cropping, grunting sound of a large grazer followed and grew steadily nearer until it was hair-raisingly close, but still out of sight. We grabbed torches and crept forward.

On the periphery of the bush camp, a mere 40 paces from where we stood, grazed a herd of six white rhinos. No stout-walled boma divided us from these hulking, prehistoric creatures, no car window intruded. A large bull lifted its head, scimitar horn and wide, grass-cropping lips clearly visible in the torch light. Then he, with the rest of the herd, resumed grazing, accepting our presence.

It was my first night in the bush, but at that moment my city fear of all things wild melted away. I felt part of their world, unthreatened and in harmony with Africa's dangerous mammals. For the first time I understood the mad impulse which compelled writer Laurens van der Post to approach within three metres of a black rhino one morning while on a film shoot in the African bush: 'He belonged, of course, to one of the oldest forms of mammal life,' van der Post had written of the encounter, 'and many hunters regard him as one of the most dangerous animals, one of the ugliest. Yet, as I stood and looked at him there, I thought I saw through all that was considered inelegant and ugly in his appearance.'

'Suddenly it was as if not only the gap of what we call time between him and I had been closed, but that a powerful feeling of emancipation was illuminating my war-darkened and industrialised senses.'

It was Ian Player, a protégé of van der Post, who made a link between the need each of us has for wild places and its practical realisation. A wilderness experience, he wrote, gives people a great capacity to understand themselves and rediscover that part of ourselves which has been guttered by a materialistic and industrialised lifestyle.

In 1959 Player, who was then officer in charge of the Umfolozi Game Reserve, and his Zulu mentor and companion, Magqubu Ntombela, led the first wilderness trail through the southern part of the reserve – an area which was once the exclusive hunting ground of the Zulu king Shaka and his heirs.

That path-finder expedition almost ended in disaster on the tip of a black rhino horn, but the omnipresent shades of the Zulu kings saw fit to spare the party, and wilderness trails became an important aspect of modern conservation, not only for the preservation of animals, but for the sanity of people as well.

My wilderness-trail experience began on an overcast evening at Mndindini base camp. Two warthogs, which had made themselves at home on the camp lawns, bid us welcome and a parade of waterbuck crossed the White Umfolozi in step with the gurgling notes of coucals in the reed beds.

Already I could feel the whisperings of sanity returning to my city-habituated soul.

The following morning our party of five trailists, led by senior trails officer Russell Crossey, started out on the myriad game paths which, over the next three days, would lead us on a criss-cross course over the wilderness area of Africa's oldest game reserve. Making sure nothing attacked us from the rear was game guard Ernest Ncube.

We walked mostly in silence, absorbing the sights, smells and sounds of the bush. Our progress was halted here and there by Russell who would point out such gems as the buffalo thorn (*Ziziphus mucronata*), a sacred tree to Zulu people, the shepherd's bush (*Boscia albitrunca*) with its wide variety of uses and a lone, giant sycamore fig (*Ficus sycomorus*) on the river bank, one of the few survivors of Cyclone Demoina which devastated the park in 1984.

While we were trying to make out a distant giraffe, the silence was suddenly shattered by a commotion of high-pitched shrieks and barks which stopped as suddenly. When we arrived at the source of the noise, white-backed vultures and crows were already staking their claim.

'I think a leopard must have taken this little fellow,' said Russell, holding up the remains of a baby baboon. 'Ingwe,' confirmed Ernest, studying the spoor. All that remained was the skull, still with its grey-green eyes wide open in terror and two little black ape feet curled in death.

Kudu and wildebeest looked down on the scene – relieved, perhaps, that their young were not the victims this time. Six giraffes were putting in a safe distance with a long-limbed gait resembling a slow-motion wildlife movie.

Half way up a hill Russell picked up a stone. Why does he need a stone if he's carrying a loaded rifle, I remember thinking. But at the top of the hill he spat on it and added to a cairn.

'This is an isivivane, a sacred spot of the Zulu people,' he explained. 'No Zulu will pass this spot without adding a stone – or the 'shades of the dead' will haunt him.'

We all followed his example and passed without further thought, but our stop at the isivivane may well have tipped the balance of fate on the final day of our hike.

This first afternoon, however, belonged to rhino, beginning with a distant white-rhino-and-calf sighting during lunch.

Well fed and on the trail again, it was the cackling hiss of oxpeckers which alerted us to the presence of big game just before two 'teenage' white rhino careered through the undergrowth in a semi-circle around us.

We pressed on, senses alert, hearts pounding, the previous night's safety briefing foremost in our minds.

Then we saw it. Not 50 metres away, in the shadow of a tamboti (*Spirostachys africana*), stood one of Africa's rarest animals: a black rhino. His ears strained forward as he tried to get a fix on the intruders whose strange smell assailed his nostrils. We could sense the rhino's dangerous confusion as fight or flight responses bombarded its prehistoric brain. But flight prevailed and he thundered off, cracking twigs in noisy retreat.

We exhaled as one, and then burst into excited chatter. Had the trail ended there and then I would have been satisfied. But there was more to follow.

As evening light spread its Midas touch over the savanna grassland, two sun-gilded lionesses with cubs provided the finale to a day already rich with bushveld significance and an almost constant parade of animals.

At the Ngilandi (England) bush camp – so named by the Zulu game scouts because you have to cross water to get there – hot tea and apple-and-cinnamon fritters were waiting.

The ablutions consisted of a spade plus toilet roll and a bucket shower hung from a tree, but we preferred to let the White Umfolozi gently cleanse our dusty bodies.

Later, as the night sounds were beginning to tune up, the camp cook proudly dished up buffalo stew from his huge, iron cooking pot.

'There's a lion down there,' said Byron, pointing to an open patch of grassland across the river. 'And there's another.'

'Look, it's a whole pride lying under that tree and they've killed a buffalo,' said Russell, training his powerful binoculars.

It was lunch time on day two. We'd stopped on high cliffs over-looking the river, which gave a sweeping view of the surrounding terrain. On our rocky perch we, another major predator, tucked into buffalo burgers, then spent a lazy few hours observing a bloated lion bloodying his mane as he picked selectively at buffalo innards.

Further downstream an old male buffalo lazed in the reed beds, biding his time before natural selection sealed his fate.

Day two was lion day: during our late afternoon meander back to Ngilandi, we spotted the two lionesses and cubs we'd seen the previous evening.

They had bagged a warthog, having chased it into the river until the little pig's trotters sank into the soft sand and it could go no further. The hog was clearly dead, but the two cubs were playing a cat-and-mouse game with the feast-in-waiting.

In the mellow time around the camp fire after supper that night, a white-tailed mongoose dropped in to pay respects. And later, when some weary hikers were already in their tents, a hyena came foraging through the camp.

When we returned to the cliffs above the buffalo kill the next day the carcass had been picked clean and not even a hopeful vulture lingered. But the stuffed lions were still lurking in trees nearby.

'Let's go down and investigate,' suggested Russell, who was assailed by dubious looks from his trailists.

The day had already provided plenty of excitement: on our walk from Ngilandi to the cliffs we'd come upon two white rhinos and had tracked them for some way through the dense riverine bush, getting a little too close for comfort.

The exhilaration of this stalk carried over into our next sighting – a large herd of buffaloes coming down to the river to drink, so we were already adrenaline-charged as we neared the buffalo kill.

'Remember, if a lion charges, stand still, don't run,' Russell reiterated the safety briefing. But lions remained out of sight, so we headed upriver, walking in the sandy bed.

Having given up on finding them, the next encounter took both us and the lions by surprise. As we rounded a bend in the river, there they were, walking down to drink.

They backed off slowly, but not before the leading lioness had sneered menacingly, her tail switching all the while.

Further upriver I thought I saw a crocodile leap off the bank. 'Probably a leguaan,' Russell surmised, 'we seldom find crocs in the White Umfolozi because it dries up in winter.'

Whatever it was, it didn't stop us swimming during the lunch break, watched from a safe distance by the now-familiar lioness-and-cubs group which were surrounded by a few warthog bones.

We did see crocs later though, sunning themselves above a deep perennial channel which feeds the Umfolozi. This was en route to Momfu Cliffs, which are the highest point of the trail.

It's a slog up to these flat-topped rocks which tower above the river, but their height ensures an uninterrupted view of the whole of the Umfolozi Wilderness Area and into the hazy beyond.

From here it was downhill all the way back to Mndindini base camp where hot showers and cold drinks awaited. I was trudging along, lost in my own world, when suddenly the four people ahead of me scattered. A buffalo charge was my first reaction as I ducked behind a tree.

But then I saw it – a black, menacing, hissing coil which leapt into an acacia branch a full two metres above the ground, then dropped from the tree and slithered off – all four metres of it.

The black mamba is probably Africa's deadliest snake; its nick-name, the three-minute snake, alludes to the speed with which the venom dispatches its victim. It was a close call for Russell who'd just missed standing on the sleeping reptile, whose response to that indignity would almost certainly have been the fangs of death.

I remembered Russell's belief in the isivivane and I silently thanked the spirits.

Back at Mndindini, an orange evening sky provided a dramatic backdrop to cold beers. Aromatic tamboti smoke wafted up from the fire while we reflected on the past three days in the bush.

From a game point of view we'd been extremely lucky – more so than most, Russell confirmed. But there were so many other bushveld images which flooded my mind as I lay in the tent on that final night: a flock of white-helmeted shrikes adorning a bush; a hovering bateleur eagle; morning light on a sycamore fig; the intense smell of the potato bush; the highway of spoor in the riverbed ….

The Hluhluwe-Umfolozi Park has been credited with saving the white rhino from extinction. A quick visit to the capture bomas the next day confirmed that the future of rhinos – both black and white – is in good hands here.

In the old days when Africa was a dark continent and hunters like Cornwallis-Harris and Selous made a name for themselves, the challenge was to conquer and tame the wilderness. Now the quest has become, in the words of Player, to preserve these 'islands of sanity in a rising sea of madness'.

Only time will tell whether humanity is as adept at preservation as it has been at destruction. On the banks of the White Umfolozi I saw, for the first time, reason enough to know the challenge is not only worth fighting for – it's crucial to the survival of both man and beast.

Kaokoland – Lords of the Namibian desert
David Rogers – October 1997

Along the dry rivers and dusty plains of Kaokoland, David Rogers went on a journey in search of desert elephants. The dung which lay in the sand of the Ombonde River was the first real clue that the desert elephants of Kaokoveld were near at hand.

It was almost dusk on the first day of our Namibian adventure and we resolved to follow the spoor the next morning. With great expectations, we set up camp in a gully beneath tall cliffs of orange sandstone.

Our group had gathered the previous evening in Wilderness Safari's luxurious Ongava Lodge near Etosha National Park. But it was here, as we collected wood, pitched our tents and prepared an evening meal beneath the cliffs that our fireside friendships were forged.

There were seven of us in the group. Our guide was Tas van Solms, a Namibian who had worked in the Kaokoveld region for many years. He was a tall, quietly spoken man, an expert tracker and a fount of knowledge on the fauna and flora of the region.

Hannes Grobler was equally suited to his role. A four-time South African rally-driving champion, he was as happy in an overall with a spanner in his hand as he was in an apron listening to a potjie simmering on the fire.

The other manne included Juri van Leeuwen and Max de Wit from Nissan, and Peter Lamberti and his assistant, Tyrone Haddaway, who were filming for *The Getaway Explorer.*

Tas and Hannes were the only two in the group who had previously been to the area. As we sat warming our knees around the glowing mopane logs on that first night, they hinted that we could expect spectacular scenery – and, if we were lucky, elephants. Next morning the noisy cackle of francolins stirred us from sleep. After coffee and rusks we packed our gear into the two 2.7 turbo-diesel Nissan 4x4s. One was the new-shape Sani, the other an SE double cab fitted with fridge, water tank and rooftop tent. They were great looking vehicles – but more importantly they were to prove unfailingly reliable and exceptionally comfortable to drive.

Once we were packed, we followed the spoor west down the Ombonde to its confluence with the much larger Hoanib River.

The meandering river was dry for the first part of our journey but a rich cloak of foliage, including ana trees (*Acacia albida*), leadwoods (*Combretum imberbe*) and false umbrella thorn (*Acacia reficiens*) hinted that water flowed just beneath the sand.

'It's not always this way,' said Tas as he pointed to the tangle of rooted trees high on the bank. He explained that these had been tossed there by floods and were reminders of the dangers of camping in rivers during the rainy season. In these rivers (where rain falls only in the headwaters) flash floods can wash through areas without the hint of a cloud in the sky.

Soon the temperature rose beyond 30°C and our tyres laboured through the powdery sand. To get through these patches, Hannes recommended that we stayed permanently in four-wheel-drive, deflate our tyres to about one bar and keep the engines turning over below 2000 revs.

We followed his advice and soon our heavily laden convoy was moving steadily along the dry river bed, the diesel engines offering excellent torque to power through the sand.

As we rumbled beyond the limits of civilisation more and more springbok, gemsbok and ostriches appeared, most dozing under trees.

Because the animals became alarmed and ran as our vehicles approached, Tas stopped the convoy and led us upwind on foot for the best views and photographs.

We also stopped frequently to watch birds. Ostriches, tawny eagles and interesting endemic species such as Rüppell's korhaan made bird-watching a varied and interesting distraction in the Hoanib River, particularly as we approached the western areas.

Our search for elephants eventually led us through the Khowarib Schlucht. This is a dramatic gorge where high cliffs of twisted, layered sandstone tower above the sandy river bed. It was in this spectacular setting that we first encountered dribbles of waters oozing up from beneath the sand.

On the fringes of these oases were settlements. Tas greeted a few of the children and enquired whether they had seen any elephants coming through this way. They shook their heads and pointed beyond the distant haze of mountains, suggesting that they had headed in that direction.

We spent that night at Khowarib Camp at the eastern end of the ravine. This community project, sponsored by Save the Rhino Trust, is a worthwhile stop. We were allocated an exceptional site on the edge of the river, a wagon-load of wood, and helpful hands to set up our tents.

The added attractions of Khowarib are excursions in donkey carts and on camels. We'd all had quite enough off-road travelling for one day and, rather than taking them up on this offer, flopped into the river for a refreshing swim. The next morning, before our convoy of vehicles headed north towards Sesfontein, we could not resist a quick trot up the river on the Khowarib camels (mine was quite a friendly mount named Nelson). Our plan was to rejoin the Hoanib River beyond this town and track the elusive elephants from the perennial Dubis Fountain.

We drove northwest from the river along the gravel highway entering into the heart of the Kaokoveld. It was a rocky, barren place with low mopane scrub and purple mountains which cut a jagged line across the dusty, blue-black skies.

On our way we passed small villages where the Herero scratch a meagre subsistence from their goats and crops. These days an increasing number are also finding ways of making a living from tourism.

On our way we saw 'courtesy stops' boldly advertised where women, dressed in traditional Victorian-styled regalia, sold hand-made leather dolls, crystals and ivory-palm necklaces. Support for these informal entrepreneurs was rewarded with wonderful opportunities for photographs.

A less well-advertised attraction of this rocky region is Ongongo Campsite. It lies some distance from the road – but if you venture into its barren, rocky midsts you'll find a glorious oasis with a hot spring ringed by trees and reeds. It was wonderful to sit in the sparkling pool listening to the birds and feeling the warm, subterranean water gush through the rocks.

There is a more sterile, chlorinated pool – and cold beers – a little further to the north at the crenellated Sesfontein Fort. This 1902 German outpost, which has been renovated as a hotel and campsite, proved to be a good place to pick up snippets of information about the area.

Between rock shandies gulped beside the pool, we spoke to other travellers who had been in the area: some of them had seen elephants – others had not.

One of the most interesting characters in the surprisingly cosmopolitan Sesfontein Hotel was local legend Basjan van Niekerk. A tall, bearded man with a gravelly voice, Basjan is well known for the fascinating fireside yarns he delivers to Afrikaans-radio listeners.

When we mentioned we were interested in seeing elephants he nodded politely. But when someone happened to add that we might also pop into the Ougams area to the north of the river, his blue eyes twinkled brightly.

'Let me tell you a story', he said, sucking deeply on his pipe, 'about Ougam's water. Many years ago my brothers and I broke an axle while travelling in the Ougams.

'I, being the youngest, was given the task of fetching water while they made the necessary repairs.

'Now the only thing more difficult than seeing elephants in the Ougams, is finding clean water. The one fountain I located was used by every animal in the area and was full of green moss and bokdrolle. Knowing the boys would be getting really thirsty and give me a klap if I returned empty-handed, I strained it through my hat.'

According to Basjan, the horrible effects took grip later that afternoon when the family was travelling home in the cart.

'We kept getting stuck', he explained. 'Each time we hopped out to push, Ougam's water also started to work. It got so bad that by the end of the day all us brothers were walking round with our trousers hanging round our necks!'

We roared with laughter. But all stories have an element of truth, especially those told by Basjan van Niekerk. Before we left Sesfontein for the Hoanib, I noticed Hannes and Tas carefully checking our water and petrol supplies. The road from Sesfontein to the Hoanib River crosses the Okambondevlakte through the so-called stofgate. As we set off through this wide flood plain our tyres kept sinking into deep pools of talcum-textured dust which created plumes behind our convoy for two kilometres or more. It's a terrible place to drive – but our vehicles had excellent seals and air-conditioning, and raced through clouds of dust without a care.

Eventually we escaped the dust bowl and arrived at the verdant Hoanib River. Once more thick green ana trees crowded the banks and high cliffs of sandstone created long slabs of shadow where we could relax and escape the sun.

The track joined the river very near to the fountain at Dubis. Just as we had hoped, plenty of elephant spoor peppered the sand – including some tracks which Tas told us were just a few hours old.

Unfortunately night was closing in and we realised that once more we would have to wait to catch up to these great desert animals. Reluctantly, we moved well away from Dubis to set up camp beneath tall cliffs of sandstone (it's important not to interfere with elephants when they drink at night).

That night as we slept under a clear, star-filled sky with the smell of dust and dung in our nostrils, we dreamed of elephants. Early next morning our persistence was rewarded. Just as we climbed out of our warm sleeping bags a huge, long-legged desert elephant bull loped past the camp. He seemed as old and weathered as the landscape itself, with brittle ivory and leathery skin which had been cracked and baked by decades in the sun.

I watched this wonderful old-timer through my telephoto lens as he walked along the river, plucking at the wild tamarisk leaves (*Tamarix usneoides*) in the soft, early-morning light. It was thrilling to see this great survivor so at home in his unusually dry habitat.

It proved to be the omen of an exceptional day. As we chugged slowly along the river we enjoyed a veritable menagerie of desert-adapted animals which were making their way along this tree-lined sand corridor. These included several small herds of giraffe, gemsbok, springbok, jackals and ostriches.

But most of our attention was on the elephants which we had come so far to find. We saw nearly 30 during the course of the day. Sometimes we sat in our vehicles and watched as they stood swaying gently beneath the trees, while on other occasions it was possible to clamber onto the high cliffs and watch them moving like toy creatures on the valley floor.

The elephants (particularly those herds with young calves) are easily stressed in the confinement of these cliffs and we took care not to bother them in any way. These creatures move freely up and down the Hoanib for hundreds of kilometres from the escarpment to the sea.

At Amspoort, however, where the river enters into the Skeleton Coast National Park, the river route is closed to vehicles.

Satisfied that we had seen the very best of the river and more than our fair share of desert elephants, we decided to reward ourselves with a visit to the enigmatic Ougams rather than return the way we had come.

At Amspoort our convoy drove out of the river and headed north along the eastern fringe of the Skeleton Coast National Park, past gravel plains which stretched endlessly to the horizon. Many vehicles had driven off the tracks to find a route that was less corrugated and it was sad to think that it would take hundreds of years before nature could repair the resulting damage. Hannes was quick to point out that you can travel in comfort on these corrugated roads if you simply let a little air out of your tyres.

We stopped for the night at Purros and decided to stay at the nearby Ngatutanga Camp. This community project, sponsored by Integrated Rural Development and Nature Conservation and the World Wildlife Fund for Nature (WWF), means 'let us all work together'. It offers camp sites, wonderful opportunities to photograph Herero people, a shop selling cold beers, and the unexpected luxury of flush toilets and showers.

'Kyk hy stink nie,' said the cheerful camp attendant as he lifted the lid of the toilet showing off a sparkling clean, porcelain interior. It was a convenience almost too good to be true. The next day, feeling clean and refreshed, we explored the nearby reaches of the Hoarusib River. It was much narrower than the Hoanib with twisted rocks, mossy waterways, and an array of fairly common water birds including Egyptian geese, white-fronted plovers and sandpipers. After a scenic drive through its cool gullies and gorges we drove out of the river and followed the road north towards the Ougams plain.

As we approached, clouds of thick fog swept off the Atlantic. The cold Benguela Current is responsible for this condensation and also the frigid conditions which make this coastal strip one of the driest deserts on earth.

The inselberg-studded Ougams, which lies only 30 kilometres from the sea, was spectacular. The desert plains were an exquisite mosaic of gravel stones which seemed to have been laid by an artist's delicate hand. Equally dramatic were the massive piles of round, granite orbs stacked upon the surface.

The raw beauty of this ancient, arid world was quite bewildering. It was startling to find it decorated with fascinating plants. The most easily recognisable of these were the welwitschias (*Welwitschia mirabilis*) which sprawled like thirsty, green tongues on the parched valley floor, waiting to lap up moisture from the incoming fog.

Tas also pointed out ancient lichens including the leafy foliose variety. With a careful hand he poured a few drops of water on their brittle olive-green folds and we watched them double in size. Equally fascinating were the Commiphora trees. Each of them was stunted by lack of water and a fraction of their normal size. With their perfectly proportioned shapes they would have pride of place in the finest bonsai collection. That evening, just before sunset, I walked onto the open plains to absorb the magnificent isolation. Far from the fire and the sounds of voices, I sat alone and reflected on the wonders of this magical land. Across the apricot-tinted plains towards the south, I imagined the processions of desert-adapted elephants and other game journeying slowly through the sandy Hoanib River.

Sadly, my journey was over. As the sun was dipping over the horizon I made my way back to rejoin the others at the fire. I looked down at the gravel plains and noticed with alarm that even the gentle fall of my feet had scarred nature's delicate design.

Something deep inside me was troubled by my intrusion. It reminded me that the wonders of the Kaokoveld are very fragile indeed. If ecotourism is to contribute to the survival of its people, wild animals and habitat, we must tread very lightly indeed.

Poachers to protectors

Most of the game scouts employed to protect the elephants of the Hoanib River were once well-known poachers.

'Men such as the infamous Piet Renoster are now doing an incredible job to safeguard the future of these rhino and elephants,' Garth Owen-Smith of Integrated Rural Development and Nature Conservation told *Getaway*. 'They are involved in educating, patrolling and monitoring rhino and elephant movements through the area.

'Game numbers have risen 15-fold over the past few years as the local communities have started to realise the benefits of conserving their natural resources.

'At present the Hoanib is community land and people are allowed to graze their cattle freely. But good news for the locals is that the government recently passed a law whereby they can benefit directly from tourism as well. In time, tourists will be issued with permits and required to use either a local scout or a guide qualified to lead parties into the area,' he said.

The great survivors

The elephants which live in the dry Kaokoveld areas of Northern Namibia are not a separate species from those found on Africa's savanna plains, but an ecotype – a race superbly adapted to the harsh, arid environment.

These mighty desert creatures have learned to be frugal eaters and, unlike their savanna relatives, seldom topple trees, or even waste a leaf. They are also excellent climbers capable of negotiating steep inclines and narrow ledges to reach inaccessible plants. They travel mostly at night to conserve their energy, often covering up to 80 kilometres in 24 hours.

In the years before fences and burgeoning rural populations, these elephants migrated freely between the Kaokoveld and Etosha Pan. Despite the new limits to their range they are surviving remarkably well.

During a severe drought from 1977 to 1982, when animals such as springbok and gemsbok dwindled to one fifth, the desert elephant population held its numbers. Since then their tally has grown from around 250 to more than 450. These animals are now extending their range hundreds of kilometres south to the Ugab River.

Such successes are largely a consequence of the tolerance of the local community as well as the efforts of Integrated Rural Development and Conservation, Save the Rhino Trust and new ecotourism concerns such as Wilderness Safari's new Damaraland Camp.

Trains and boats and planes in the northern Red Sea
David Steele – June 1998

In the first of a three-part series on the wrecks of the northern Red Sea, David Steele recounts the dramatic story of the sinking of the SS Thistlegorm – then descends onto this remarkable Second World War time capsule.

❧

I t was a hot night … the sort of night you choose to sleep on deck. Little did the sailors in the convoy of 20 ships, waiting at what they thought was a safe anchorage at the southern tip of the Gulf of Suez, realise what was about to happen.

The quietness aboard the Thistlegorm was shattered for bridge-man Angus Macleay, lying naked and half-awake on his bunk, when he heard a 'terrible explosion' and shouting on the deck.

Unable to find his clothes in the dark, he rushed up wearing nothing but a lifejacket. There he found 'an inferno of flames and flashes' and decided to escape the boiling heat by diving into the water. He ran to the railing and was just about to jump overboard when he noticed one of the gunners unconscious in the flames.

The deck was burning and covered in broken glass, but Macleay managed to get to the man and hoist him on to his shoulders. Then, as he struggled barefoot across the deck to a lifeboat, some men came to his assistance and they helped him into the boat. (Macleay's bravery was later rewarded with the George Medal and the Lloyd's War Medal for Bravery at Sea.)

Although most of the Thistlegorm's crew had been asleep when the bombs struck, the crew of nearby HMS Carlisle had been at action stations and some of them saw the attack. One was marine gunner Dennis Gray who vividly remembers the moonlight as being so bright he could have read a book on deck.

'We saw the aircraft flying low across the ships at anchor and I remember how big it seemed,' he said in a recent interview, adding that it had flown so low the gunners were unable to depress their guns far enough to get a decent shot.

'We had a grandstand view of the terrific explosion as the 15-inch shells blew up. The flash lit up the shores on both sides of the Red Sea and we were paralysed as we watched a red-hot railway engine flying through the air!'

With the engine heading straight for him, and other scorching debris flying about, Gray and his oppo dived into – of all places – an ammunition locker for shelter. When they looked out again the engine had disappeared in a cloud of steam and they could hear loud cries for help in the water. At this stage HMS Carlisle's boats were lowered to pick up survivors.

The ill-fated, 415-foot long Thistlegorm (the name means 'blue thistle' in Gaelic) had been built in 1940 and was on its fourth voyage as an armed merchantman a year later when it sank.

That year was a bleak one for wartime Britain. The Axis powers had virtual control of the Mediterranean, and convoys supplying the Eighth Army in North Africa had to sail via the Cape and up through the Red Sea. This is the route the Thistlegorm took. She was heavily laden with all sorts of military equipment for the Allied troops preparing to relieve Tobruk: Bedford trucks, Morris cars, BSA motorcycles, Bren-gun carriers, bomb trolleys, Lee Enfield rifles, aircraft wings, tyres, medical supplies, generators, torpedoes, shells, landmines, ammunition, fuses and something only the British could need in the desert – dozens of Wellington boots! On deck were two railway locomotives complete with tenders and tanker wagons.

The Thistlegorm had nearly completed her arduous journey when she dropped her starboard anchor at Anchorage F in the entrance to the Straits of Gubal, waiting for permission from Alexandria to proceed further north up the Gulf of Suez.

She was within sight of Mount Sinai, coincidently at the spot where some people believe Moses parted the Red Sea to let his followers through.

At about 01h30 on 6 October 1941 the convoy was discovered by four long-range German Heinkel HEIII bombers flying from their base in Crete. Two bombs hit her number four hold, crammed with munitions, and this prompted a second, massive explosion some 20 minutes later. This all but tore the Thistlegorm's stern section from the rest of her hull and caused her to sink onto the sand 30 metres below. Historians and writers disagree on whether the Germans were just plain lucky in coming across the convoy and hitting the right ship in the right spot, or whether the Thistlegorm's sinking was the result of a carefully planned and skilfully executed operation.

Whatever, the heavily overloaded ship sank very quickly and nine of her 49-man crew perished – eight aboard the ship and one who is thought to have been taken by a shark. The dead included five gunners who, in all probability, had been sleeping on deck and were unable to get a return shot from the anti-aircraft gun mounted near her stern.

For many years after the sinking, ships of the Royal Navy would lower their ensigns to half-mast as they passed the spot … then the Thistlegorm passed into history and lay forgotten in her watery grave.

In 1955 she was discovered by Jacques Cousteau and the crew of the Calypso, who recovered one of the now-famous BSA motorbikes, the ship's safe, and her bell from the foredeck. The story of the discovery is recounted in Cousteau's book *The Living Sea*.

After Cousteau's exploration, the wreck lay frozen in time until 1992 when she was rediscovered by some liveaboard divers who had noticed Bedouin fishermen casting their lines over her. (The divers knew that wrecks create artificial reefs which attract fish and considered the spot worth investigating.)

With her interesting cargo – one of the best collections of war memorabilia outside any museum – the Thistlegorm soon became a scuba legend and gained the reputation of one of the greatest wreck dives in the world. But her popularity has not been without its problems and it is more than just time that has taken its toll.

Perhaps 100 divers visit the wreck each day, most of them undertaking at least two dives. Some have taken small souvenirs – items such as corroding motorbike handlebars or saddles – which are absolute junk on land but irreplaceable on the wreck.

Not only are these looters spoiling this remarkable site for future divers, they are also desecrating a war grave.

Worse still, diveboats have damaged the wreck in the strong current by mooring onto weak parts of the sunken ship. Because of this a railway tanker wagon now hangs dangerously over the entrance to number one hold.

Fortunately the rape of the Thistlegorm seems to have abated. Divemasters are far more careful about where they tie their mooring lines and divers' attitudes to souvenir hunting seem to have changed.

The Thistlegorm is more difficult to dive than most other Red Sea wrecks: a strong current usually flows as far down as her deck, her vast size tempts divers to push the limits of time and air consumption, and the visibility is normally only about 10 to 15 metres.

Conditions, however, were near perfect for my first dive on the wreck, in April last year, with visibility at 25 metres and a current noticeable only on the surface of the water.

Our Egyptian divemaster had attached our mooring line onto the wreck and a second floating line ran from the mooring line along the port side of our boat, the Shalakamy Explorer, past the diving platform at her stern.

We jumped in and used the floating line to pull ourselves – up current – to the mooring line and then descended down this line to the wreck.

Pausing at five metres, I realised the current had all but disappeared. The water was a comparatively cool 22°C but the visibility looked good. Scanning the area below me I noticed an irregular greyish-blue shape through the even, blue curtain of the sea.

Excitement welled as I descended further and the shape resolved itself as the well-preserved foredeck of the Thistlegorm.

After finning to the bow to get a general impression of the wreck, I made my way towards number one hold. Parts of the wreck had become encrusted with hard and soft corals and a variety of brightly coloured fish had taken up residence in the comparative safety of this artificial reef.

A shoal of fish circled overhead and game fish – including an enormous tunny – hovered expectantly, waiting for their next meal. Watching them I nearly missed a crocodile fish which scurried along the deck in front of me.

The hold had lost its cover and could be entered safely. Rows of carefully parked BSA motorbikes and Morris cars appeared before me.

Aware that most first-time divers on the Thistlegorm are like children let loose in a chocolate factory, dive buddy Lawrence Dale and I concentrated on this hold, photographing and videoing the vehicles.

Time flew, as it does on great dives, and all too soon it was time to ascend. As I slowly moved up the mooring line, I looked down and noticed streams of bubbles rising from cracks in the wreck as divers from other boats took our place.

Later, while enjoying breakfast and steaming cups of coffee, we all agreed that although we'd seen only a small part of the Thistlegorm, it had been one of the best dives of our lives and we excitedly discussed which parts of the wreck we'd explore next.

It would take several dives to see the wreck properly, but that is exactly what makes the Thistlegorm so popular. Most divers concentrate on the front half of the wreck, often starting at the bow. Here the large port anchor is still firmly in position while the starboard anchor chain stretches away from the wreck, confirming she was lying at anchor when the bombs struck.

The foredeck and anchor winches are well preserved and it is possible to enter the chain room through the doors facing number one hold. Although there's not much inside, it's an easy penetration which provides all the excitement of being inside a wreck.

Immediately behind the foredeck is the large opening to number one hold, with an imploded railway tanker truck mounted on the deck on one side of the opening. The port tanker has shifted and is dangerously balanced over the edge of the hold, so you should avoid swimming underneath it. All the holds have two levels and number one hold has motorcycles and cars parked on the upper deck and medical supplies, rifles, generators, aircraft parts, camp beds for field hospitals, Wellington boots and tyres below.

The main mast stood between the two forward holds, but has toppled over and now points towards the port quarter. Near its base are the winches which were used to manoeuvre the cargo booms.

Also in this area, against the railings on both sides, are two paravanes (mine-sweeping drones) and their davits. Many divers mistake the paravanes for torpedoes, but their real use was to sever mine-mooring cables while being towed by their mother ships.

The upper deck of number two hold contains BSA motorcycles and Morris cars, while lower down you'll find Bedford trucks laden with more motorcycles. There are railway tenders on either side of the hold and, since their weight has caused damage to the deck structure, caution should be exercised when exploring the hold.

The collapsed remains of the bridge are behind number two hold. Here the decking has all but disappeared and it's possible to enter the captain's quarters through gaping holes. His comparatively undamaged bathroom, complete with toilet and bath, are a popular attraction and an interesting photographic subject.

Number three hold – packed with boxes of ammunition, mines and grenades on the upper level and bombs, shells and anti-tank mines on the lower level – is situated behind the bridge.

One of the most exciting dive options is to enter this hold, then swim underneath the bridge and deck all the way to number one hold. However, this should be attempted only by properly equipped and qualified divers led by an experienced divemaster who knows the way.

Behind the bridge lies the collapsed remains of the sheet-metal roofing which once protected this area from the tropical sun. Here you'll also find a large hole where the funnel once stood.

Nearing the stern, number four hold is where the two bombs hit the ship, triggering the explosion which all but tore the Thistlegorm in two.

All that remains of the hold is a pile of tortured metal which slopes to the sand. It's difficult to distinguish various items in the rubble and even the two Bren-gun carriers can be missed from a couple of metres away.

One of the locomotives which was blasted from the deck lies near the rubble on the port side. It's possible to explore this and the one on the starboard side (situated slightly further forward) in a single dive, but you have to be careful not to go into decompression time. Both are well worth the visit.

Finally, there is the stern section lying tilted towards the port side. The propeller and rudder are visible above the sand on the starboard side, making interesting photographic props.

Higher up, on the deck, are two fascinating relics: an anti-aircraft gun on the poop deck and a 3.5-inch gun immediately in front of it.

The sinking of the Thistlegorm was a tragedy but, by going down in shallow, diveable waters near what are now the diving centres of Hurghada and Sharm el Sheik, she is a boon for underwater adventurers. In fact, she can be reached even by day boats operating out of Sharm.

In addition, there are several other historical wrecks in the area including the easily accessible Carnatic and Dunraven. And then there are the remains of the wreck of the Jolanda at Ras Mohammed, arguably the greatest dive site in the world.

Happily, these wrecks are little more than an overnight flight away from Johannesburg and increasing numbers of South African divers are taking the plunge.

Fort Beaufort – A town built for battle
Cathy Lanz – July 1998

*Most passing travellers would give the
Eastern Cape town of Fort Beaufort a
30-second write-off. This would be an injustice,
Cathy Lanz discovered.*

A ny town that has been through four wars can be forgiven for looking like it's lost the battle. Drenched in autumn rain, Fort Beaufort looked thoroughly beaten.

The main business district was a fusion of neon signs and freight trucks. Rain fell unceasingly on bedraggled pedestrians and kerbside cabbage sellers. Down side streets once-magnificent Victorian homes dripped water gloomily from cast-iron fretwork. A shop advertising afval shared premises with a florist. There seemed to be an inordinate number of funeral parlours.

Before I'd finished parking I was accosted by a fellow brandishing an ink-smudged donation form; next came the parking attendants. To make matters worse, the museum's curator, Moose van Rensberg, had phoned the day before to say that his conference in Grahamstown had been extended and he wouldn't be able to show me round.

It was the kind of situation which makes a journalist want to head for the nearest bar and get snot-flying drunk. Only there didn't seem to be any bars – just a rusty sign to the museum. I wasn't hoping for enlightenment but rather an escape from extortionists.

At closing time I was still there, browsing through nearly two centuries of memorabilia, in a tin-roofed cottage which once served as an officers' mess. I emerged with a head full of exploration plans and entirely different feelings about Fort Beaufort. Take white settlers heading north, Xhosa pastoralists heading south and a fertile valley in between – and you've got a recipe for conflict. This conflict manifested itself in nine frontier wars starting in 1779 and spanned the next 100 years.

Fort Beaufort entered the fray in 1822, soon after the Fifth Frontier War. Named after the Duke of Beaufort, father of the governor of the Cape, Lord Charles Somerset, it was one of several strongholds built to repulse the Xhosa.

For the British, the defensible position of Fort Beaufort was ideal – built on a tongue of land surrounded on three sides by a natural moat provided by the Kat and Brak rivers.

Don't go looking for a fort named Beaufort in the town. There isn't one. There never was one. There was a Fort Boyes though, which later made way for the magistrate's court.

The original fort was a Martello tower, a cylindrical stone construction used to great effect by the English for coastal defence after the French Revolution.

The Fort Beaufort tower is one of only two in the world built further than three kilometres from the coast. And just why the British needed a Martello on the banks of the Brak is anyone's guess.

Martellos were specifically designed to withstand heavy cannon fire – something blissfully absent from all Xhosa assaults. Unsurprisingly, the cannon – which swivelled through 360 degrees on top of the tower – was never fired.

I climbed the iron stairs into the tower and was greeted by generations of human faeces and a stench to match. It's a strange human habit that defies understanding – that people will climb a precarious ladder to perch at a dangerous height on a rickety wooden floor in order to leave their mark.

Perhaps it's just a simmering continuation of the centuries-old Xhosa-colonist conflict. The Tenth Frontier War – War of the Turd. Back to the real frontier wars, the War of the Axe (or Seventh Frontier War) started right in town, a little way up the road from where I was staying at the Savoy Hotel.

In 1846 a tribesman called Tsili stole an axe from Charles Holiday's shop (now the Emgwenyeni Flats) in Durban Street. The culprit was caught and sent for trial in Grahamstown, chained to the hand of another prisoner. En route sub-chief Tola (one of paramount chief Ngqika's men) decided to rescue his subject. The prison party was attacked and Tsili was liberated by hacking off the hand of his fellow prisoner.

Demands and ultimatums were issued, ignored and, bang, there was soon a whole new war.

Over time about 2000 British troops were stationed in Fort Beaufort. Because of its strategic importance, the country's first telegraph system was established between Grahamstown and Fort Beaufort. Fort Beaufort later became the chief telegraph transmitting station for the whole Cape Colony.

Most of the old military buildings still exist, although in dubious states of repair and usage. The Infantry Barracks now has a green and blue payphone inserted into one wall. The Military Museum, housed in the old officers' quarters, has been closed for some time (a residents' committee is working to reopen it). And the old Military Hospital is now a storeroom.

Between doing duty as a hospital and storeroom, the cavernous building, with its yellowwood rafters, ceiling and floor, served as the magistrate's residence. It was here that the young Iris Vaughan penned her diary, which has become a classic of South African literature. The name of Iris's brother is still visible carved on a back wall, along with those of hospitalised soldiers. Iris's name doesn't appear. She obviously heeded her parents' warnings about writing on walls.

The Xhosa may never have penetrated Fort Beaufort's defences, but aliens had more success.

In June 1972 the town made international headlines when a local farmer spotted a UFO. He called the police who verified the sighting by taking pot shots at the strange light. It came and went over a few days, scaring the wits out of lovers who used the overlooking hill for surreptitious 'nookie'.

I learned about the alien visitation from press clippings in the bar at the Savoy Hotel. Ah, so that's why the place was called the UFO Bar and had flying saucers painted on the walls.

There's nothing alien about the Savoy (except perhaps its name). It's related in type to all those Royals and Commercials which faithfully served travellers in small towns before the B&B revolution.

The dining room was empty, the bar full. Pizza is served on Wednesday's, Friday's and Saturday's. It was Wednesday so I had pizza. My conclusion – the Savoy is a fine place for pizza and for mingling with locals. You might even find somebody who saw a UFO landing.

UFOs and military memories are not all Fort Beaufort has to offer. About 10 kilometres from town, a rural road winding through aloe-studded hills delivered me into the gates of Healdtown College.

Founded in 1853 as a Methodist mission school, Healdtown has survived financial collapse, Bantu Education and the fires of political protest to become a bastion of black education.

Nelson Mandela was a Healdtown boy. So too were Robert Sobukwe, Govan Mbeki, Ray Mhlaba and rugby board president Silas Nkanunu. Several present and past leaders of other African states were also educated at Healdtown – including one neighbouring president they're not too proud to have on the list!

Healdtown is in the throes of major restoration of the historical estate and boarding facilities. The next step is a state-of-the-art library and resource centre in the boys' hostel where Madiba spent his high school years. No prizes for guessing who it'll be named after.

Nelson Mandela, Lord Charles Somerset, Sir Benjamin D'Urban, Sir Harry Smith, road-builder Andrew Geddes Bain, painter Thomas Baines and Xhosa paramount chiefs Ngqika, Sandile and Hintsa: all prominent figures in South Africa's history; all associated in some way with an all-but-forgotten town named after a fort that never was.

I wouldn't wish a century of conflict on any town. But then again, wars do throw out the best stories.

Doubling the wintery capes
Justin Fox – August 1998

*Justin Fox takes the long way round on
a passenger berth on one of Safmarine's
container ships from Durban to Cape Town.*

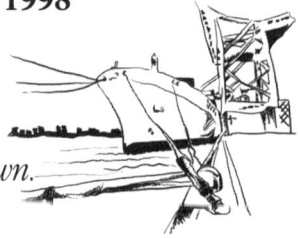

A t last.
'Gangway up!' calls the captain.

The blue of the radar screens casts the only light on the bridge.

'All clear aft,' crackles the voice on the walkie-talkie as hawsers snake onto the deck.

'Slow astern starboard.'

We ease away from the wharf. A gap of black water opens inexorably. Like a loss. Like a mountain moving, and almost as surprising. Tugs boil fore and aft, heaving at our hull. The nose comes full round, slowly.

'Stop the bow thrusters,' says our pilot.

'Slow ahead two,' calls the captain.

'Watch those trawlers at anchor. Otherwise you should be clear. Have a good voyage Bill,' says the pilot and, shaking the captain's hand, leaves the bridge.

Now we're facing the harbour mouth and the tugs release us. Squeezing a skyscraper through the eye of a needle. The screws begin to turn, lathering our stern. The deck begins to pulse like the skin of a breathing leviathan. A vessel comes alongside and our pilot waves farewell as he scuttles down the ladder onto a bucking deck. It peels away and describes a sharp turn, back into the port's safety. Soon we're free of the container port, lit up behind us like a faux city.

The red-and-white leading lights lie dead astern now, marking our way. At the fairway buoy SA Winterberg swings to starboard and into the shipping lane.

'Midships.' The call is repeated by the helmsman.

'Full ahead.'

The ship shudders, building to 21 knots. The ocean is black as pitch. At sea again. At last. I'd arrived at the entrance to Durban docks on a golden afternoon in June, bound for the Cape of Storms. Safmarine's four sister container vessels, also known as the 'big whites', have a few cabins for passengers, giving the public a chance to experience life on a 'freighter'. I'd booked passage on the SA Winterberg.

My taxi drove through a dockland maze, then along wharves lined with ships.

Coming round a hill of containers I spotted it immediately: a white giant with lines as sleek as you could wish of a working ship.

The SA Winterberg was all activity. On the wharf, cockroach-like straddle carriers manoeuvred containers into place before header blocks whisked them skyward and down onto the deck. Banging, clanging, shouting.

Purser Gordon Splinter showed me round the vessel: a lift to number four deck which housed my comfortable cabin and those of the captain and other passengers. He pointed out my lifejacket store and showed me which lifeboat to muster at.

Durban's skyline lay in a wide embrace across the water. Soot-covered men administered the movement of big cargo. Painters on a floating platform finished touching up the hull along the waterline. This is as far from a cruise ship as you can get, I mused. And why not?

Dusk fell and the dockland, lit by orange lights, took on a curious glow. A maritime twilight zone haunted by cyclopean creatures servicing the sea monster. Humans appeared dwarfed, insignificant, on the container plains.

Back on number two deck, dinner was a hearty four-course affair. I sat beside the captain. There were three other passengers: the Adams family (proud parents of the ship's young third officer) and Auntie Rose, a delightful old dame from Kalk Bay who was sailing with Safmarine for the seventeenth time. Originally from the UK, she'd come to Africa as a young woman. 'Lived through Mau Mau in Mombasa, m'dear,' she confided. This was her biannual chance to escape her landward cares. 'Ooh, I just love it at sea.' Then she turned to the captain and asked. 'Tell me, dear, how does this boat of yours float?'

Laconic Captain Bill Boddington from Bedfordshire sat at the head, running his fingers over his moustache. He talked about loading times, the run to Europe, Rotterdam versus Durban efficiency, foul weather in the Bay of Biscay. 'The big whites have only got a coupla years left,' he said. 'The technology changes so fast, particularly with the new generation of refrigerated containers starting to appear.'

I sensed the nostalgia in his voice and realised that everyone round the table was chasing some nautical dream or other. After all, ships still exude an air of romance, even working ships. Rose, it seemed, had visions of the Titanic's glamour and nursed memories of cruises with her late husband; Captain Boddington saw the sad end of the line for the big whites; Keith and Vivienne talked through dinner about how the navy's not what it used to be. And me? I carry a cargo of nautical nostalgia born of a childhood reading sea stories and mucking about in boats.

'Have we left PE yet?' asked Rose as we made ready to leave Durban.

Through the night things moved about in my cabin, waking me intermittently. At first light I emerged on deck. An egg-yolk sun grew out of the sea, dripping with albumen. The bows were seesawing into it, ploughing a wide furrow in the ocean.

The Wild Coast was a thin grey smear, growing and shrinking on the starboard beam. Cape gannets cruised the swell lines in search of breakfast.

I climbed to the bridge and had a look at the radar screens, the charts, the log-book. While snooping about I met Third Officer Yael Adams: clipper-bow nose, hazel eyes, infectious smile. She's 23, from the Cape Flats and destined to become the first Coloured captain in the fleet. Yael cut a proud, tiny figure on the bridge, her single gold stripe catching the light self-consciously.

'I did maritime studies at tech straight after school, then joined Safmarine as a cadet,' she said. 'I'd never been to sea before, but now it's my home. The ports are hectic and stressful, and there's lots of responsibility. Also too little sleep. All I ever want to do is get back to deep sea.'

'The English Channel is the most nerve-wracking. You don't know where those other captains bought their licences … and most don't speak English. I always alter course to avoid them, just to be safe.' Next morning we woke to find tugs putting final touches to our Port Elizabeth berthing. Then sci-fi insects crouched over us again, working their long mandibles.

The passengers were granted a day's shore leave, but what to do with it? The Adams's and I took a taxi to The Boardwalk for some desultory window shopping, but it felt strange not to have deck under my feet and I quickly tired of landlubber nonsense. In just two days I'd come to view the ship in possessive terms and the land as something alien, threatening even. There were still six hours of shore leave left, but I grabbed a ride back to the ship, the family. The society of the sea.

By the following morning we were off Plettenberg Bay. It was a soft, wind-free day. The sea was a Tuareg cloth – endless indigo, but high cirrus spoke of foul weather in the west. As the day wore on the ruler line that separated the blues of ocean and sky began to wobble. The sea turned gunmetal grey as a cloud bank raced to meet us, the water beneath it puckering into horses.

Rose stood at the rail, the wind ruffling her purple rinse. 'You know, I have Christmas aboard one of the white ships every year … to be with me children, the dashing sailors.'

She scanned the horizon as though looking for something. 'I packed me bags last night when the ship was tossin' about,' she confided in a stage whisper. 'Just in case we had to get in the lifeboats.' Her Titanic alter ego had found some purchase. Before going below she asked, 'Are we in PE yet, dear?'

As the first rain streaked down I ducked into the wheelhouse and looked at the chart, tracing our pencil line towards the Cape. The warnings were everywhere. 'Blinder Rocks Breaks Heavily,' 'Bulldog Reef' and 'Rocky Foul Area' lay ahead. Crayfish-trap fishing grounds to starboard, oil and gas rigs to port. The weather printout read: 'Sea – rough to very rough; swell – SW 4m.'

We eased round Africa's tip, unfazed by the ocean's mood, our bulbous bow punching into a rising swell which sent water exploding over the bows. Danger Point was lost in fog.

Late afternoon and abeam of Hangklip the horizon cleared briefly to reveal the Cape Peninsula's crags, impaled by shafts of orange sunlight. Black clouds stewed above. It breathed menace.

There! A pinprick flash. I counted them: two every 30 seconds. Cape Point light.

We rounded in the dark, taking bearings off Slangkop, then Green Point light-houses. Dead slow as SA Winterberg crept into an anchorage sown with ships and the odd irritating fishing smack cutting across our course. I noticed a big blip on the radar heading for the harbour entrance.

'You don't have permission to enter,' came the authoritative command over the radio.

'Whata you tellin' me!' wailed a voice with a thick Italian accent. 'I'm acomin' in.'

Soberly: 'This is your pilot. I told you to keep well clear until I boarded you, over.'

'But I'm aheading straight for the entrance right now! Ooaah, what musta I do?'

'Well, you've got yourself in a mess. Return to your station. Over.'

We watched on screen as the bulk carrier made a hairpin turn, perilously close to the breakwater. 'The Italians are always good for some entertainment,' said our captain, chuckling.

'Probably rushing to get to some signorina with a gap in her front teeth waiting for him at the Seaman's Embrace,' I said.

We found a spot seven cable lengths from the nearest tanker and dropped anchor. Port control had notified us of a 34-hour wait for a berth in the container dock. Cape Town was so near. The upturned saucer of Robben Island too. Tangible. Swimmable even. Yet there we lay, dancing up and down on our anchor chain, waiting. On a golden morning we aimed our boxes at the port. Table Mountain was anchored in a bed of mist, like an aircraft carrier. At any moment it might let go mooring lines and sail for Argentina.

As we entered the harbour I thought of all the evocations this Tavern of the Seas represented. How many famous ships had anchored here; how many wrecks scored these shores? Africa's turning point. Adamastor. Way-station of empire. Nostalgia brimmed: Union Castle liners, Cunard's queens, the square riggers be-fore them, and the loyal working ships of this southern ocean.

Heading for the gangway to disembark, I passed Auntie Rose. 'The sea seems much calmer now,' she said. 'So I've unpacked me bags. When do you think we'll get to PE dear?'

Brunch with Mrs Pels
Robyn Daly – September 1998

A palm-fringed island in the Okavango Delta is certainly a wild take on the deserted-island theme. At Xigera Camp Robyn Daly found the solitude and romance pleasantly interrupted.

Ⓐ tiger feather.

For the rest, the island seemed deserted. Shakes had checked carefully. So had Ishmael. A grey lourie 'kwayed' as it flew overhead, but didn't stop.

Still a deserted island. How nice, I was musing, when Ishmael broke the reverie. 'Look. Over there,' he said pointing and waving binoculars at ilala palms (*Hyphaene benguellensis*). A big bird flew out and away.

'That was a Pel's fishing owl,' said Shakes.

The one that got away. Oh well.

A loud crash of palm fronds overhead.

'Look,' said Ishmael and Shakes together, determined they would have failed as guides if I did not see this intruder.

I peered up.

A giant, ginger pussycat spread its wings and with hefty flaps launched into the air.

'Pel's,' chorused the guides.

It didn't go far – just across the bulge of our little island to land in the headdress of another ilala. I squinted through Ishmael's binoculars. A close look revealed oat-cookie plumage with dark bars on the wing feathers. All was tinged slightly green from Ishmael's tinted lenses, but the bird was recognisable as the owner of the tiger feather.

'And there's a nest,' said Ishmael, moving on a few metres and pointing at a ramshackle clump of twigs in the crook of a waterberry (*Syzigium cordatum*). He tapped the trunk. 'To attract the chicks,' I was told. Nothing. 'Must be eggs,' Ishmael added and we wandered over to the palm where the owner of the nest was still sitting, watching us with gimlet-eyed intensity.

'That's the missus,' said Shakes. Then after an adulatory pause: 'It's time to eat.'

The two guides brought out chairs and tables and laid out a fine selection of fried chicken, salads and home-baked bread and hung hammocks for the afternoon siesta that would be mandatory after all the food.

We settled down to brunch – overseen by Mrs Pels.

This business of having your own island is something you don't have to try very hard to get used to in the Okavango Delta. The waterway spreading out like Medusa's hairdo from the panhandle snakes round many exposed high points – from a termite mound to a fully colonised hump replete with palms and sausage trees. Islands you can claim for yourself. But don't, like I did, think you'll have it all to yourself. If your chosen spot is not inhabited by a Pel's fishing owl, then it's a lone dagha boy buffalo, pride of lions, a breeding herd of elephants ….

Xigera Camp (managed by Wilderness Safaris) on the southern border of the Moremi Wildlife Reserve also has its own island. It's called Paradise. But the humans have compromised a little on the deserted-island fantasy, sharing it with a family of baboons that are cheeky by day and barking-scared of predators by night.

It's a beautiful forest camp with eight luxury tents reached by raised wooden walkways and a thatched bar-cum-lounge-cum-dining area that's as sociable as one of the Delta's papyrus-fringed hippo pools.

For animals and humans alike, Paradise Island is reached by a wooden bridge connecting it to the 'mainland'. By daylight, camp staff and guests make most of the crossings; by starlight it's a different matter.

Dinner was candlelit and the table set, as it usually is, with a view of the bridge. Among the guests was a tour group of Americans comprising Dennis the guide, four men called Bob and their wives, and an 86-year-old woman who proved adept at climbing in and out of Land Rovers. Two South African couples – named more variously and originally than the Americans – filled the remaining seats. Conversation was the usual chatter about the day's game viewing punctuated with occasional reminders to those seated facing the bridge to 'keep an eye out for the leopard.'

The spotted cat didn't arrive during dinnertime, but hyenas walked back and forth as though the construction was the most natural thing in the world. On one end of the bridge was a sandpit to faithfully record the spoor of each animal that crossed in the night – a useful way for the rangers to check whether predators that had gone onto the island were still lurking there.

Of course, for the likes of hippos and elephants, the bridge wouldn't do. They drift in and out of Paradise at will. Despite elephants, baboons and hyenas regularly pestering the camp, and lion and leopard spoor occasionally in the sandpit, the staff remains humble about their game viewing. 'We're not in the main game area,'

I was warned when I first enquired. 'If you want the likes of huge herds of buffalo, they're more often found on Chief's Island. They move through here sometimes, but there are no guarantees.'

What Xigera does offer, which many Delta camps can't, is a wide choice of activities. Year round you can go boating (a full day exploring the Delta waterways by motorboat with brunch on a 'deserted' island and a snooze in a hammock is highly recommended). There are also game viewing by vehicle, bush walks and leisurely trips on a mokoro which, as one guest commented, 'is just about the most relaxing thing you can do.' Mokoro are also one of the best ways to get the full benefit of the Delta's abundant birdlife.

When it comes to the birds, the experience is nothing short of magnificent when you start ticking with a nesting pair of Pel's fishing owls. And that was just brunch.

Caves of antiquity
Don Pinnock – November 1998

For more than three million years our hominid ancestors have been living around the caves at Makapansgat. Don Pinnock went along to check the accommodation. He found bones way over his head and an address with an uncertain future.

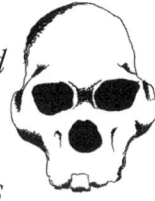

❧

'Hand axe. Banded ironstone,' pronounced Judy Maguire, flipping the rich red-brown artefact out of a Tupperware lunch box. 'Early Stone Age – about 400 000 years old. It was probably a reject; it hasn't been used.'

I picked up the glittering, 15-centimetre implement. It was a perfect teardrop, shaped and beautifully chipped to a keen edge all round, still sharp after all those years. It lay in my hand, the right weight, the right shape, utterly comfortable, undoubtedly made for a hand like mine. It seemed brand new: straight out of the corner rock shop.

We were standing below the dump at the old Makapansgat Limeworks just east of Potgietersrus. Judy zipped open a blue holdall I'd mistakenly presumed was her overnight bag, hauled out a Checkers packet and dipped her hand into it.

'Half a fossilised brain. About three and a half million years old. It's that of a child, found at Taung. Of course it's really the sediment which half filled the braincase and solidified. Professor Raymond Dart identified it in 1925. Then he found this ….'

Judy dug into another packet and produced the front of a tiny skull. It fitted perfectly over the brain. Another packet offered up the lower jaw. The even milk teeth protruded like those of a youngster in need of orthodontics, the nose area receded and there were no ape-like ridges above the eyes.

'It was unprecedented – a human-like, ape-like creature but with a brain unexpectedly large for an ape,' commented Judy, holding the skull like Hamlet and staring into its empty eye sockets. 'Dart named it *Australopithecus africanus*, southern ape of Africa. This proto-man, he said, was bipedal, cave dwelling and predatory.

'But his claim proved to be hugely controversial. He was denounced – both in public and academic circles – for daring to suggest we'd descended from apes. Detractors said he'd merely found an aberrant chimp and was over-interpreting the available evidence.

'Then Robert Broom found an adult skull at Sterkfontein – dubbed Mrs Ples – and Dart's claims were vindicated. And in 1947 James Kitching found *africanus* fossils in these dumps at the limestone mine.'

I'd phoned Judie a few weeks earlier for information about Makapansgat. 'Don't ask, come and see,' she'd replied. 'I'll go with you.'

It wasn't a chance I could pass up. Judy's part of an extraordinary geneaology of local palaeontologists who are among the finest in the world. They include such names as Broom, Dart, Tobias, Kitching, Brain, Clarke and Berger, people who have utterly changed our understanding of human evolution.

The Makapan Valley is part of a highlands system which tilted into existence when, hundreds of millions of years ago, the horizontal sediments of the Transvaal Supergroup were penetrated by a massive upwelling of igneous rock and then sagged in the middle, popping up hills on its perimeter. The northern rim of this immense soup bowl includes the Makapansgat Highlands – its southernmost rim is the Magaliesberg.

In between lies the endless-seeming Springbok Flats, parts of which would once have been marshy wetland supporting boundless animal and bird life. The highland rim also provided stepping-stones for forest plants, animals and humans to enable migration across the hot, dry surrounding plains.

Within living memory vast, lemming-like herds of springbok traversed the Flats. Samuel Cronwright, the husband of writer Olive Schreiner, described a migration in 1925: 'Over 100 miles long by 15 miles wide was covered by the trekbokken moving in an unbroken mass, giving the veld a whitish tint, as if covered by a light fall of snow.'

Time and the elements have eroded the northern edge of the sedimentary uplift. The crest of this is Black Reef quartzite; now a mist belt sheltering isolated patches of relict forest and penetrated by deep limestone caves in the underlying dolomite. The wealth of natural resources in the area, together with the availability of protection, was to be a three-million-year-old cooking pot for primate gene experimentation – a 'hominid heartland' with its history written in the rum-tumble breccia infill covering the many cave floors.

Standing in the scrubby bush in the near-deserted valley floor, it was hard to imagine this nursery of life. Three lime kilns, stoked on local hardwoods and burning day in and day out for more than 30 years, had put paid to the surrounding woodland. The trekbokken were all gone to braaivleis or biltong, the marshland had vanished, the animals had been shot out and the rivers had dried up because of climatic changes and bad farming. The silence of progress was deafening.

But the stones still sang with their memories. Behind us, row upon row of rocks had been piled into neat walls by research students and almost every piece contained fossil remains.

Judy pointed to a mountain of debris which had been removed to get to the limestone: 'It's all fossil-rich breccia.' The place was a veritable bone yard.

We climbed over the fossil dump and threaded our way into the innards of the hill, along a winding corridor of rock. It led into an immense cavern, held up in places by wood-and-cement pit props and seemingly very precarious. The miners – working from around the time of the Anglo-Boer War to the mid-1930s – had blasted out a mass of limestone, leaving a roof with heights varying from around a metre to more than 30.

Above us, embedded in what must have once been the cave floor, were fossil skulls, leg bones, teeth, blow-fly pupae and even fossilised dung balls of an ancient species of dung beetle.

The fossils of more sinister creatures have also been found there – enormous porcupines, dassies the size of large dogs and sabre-toothed cats with jawbones which could pivot downwards to an extraordinary degree to allow food to get past their huge incisors. A large number of our ancestors must have gone down their greedy gullets.

The caves were formed when rain water combined with carbon dioxide to form carbonic acid. This became progressively more acid as it passed through the surface soil and began corroding the dolomite sandwiched between harder bands of chert.

Cavities, and then vast chambers, were dissolved out of the dolomite and filled with water. But when valleys deepened the water table dropped, draining the caverns and leaving perfect habitations for all manner of creatures, including proto-humans.

Some of this dolomite contains the remains of life forms which are mind-bendingly ancient. Just outside the Historic Cave some Malmani dolomite contains stromatolites, the fossilised remains of blue-green algae which grew in a shallow sea hereabouts nearly 2500 million years ago.

From the Limeworks we threaded our way through the bush to the Cave of Hearths, so named for the discovery of ancient fire sites. The cave offers the earliest evidence of the controlled use of fire in Africa, and viewing a Stone Age hearth with the discarded remains of a meal within its blackened circle generates an eerie feeling.

The cave fill has been extensively excavated by members of the University of the Witwatersrand staff (notably archaeologist Revil Mason and his researchers) and the labels painted on the rock face go from Early Stone Age upwards to the Voortrekkers.

From there it's a short walk to the adjoining Historic Cave, or the cave of Mokopane. It was in this huge cavern, in 1854, that more than 1000 Ndebele under chief Mokopane starved to death while Boers maintained a siege at its two entrances.

What exactly started the hostilities is still subject to conflicting histories. Possible causes were the indenture by the Boers of orphaned Ndebele children as unpaid labourers (how they became orphaned is open to speculation), the killing of Chief Mokopane's brother by Boer leader Hermanus Potgieter, or a dispute over cattle.

There were also undoubtedly larger issues at stake, with the Boers appropriating the best land by force of arms, forcing labour through an inboekseling system and claiming grazing, ivory, game and skins.

Whatever the pretext, Potgieter and his hunting party were attacked and all but Potgieter were killed outright. The leader was dragged to the top of a hill and flayed alive. According to oral tradition his skin was used in rites for many years afterwards and is said to still exist.

The Ndebele then went on a killing spree, murdering men, women and children and dashing their brains out on two sturdy camelthorn trees at a place now named Moorddrift. The Boers mounted a punitive expedition and the Ndebele fled into the caves with their cattle and provisions, barricading the entrances and shooting anyone who was foolish enough to stick their head over the cave lip.

Hermanus Potgieter's nephew, Piet, died this way and his body was recovered by a brave young Paul Kruger, later to become president of the Transvaal Republic.

Attempts were made to flush out the tribe by bombarding the cave mouth with a field cannon and rolling smoking logs into the cave entrances. The Ndebele attempted to break out by stampeding their cattle, and in this way Mokopane himself escaped, lashed to the belly of an ox. There was no water in the cavern, and when the siege ended 25 days later more than a thousand Ndebele were dead.

The view from the mouth of the cave up Mokopane's Valley was spectacular. Euphorbias and acacias dominate the foreground, and at the head of the valley a towering quartzite bluff seems to hover over an ancient forest.

Was it like this when tiny A africanus skulked there with crude bone clubs more than three million years ago? Did Stone Age men prowl in the forest, or Iron Age hunters sit by the sparkling river waiting for prey?

Today the area is owned by the Potgietersrus Municipality – bought, not for its historical significance, but to ensure the town's water supply. The caves themselves, which have been declared a national monument, are curated by the University of the Witwatersrand.

But neither authority has the funds to even fence the area adequately, let alone protect the sites from ongoing vandalism. Squatters have moved into the lower end of the valley and it seems it's only a matter of time before one of the most important treasure houses of humankind – and an area of great natural beauty and heritage – is lost to browsing goats and subsistence plunder. Well, it's a valley with many histories ….

But if ever there was a place in South Africa that needs to be taken over by National Parks or declared a World Heritage Site this is it. Judy is part of a team which has been asked to plan the management of the sites and the future of the valley and its surrounds. But there's no guarantee that their recommendations will be implemented.

Standing on the valley floor again I could feel the tangible presence of the strange, compelling caves full of stories and old bones in the hillside above me – and 30-metres of bone-filled breccia told a rather disquieting tale. Humans, in their various evolving forms, killed to eat. But the Historic Cave suggested a less benign reason for bones.

Picking up Judy's beautiful hand axe and noting its deadly point, I wondered whether its maker had only food gathering in mind. Perhaps Robert Audrey, who wrote *African Genesis*, had been right when he said our propensity to kill is what made us human. On the other hand, looking at the jawbone of a sabre-toothed cat in the Bernard Price Institute's little museum at Wits University the following day, I reckoned that if the caves had been my home back then I wouldn't have let the axe out of my grasp for a moment.

Slow boat to Aswan
Justin Fox – April 1999

There are perhaps only two great journeys in life, those of birth and death. Justin Fox traced a hairline space between the living and the dead on a stretch of water as old as time itself.

ॐ

I landed in Cairo long before dawn, a city wrapped in polluted winter chill. As I climbed into my hotel bed the first muezzins began to call across the rooftops of this, the mother of all cities: 'Allahu Akbar!' (God is most great). The sound enveloped me, sending a thrill of shivers through my body. The voices dipped and wailed, swirling with the mist coming off the Nile far below my room.

I got up and stood on the balcony, watching the river muscle between skyscrapers. The call to Allah was taken up from one minaret to another until all 600 ushered in the dawn. I was swept up in the emotion of being in this ancient place of pyramids, pharaohs and 16 million Muslims rising in Ramadan prayer.

When I awoke several hours later, drugged by the sound of traffic and lack of sleep, I took the underground to the nilometer on Roda Island. Just opposite the bulrushes, where Moses was found in a basket by the pharaoh's daughter, stands a curious structure housing a stone yardstick used to gauge the level of the Nile. During the annual inundation the water level used to be measured to determine whether the valley would be fully irrigated, drought stricken or badly flooded – and so determine taxation. I spiralled down the stone staircase, cubit by cubit, to the very base where river water was originally allowed in. Since the building of the High – but ecologically disastrous – Aswan Dam in the 1960s and the termination of the flood waters, this 'well' has remained dry.

I listened for the sound of the great river, but registered only the eerie silence of the pit. This, I decided, would be the starting point of my quest. Metres away from me I could sense the awesome tonnage of water surging out of the interior: inexorable, timeless, unfathomable in its power and its weight of history. I was humbled, cowed even, in this spiritual place and resolved that in the coming days I would consign myself to Hapy, the hermaphrodite deity of the Nile in flood, and In sha' Allah (God willing) I would be blessed by the greatest of all rivers.

The plane banked round the town of Luxor and I glimpsed the fragile thread of life sandwiched between limitless Sahara sand to the west and mountainous desert to the east.

Soon I was stepping up the gangplank of the Sun Goddess, my luxurious home for the coming voyage. The senator's suite was well appointed with a lounge offering views over the bows to where the Nile unspooled before me.

Life on board, I quickly realised, was well organised; our days planned to the finest detail. We were to visit the sites in the mornings and late afternoons, while through the heat of the day the ship cruised further upstream, affording ample time to flake out on the upper deck.

In the evenings there were various forms of entertainment: belly dancing, a Nubian folk evening, the Captain's formal dinner and 'galabia night'. The latter was a raucous event in which guests dressed in traditional Arab costume (and ended up playing silly games such as mummifying each other in toilet paper and the more risqué 'pass the banana').

Lunches and dinners were at waterline and turned out to be five-course affairs. But the finest meal was an Arab barbecue on the upper deck. We cleaved upstream, trailing a line of cruise ships, and threaded a course between the quill sails of feluccas as we sampled delicious hummus and tahina (sesame seed) dips while the smell of kofta (spiced mince patties) and kebabs wafted across the deck.

Our first encounter with the genius of the ancients was on a visit to the two famous monuments of the east bank: Luxor Temple and Karnak (or Thebes, capital of the New Kingdom, as it is known in the Bible). The sheer size of the latter leaves you both spell-bound and utterly drained. Karnak's Temple of Amun is a grand succession of pylons, courts and columned halls, obelisks and colossi. Mighty stone lotus blossoms are suspended on high, soft light shines through the capitals (some still showing the colour from millennia-old paint) of the forest-like columns in the Great Hypostyle Hall, while the remains of a two-kilometre avenue of sphinxes leads from Karnak to Luxor Temple. And everywhere there was iconographic evidence of the great river, the object of my fascination: ubiquitous boat motifs in the reliefs, papyrus and palm columns, images of crocodiles and hippopotamuses.

The second day in Luxor was the 'big one' – the Theban Necropolis, arguably the greatest open-air museum on earth and testament to the ancient Egyptian's obsession with the hereafter. We crossed from the land of the living, the east bank, to the world of the dead, the realm of chaos, the desertscape on the west bank. It was here, in the Valleys of Kings and Queens, that the pharaohs, queens and noblemen were buried in lavish tombs. The cult of the dead resulted in the whole society being geared towards the hereafter, pharaohs spending their lifetimes preparing for their deaths.

The embalming took around 70 days, during which the mummies were prepared: brain and viscera removed, the cadaver dehydrated in salts then wrapped in gum-coated linen bandages. The mummies were hidden in underground warrens (such as the famous tomb of Tutankhamun) in the hills of the west bank along with all the treasures they would take into the afterlife. I was amazed – upon descending into this spectral underworld – at the vivid colours of the paintings and hieroglyphics on the walls of the tombs: so bright and, ironically, so full of life. And such imagination – three-headed snakes with feet and wings, astronomical ceilings dotted with stars, 'solar' funerary boats, sun-worshipping baboons, winged suns and ram-headed beetles.

But heaven had its downside. At every monument I was surrounded by the baksheesh hunters of the Upper Nile, those insistent salesmen who hound tourists from bus to tomb and back again: 'Miester, miester, how much you pay for my statue? I give you special price; no tourist price. Free! I give it to you for free!' But don't be fooled by these ruses. Just keep looking ahead, and keep walking.

The last mooring line snaked aboard and the vessel slipped astern on the tug of the current. Then the engines lathered the water, our bows swung into the stream and the ship shuddered into life. Southward, upriver and deeper into the heart of Pharaohic Egypt.

We coursed through an ancient world where fellahin worked the fertile 'black soil' on either side of us as they had done for millennia. The Sun Goddess glided past sugar cane and banana plantations, dom palms lining the fringes, cattle standing knee-deep and fishermen beating the water to chase fish into their nets.

There was a play of startling colours: deep blue of the Nile, viridian green of the banks and gentle light turning the desert sands to fiery gold. We were moving at exactly the speed of the prevailing northerly whose constant breath has propelled craft upriver for as long as sails have been unfurled to trap it.

The day began to wane and lilac mountains adorned the west. I looked into the thread of light marking the highway of water down which the past came flooding. I could almost see the great three-tiered, obelisk-laden barges from Aswan towed downstream by spans of rowing boats, or funerary craft bearing the pharaohs across the river to the world of the dead. In the soft Saharan sunset all seemed possible, time a strange and malleable thing.

The Sun Goddess was bound for Edfu, somewhere upstream in the gathering darkness. Here, on the upper deck, we seemed to hold both day and night in our grasp. We were the fulcrum on a giant scale of light and shadow, the realm of the living slowly tipping into darkness. There was a disco throbbing in the bowels of our ship, but no one was interested, given the majesty of this star-and-minaret-spangled night into which we slid.

We approached the locks north of Edfu after dark. There were voices from below and I could make out children in rowing boats fighting against the current, others standing up in the tossing cockle shells holding up their wares. A faint echo came up from the waterline: 'For you, miester, very special price!'

The sun goddess docked beside the famous 'dual temple' of Kom Ombo (dedicated to the worship of the falcon-headed Haroeris – the Good Doctor – and the crocodile god, Sobek). The temple watches over the first bend after a long straight stretch of Nile, a place where crocodiles once basked in great numbers on the banks. Our guide showed us where the first reptile of the inundation (harbinger crocodiles preceded the flood waters downstream) used to be let into the temple through a water gate to a well where it was starved to death, then mummified.

To port, the temple was lit up like an ancient Cape Canaveral and to starboard the sky bled to death as we slipped our mooring and stole southward. The Sahara was pressing in: we could smell its dryness, feel its implacable presence beyond the curtain of palms. It was impossibly romantic, monstrously freighted with history and unnameable emotions. No one spoke on the upper deck. Despite the fact that the crocodiles have all been exterminated, the cult has perished and the High Dam has stopped the flooding, we had all been touched by Kom Ombo and the spirit of the flood-giving crocodile god.

Docking in Aswan, the final port of our cruise, we stepped ashore to explore this languorous town. The Corniche is a delightful place to promenade in the evening, but don't miss the bazaar on Sharia al-Souk, one street back from the waterfront. In centuries past you could buy the many products of Africa there as they passed through Aswan from the south: incense, ebony artefacts, war elephants, leopard skins and beautiful Ethiopian slave girls. Today the streets are still a maze of shops with spices and perfumes issuing their 'lotus' and 'Arabian night' scent into the alleys.

In the afternoon we glided across the Nile on a felucca, circling Kitchener's Island. Camels were arriving from the desert on the west bank, loping down the slope where noblemen's tombs had been sunk deep into the cliff face. We lay, becalmed, off Elephantine Island and the sailors sniffed for the breeze as the tall lateen sail responded to occasional cat's paws.

The first cataract – just outside Aswan and an obstacle to further navigation – was the gateway to Nubia and the rest of Africa, the last outpost, the 'edge of civilisation' from where trading parties could venture into the Sahara, the Sudan, Ethiopia or beyond. From Hatshepsut to Kitchener, all expeditions started here.

On the day of my departure I decided to have tea on the terrace of the Old Cataract Hotel, famous from Agatha Christie's *Death on the Nile*. I sipped my thick, black, cardamom-flavoured ahwa (Turkish coffee) and surveyed the scene. Arabic music drifted on the breeze and feluccas tacked between the hotel and the Yebu ruins across the narrow stretch of water, scrawling their wakes like hieroglyphics on the blue parchment of the Nile. It was an ancient tableau, with Nubian houses and ruins jumbled upon rocks in the middle distance and the Aga Khan mausoleum rising on the far bank. Beyond them desert sands stretched all the way to Mauritania.

Near this spot dwelt Hapy, god of the Nile in flood, in an island cavern from whence the hermaphrodite poured the water of the mighty river from a bottomless pitcher. It is said that on Elephantine Island one used to be able to hear the 'voice of the Nile', caused by a natural whirl-hole in the rock – now silenced by the High Dam. How many tales would it tell if only its mouth could be opened again?

On a boulder opposite me I could make out inscriptions of an early nilometer – far more crude and ancient than the one in Cairo – etched into the rock near the waterline. I looked at the spot and felt a curious nostalgia: it was the end of my voyage, and this was a place that marked many endings. Never again would the cubits be ticked off by an official of the Pharaoh, eager to send the good tidings of a healthy flood by fast felucca to Thebes.

Monkey business in Uganda
Don Pinnock – April 1999

In a dark, almost impenetrable forest in southern Uganda, live huge, near-mythical creatures which remind us of ourselves. Don Pinnock followed a tangled trail to the feet of a silverback, and to some disturbing questions.

ço

Gorillas are outrageous! Nothing prepares you for meeting one on the greendripping, mosscovered, butterflied equatorial forest floor. They look up at you from their wrinkled black leather faces and it's ... it's ... well, it's extremely difficult writing about mountain gorillas. Words seem woefully unable convey the emotional impact of the experience. When one first locks onto your gaze with its beautiful, wise, hazel-brown eyes your ears ring. It's a sort of First Contact – it thwacks you in some ancient corner of your animal brain and comes out as tears. When the gorilla looks away you feel instantly lonely.

I didn't know that about gorillas until I met one, of course. What I was thinking about when I boarded Air Uganda's only plane and headed for Entebbe was people. I'm not sure when it first occurred to me that human beings might be an evolutionary mistake: probably while watching the eight o'clock news. Sure, we've taken over the place, but judgment about the path we're on really depends on whether you rate success as the ability to loot, burn and landgrab or live in harmony with earth's other life forms. If we are on the wrong track, I got to thinking: where and when did we branch off?

There's heated debate in some scientific circles about whether we stepped onto the savanna and stood up because the forests receded and the grass was high, or became a semi-aquatic, hairless, dolphin-like creature able to hold our breath because the forests flooded and stranded us on soggy islands. But, either way, we probably began the stooping march to cell phones and hamburgers in the equatorial forests of the Great Rift Valley.

We left them, conquered space and invented paper clips. But gorillas and chimpanzees stayed put, almost unnoticed by the human world until fairly recently. With logging operations and banana shambas hacking away at their ancient forest home, however, these distant cousins of ours are now under terrible threat.

Before leaving I wasn't sure if looking into their eyes would count for much, but I wanted to visit them in the wild before we turned their habitat into a coffee plantation – to somehow say sorry and to see if, maybe, it was they (and not we) that had taken the more sagacious road.

My introduction to Uganda, however, was not primates but lake flies. Around the Great Lakes they're not measured in billions but in kilotons, and form the base of those food-chain pyramids you see in biology books with humans perched at the top. From the aircraft they look like brown mist floating over the water and their swarms are so dense that people have died in their midst, unable to breathe. When you swallow them by mistake they won't go down, but seem to stick in the back of your throat.

Entebbe is notable for its international airport, the gracious Windsor Lake Victoria Hotel and monstrous Nile perch which get dragged out by locals (who think a 30-kilogram fish is not worth mentioning at the sailing club). From there we joined a reasonable tar road carrying a veritable river of taxis, little Japanese motor bikes and hurtling buses towards the equator and (for those that persevered) the Ruwenzori Mountains on the Congo border. First stop was not gorilla-type jungle but Queen Elizabeth Park to see wild chimpanzees, the sort that didn't ride round on bicycles wearing sequined fezzes.

Mweya Lodge is a magnificent place overlooking both the Kazinga Channel and Lake Edward. Hippos and warthogs keep the grass short and a nosy family of banded mongooses patrol the chalets searching for rhino beetles and lesser insects which they crunch, somewhat disgustingly, under your table or chair. But its value, for me, was its proximity to a secretive primate haven.

Chambura Gorge sneaks up on you and its appearance – a deep forested gash in the Rift Valley floor – can take your breath away. Its name means 'search and fail', an appellative it earned because of the many local people who entered it never to return. As I peered over its rim onto the top of the gallery forest below, a violet-blue Ross's turaco, perched on a towering Uganda ironwood, kkkowed in fright and took to the air, flashing brilliant red underwings. Black and white colobus monkeys, looking like little bearded men in dress shirts and tailcoats, squinted up at us from the top of the canopy, and then went on foraging.

A steep path led into the gorge and, as guide Tushabe Venantius shepherded us down, a red-eyed dove took up her usual complaint: 'Oh dear, my eyes are red. Oh dear ....' Like all other guides I spent time with in Uganda, Tushabe was absolutely first class – committed, knowledgeable and easily able to identify animals, birds or plants in both English and Latin. 'Take photographs,' he told us with a wide grin, 'but leave only footprints.'

Down at river level a troop of yellow baboons crashed across the path, trotted along some horizontal boughs and lowered themselves into the abundant undergrowth. Soon afterwards we heard the chimps.

'They're eating sabu folonda,' chuckled Tushabe. 'It's a fruit – a bit alcoholic – and it makes them talk a lot.'

The hard, tennis-ball-sized fruit thudded down almost at my feet before I realised we were beneath the band. For a moment I couldn't make out what my binoculars had focused on as I swung them upwards, then realised I was looking at the hairy backside of a huge primate perched comfortably above me scoffing bright yellow fruit.

The chimp leaned forward and peered down, looking slightly peeved, took a bite then peered again, as though he had second thoughts about the bug-eyed creature gaping up at him. It could have been my imagination, but his expressions seemed both human and understandable.

His next action was so elegant that if I wasn't glued to my binoculars I'd have applauded. He stood up, grabbed the branch he was standing on with one hand, swung under it (still holding with one hand), let go at precisely the right point in his swing to catapult himself, spread-eagled, onto a lower cluster of leaves way too thin to hold his weight. But he merely held on as the branch bent, then let go as his feet were deposited neatly on a lower bough. Then he sat down, gave me a hard look and peed loudly onto the leaf-covered forest floor. His last action left me in no doubt who the alpha male was around that neck of the woods.

As we left the gorge a large male lion broke the cover of a euphorbia thicket, bounded across some open grassland and dived down a path into the gorge we'd just vacated. Somehow I hadn't reckoned on lions, but it made me remember the place's name – Chambura, where people go but do not come back.

From Queen Elizabeth Park the tar headed east but we soon turned south into a maze of un-signposted tracks which had more in common with river beds than roads. I can't imagine how anybody not born and raised in the area can make sense of them. Side roads constantly veered off, particularly just before blind bends and it took a while to work out that they were part of an ingenious system of splitting roads round bends to prevent accidents. An unwary traveller taking one by mistake would be almost assured of a head-on collision with one of the careening vehicles which hurtled past from time to time.

'Godammit!' yelled tour guide John Addison as the umpteenth oncoming minibus refused to vacate its mid-road position. 'They think they bought the bloody road with their license!'

A bakkie, with what seemed to be an entire village on the back, roared up behind us, hooting urgently. There was no room to pass but the hooting continued until it managed to ram past on the obligatory blind rise. We looked in wonder at the massively overloaded vehicle – a moving tribute to both Toyota and mango-tree mechanics.

The villages we passed were mostly neat rows of mud houses amid seemingly endless banana fields. Many doubled as shops and sported signs such as Another Life Saloon, New Vision Off-Sales, Set-Set Hair Salon, Tender Teapot Hotel and, along a particularly nasty stretch of road, Doctor of Broken Bones.

At one small town we needed to make a pit stop and pulled in at a neat little hotel and went in search of a loo. It was a pit all right, a squat and swat which seemed to have been positioned so locals lining the veranda could watch mzungus staggering out with expressions of shock on their faces. 'There are probably so many diseases down there,' commented one of our party in his broad Scottish accent, 'they'd scare the shit out of penicillin!'

After hours of chassis-punishing lurching and banging southwards towards the northern border of Rwanda the scenery suddenly rose up ahead of us, impossibly green, and we turned down a side road (I use the term loosely) marked by an alluring sign: Bwindi Impenetrable Forest.

At Mantana tented camp we were greeted with a tray of iced lemon drinks and another of cool, rolled face-cloths with which to scrape off the dust. Birdsong filled the forest and the smell of cooking drifted up from the kitchen. From the camp we could see the undulating canopy of the brooding forest, threaded through with wraiths of mist. A tropical storm rumbled ominously in the mountains and the damp, warm air felt like the breath of a living creature. It must have taken an awful cataclysm to force our early ancestors out of such a paradise. From somewhere a phrase was downloaded into my mind: Here Be Gorillas.

There are three sub-species of gorilla: western lowland, eastern lowland and mountain gorilla. The last – *Gorilla beringei beringei* – is by far the rarest, with only around 600 in existence, and is found only in the high, afromontane rain forests around the Virunga volcanoes in Central Africa. They were 'discovered' when two were shot by a German army officer, Oscar von Beringe, on the slopes of Mount Sabinyo in 1902. Now, ironically, the sub-species bears the name of their assassin.

Their habitat, overlapping Uganda, Rwanda and the Congo Republic, is politically volatile: until recently it was a battle zone, with thousands of refugees and soldiers trampling through the forests, exposing gorillas to gunfire and human diseases (gorilla DNA is 97.7 per cent human so they're susceptible to most of our ills).

Their lowland cousins, though more numerous, are increasingly falling prey to effects of mainly European-based logging companies which cut roads into the virgin forest, and from hunters who use the roads to access their habitats. 'Bush meat' is the main source of protein for people in the region (and for the loggers) and it is estimated that some 40 000 tons of it are consumed each year in the Congo alone. Primates are part of this plunder, and around 600 gorillas and 3000 chimps a year end up in cooking pots. Given their genetic proximity to humans (chimp DNA is 98.6 per cent human) this virtually amounts to cannibalism. It's like eating your grandparents.

Situated in now-peaceful Uganda, however, Bwindi Impenetrable Forest is a safe haven. There, in relative security, the great, lazy primates wander, rest and sunbathe between bouts of eating and sleeping. Apart from the occasional luxury of ant hors d'oeuvres, gorillas are gentle vegetarians, nibbling the leaves and stripping the bark from around 58 plant varieties, then belching luxuriously as they rest their bloated stomachs in supine majesty.

After formalities with permits, and the selection of trackers, we met with our guide, Richard Magezi, at the entrance of the park. In 1991 he began the two-year task of habituating the Mubare group to human presence, and now considers them virtually part of his own family. He outlined the rules: no more than six people on the trek; nobody with illness permitted near gorillas; approach no closer than five metres; and maximum contact time one hour.

As we entered the forest a red-tailed monkey dropped from a shepherd's tree (*Boscia albitrunca*) branch in the high canopy, its tail streaming out behind like the cord of a bungi jumper. A chimp – dissecting nuts along another branch amid a flap of great blue turacos – took no notice.

A squelch of earth in a rare shaft of sunlight had attracted a crazy whirlwind of butterflies. Gaudy swallowtails, blue mother-of-pearls and brown chocolates dominated a melee of smaller white, orange, red and speckled flutterers, all competing for places to slurp the ooze with their outrageously long tongues.

The Mubare group had been spotted in the next valley the day before and we made for that point, following the machete-swinging trackers through impossible-looking tangles of branches, leaves, ferns and wicked stinging nettles. At times we were moving on packed foliage up to a metre above the forest floor.

When we arrived at the place where the gorillas had rested the previous day, I picked a half-eaten leaf and a chewed stick and tucked them into my daypack. Somehow it seemed significant to keep the leftovers of a gorilla lunch. From there the tracking began in earnest and I soon discovered the good sense of walking on your knuckles: where gorillas had passed with ease we humans slashed and cursed, got caught by vines and were smacked by overhanging boughs. In the jungle, bipedalism was bad news!

'Shh! The gorillas are here!' whispered Richard suddenly and everyone froze. I detected the movement of a dark shape ahead and stared fixedly at it. Then, glancing to my left for no particular reason, I found myself in the gentle gaze of the most thoughtful brown eyes I'd ever seen. The female gorilla was sitting like a silent, furry Buddha only a few paces from me, exuding a peacefulness which offset any possible fear I might have had in the presence of such a powerful, near-mythical creature. Then she tipped onto her knuckles and loped to the base of a giant ebony tree (*Diospyros abyssinica*), lay on her side and began fishing for termites, licking them off her fingers and grimacing comically when they bit her.

We moved a few paces and were halted by the presence of an enormous silverback. I remembered Richard's instructions if he charged: crouch down and don't make eye contact. But I couldn't drag my eyes away from him.

Beneath his huge topknot were two penetrating eyes, a shiny black leather face, enormous air-scoop nostrils and a mouth you'd have to describe as quizzical. His muscular arms reminded me of Popeye and his chest would be the envy of a Sumo wrestler, but my startled gaze was drawn to his fingers: they were the size of huge, tropical bananas. Heaven help anything that fetched a clout from a silverback! He rumbled deep in his throat, causing me to fear the worst, but then ambled off, with us skulking in his magisterial wake.

'Come quickly,' hissed Richard after a few minutes of trying to tiptoe through underbrush with the consistency of newly boiled spaghetti. We peered round a bush and there the great creature was, comfortably scratching his broad buttocks with an expression of complete contentment. Beyond him were three females, another young male, some adolescents and two babies.

A youngster – looking for all the world like a cuddle-toy – bounded towards the scratching patriarch, sat down beside him and pounded his little chest, then looked up at pop for approval. Having secured that, it leapt for a branch, hung by its feet with its arms dangling and offered us an upside-down grin.

The silverback glanced at his gawking audience with not a trace of interest – we could have been forest butterflies for all he cared – then rolled onto his giant knuckles and was gone.

Our paths had parted. But where they would ultimately lead remained an unanswered question. By the time we'd bone-lurched our way back to the howling madness of downtown Kampala, however, I had no doubts about which branch of the family tree I'd choose to be on.

Towers of the southern storms
Justin Fox – December 1999

Pursuing a fantasy of lighthouses, Justin Fox set off on a route following the great 'fire towers' from Cape Recife to the Cape of Storms along a coastline known as the 'graveyard of ships'.

Lighthouses are places of loneliness, drama and romance. People seem to respond instinctively to their allure. As a child on holiday in Simon's Town I used to stare out into False Bay and wish I was the lighthouse keeper on Roman Rock, that storm-ravaged lighthouse beyond the harbour wall. When the southeaster raged, the tower would be buffeted by huge waves. No boat could get near it and I pictured the keeper cut off from all contact with land for days at a time.

I imagined him as an old man with beard and pipe (he had to have a pipe) wearing sea boots, a sailor's cap and thick woollen fisherman's jersey. He smelt of tobacco and salt and peppered his speech with nautical terms. He had tattoos of anchors and mermaids and could tell a yarn or two about shipwrecks and gales, drownings and brave rescues.

Lighthouses symbolise hope, something steadfast in the chaos of a stormy night. They seem even to have a spiritual air: a guiding 'house of light' – almost like a place of worship – for those in peril on the sea. And the lighthouse keeper is our maritime Samaritan.

My expedition was to be a journey from Port Elizabeth to Cape Town – the co-ordinates being the major lighthouses along the way. I was most interested in visiting the elegant 19th-century edifices, the quintessential lighthouses (not the purely functional metal structures of today) and meeting some of South Africa's last maritime Samaritans.

It was early September when I arrived in a stormy Port Elizabeth, where the winter was having a last word. I headed straight for Cape Recife. As I stepped from the car, the wind took the door and nearly whipped it from its hinges. These were the conditions lighthouses were built for, I thought ruefully as I made my way across the sand-blasted beach, bent double.

The structure, built in 1851, stood squat and redoubtable in its black-and-white livery on the sand flats of Cape Recife Nature Reserve. Terns, seagulls and sandpipers were battling with the blow, either ground scurrying or struggling in spastic, feather-flailing flight. Flotsam and jetsam were slung along the high-tide line, testament to the dangers thereabouts. As if to highlight the point, a cargo ship laboured out at sea, its deck tilting exaggeratedly in the swell.

I was soon frozen to the marrow and retreated to Pine Lodge, where I'd booked a log cabin for the night. All the accommodation I had arranged for the trip fulfilled the criteria of being as close as possible to the grand old lighthouses of the Cape.

Next morning I returned to Recife and the scene was utterly transformed. The wind had died and there was a breathlessness in the air as the sun rose out of the Indian Ocean. A sea snake lay stranded by the tide, its black-and-yellow markings glinting in the sun. I was about to touch the strange flattened swimming tail when it opened its mouth – sea snakes are extremely poisonous, so I backed off.

I went to pay a call to Roland Black in his office at the light. Roland is Lighthouse Area Manager for the Eastern Cape coast and he has a passion for lighthouses. 'A life in lighthouses offers such diversity,' he enthused. 'We're forever in boats, helicopters and 4x4s inspecting remote places. It's not a job, it's more a way of life.'

We climbed to the top of the octagonal tower, all ship-shape with Oregon-pine panelling and brass fittings where Roland showed me how the beehive-shaped lantern ran on rollers (some float in a mercury bath).

'You see the light gets refracted back into the centre,' explained Roland while standing in the middle of the glass dome, 'and is concentrated by means of lenses and prisms into a strong beam. Apart from the big rotating light there's also this sector, a shaft of red light which marks the dangers of Roman Rock.'

He explained how every lighthouse has its own particular sequence of flashes to identify it from other lighthouses (a sailor simply has to look up the sequence on a chart to determine where he is). The foghorns – or nautophones, as electrically operated horns are called – also have their own sequence of blasts, or 'character', to identify them. In addition, many lighthouses have transmitters which send out a specific coded radio signal. The structures also have different shapes and are sometimes painted in distinct patterns so as to be easily identified from far out at sea.

'Recife has these big black-and-white horizontal stripes to distinguish it from the sand-dunes behind,' said Roland. 'Seal Point is all white, which stands out against the dark fynbos.'

That afternoon I took the N2 to Humansdorp and arrived at Seal Point's Cape St Francis Lighthouse (1878) where I introduced myself to Eddie Crafford, the senior lighthouse keeper.

'It gets stormy here, I can tell you,' said Eddie. 'Just a few months ago a trawler went aground on the rocks and all the crew were drowned. This is the only part of the coast where just one kilometre from the shore you have 100 metres depth. I've seen an eight-metre swell coming in here. It's an awesome sight.'

Cape St Francis is the tallest masonry lighthouse in the country and the spiral staircase up which I panted is actually within the thick stone wall. The view from the top was magnificent, with the craggy cape below and rows of breakers passing from right to left, the nearest peeling into white where surfers carved the faces.

The twilight drained away and waves hammered the rocks, creating a din to wake Neptune. The globe came on, sending a shaft of light into the dusk where a flotilla of trawlers sea-sawed on the swell. A thin mist hung above the breakers, giving the beams an eerie purchase. The air was spring-crisp, clear after the previous day's big blow. A dog barked and the vygies closed their faces.

After a night in a cosy thatched chalet at Cape St Francis Resort I sped west, not stopping at the playgrounds of Plett and Knysna, for lighthouses were my primary goal.

Hendrik Swart kept a tight ship at Mossel Bay's Cape St Blaize (1864). It was all white-washed stone and painted timber and reminded me of a spit-and-polish navy training unit. The maintenance of a lighthouse requires dedication, and keepers have to be handymen, seeing to chipping and painting, dealing with chronic rust and of course making sure the lens is clean and the lamp's mechanism functioning.

I climbed the bluff behind the light where dassies watched my stumbling progress, a touching concern for my safety etched on their faces. Whole mountain ranges of water were throwing themselves at the cape and an icy wind shivered the fynbos. An orange sun left a few rinds on the western horizon to wither. The westerly was building and soon began to howl, tearing streaks off the breakers.

As I sat on the cliff I remembered a dark night 12 years ago when a lookout on our replica caravel (re-enacting the 15th-century voyage of Bartolomeu Dias from Lisbon to Mossel Bay) spotted the light at St Blaize. We had been living aboard the cramped vessel – 14 of us in one cabin – for six months. The light of St Blaize, a powerful stab in the night, marked the end of thousands of miles of slow tacking down the Atlantic. We sailed towards the flash, our hearts brimming with the euphoria of landfall. It was 3 February, the festival day of St Blaize, after whom Dias named the place.

When the beam came on I escaped the wind and climbed the tower's ladders to the droning lamp. The beautiful, blinding, turning thing held me enthralled. Part clock, part lens, part Cyclops, it was all glass and brass with a compass rose on the ceiling attached to a weather vane above. The beams wheeled through the darkness, great swirling spokes of light. They seemed to make an ethereal humming noise – the low swish of an arcing blade.

That evening I sipped a glass of port on the sofa in Huijs te Marquette Guesthouse from where I could watch the lighthouse. The stormy night thickened and congealed round the headland, but the pale beams kept up their pulse. And I thought of the first Mossel Bay shipwreck, a Portuguese vessel run aground on the rocks below St Blaize on a night probably just like this back in 1504. What would the captain have given for a guiding light?

Driving westward the next morning my Golf sped past the horror of Mossgas and a Langeberg range dusted with snow. I turned south at a sign pointing to the tip of Africa. The land grew flatter and the cattle fatter as I neared Agulhas. But the landscape seemed a distraction. There was something bigger going on out there: the drama of the end of a continent and the grappling of mighty ocean currents.

At Struisbaai wooden fishing boats were preparing to go to sea. For their crews the lighthouses of the southern Cape were a matter of life and death, I thought, as a stubby vessel nosed into the swell.

Agulhas boasts an excellent museum with descriptions of the optical systems, mechanisms and construction of lighthouses. There's also a big driebeenpotjie that was used to boil sheep's tails to produce fat for fuelling the lamp.

Within the 30-mile range of Agulhas light the coast is fringed with dangerous reefs on which more ships have been wrecked than on any other part of the South African coast. The following impassioned plea for a lighthouse came from a farmer in the district:

'I have been painfully called upon to witness ship after ship cast away, valuable cargoes strewed along the beach, and hundreds of human beings at a time washed up dead upon the shore. There was the Arniston on 30 May 1815, a total wreck with no less than 372 bodies of men, women and children washed up, their corpses torn and partly devoured by preying vultures. Had a lighthouse been near, this incident would probably not have happened.'

The limestone lighthouse at Agulhas was finally completed in 1849, built in the style of the Pharos in Alexandria – one of the seven wonders of the ancient world. That greatest and tallest lighthouse of all was erected in 279 BC. Built of white marble it stood more than 125 metres high. On the summit was a statue of Poseidon where log fires burned perpetually, producing a warning light at night and smoke by day (the Afrikaans word for lighthouse, vuurtoring – literally 'fire tower' – more accurately describes early lighthouses).

Exploring the shore it didn't take me long to find the first shipwreck, a Taiwanese trawler – the Meisho Maru – lodged between rocks and being pummelled by

waves. At Agulhas Guesthouse that evening, owner Phil Fenwick entertained me
with tales of another disaster at sea, the sinking of the passenger liner Oceanos. He
was one of the helicopter pilots of 15 Squadron involved in rescuing the crew and
passengers from the heaving deck in a 12-metre swell and 35-knot wind.

My route led via Die Dam towards Gansbaai. I glimpsed the lattice-structure of
Quoin Point Light on the road to Buffeljagsrivier, then trundled into Pearly Beach
where the sand lived up to the name and half a dozen whales breached for joy in
a green sea.

At Danger Point (1895) I met Mervyn White, a charismatic keeper who came
close to my childhood conception of this strange breed of men. He was a headstrong loner with a devotion to his calling and a love of the sea.

'Except for Bird Island, I've worked every lighthouse on the Southern African
coast from Swakopmund to St Lucia,' said Mervyn. 'This is one of my favourites.
It's my home, you know, and I treat is as such.'

Arguably Southern Africa's most famous wreck lies just 1.5 kilometres off
Danger Point and a plaque at the lighthouse commemorates the bravery of those
soldiers and sailors who stood to attention on a tilting deck as women and children
rowed ashore. HMS Birkenhead lives on in the annals of naval history as the first
time the command 'women and children first' was issued.

The loss of the Birkenhead in 1852 prompted renewed calls for a lighthouse at
Danger Point, but it was only after another 22 ships had run aground there that
it was finally built. The coast is dotted with hundreds of graves, drowned victims
having been buried where they washed ashore.

From the tower the Cape of Good Hope and Hangklip peninsulas looked like
islands, perfectly water-coloured in grey silhouette on the horizon. Behind them
a massive cold front was brewing. 'If you're going to Cape Point tomorrow, you're
in for one hell of a storm,' warned Mervyn as I headed for my refuge in Kleinbaai,
the Marine Guesthouse.

From the Cape Point Nature Reserve entrance I drove to the famous claw of rock
through horizontal rain. Mervyn was right: it was going to be an ugly night at the
Cape of Storms. As I struggled down the path towards the lighthouse, I remembered
what I'd read about its construction. The first light was built in 1860 (today it's used
as a control tower), but was too high and often shrouded in fog. That's why a light
closer to the waterline was constructed in 1919. It's South Africa's strongest lamp,
emitting a beam of 10 million candle power with a range of 35 miles.

I negotiated the slippery aluminium ladders down the cliff past a once top-
secret Second World War radar station, now in ruins. Up in the control tower

the keeper on duty – this is the only lighthouse which is manned round the clock – was watching me through his binoculars. These men have to be hawk-eyed, and nothing escapes them. I sneezed and imagined him noting diligently in the logbook: 'Journalist sneezing, bearing SE at one knot over boulders (foolish). Barometer falling fast.'

It was almost sunset and the tourists had left. Enormous waves broke against the rocks below my perch and sheets of rain streaked across the ocean. Just then the sun broke free of the clouds and transformed the rocky cliff into an ingot of gold. That moment of sublime light in the gathering storm was one of the most beautiful things I have ever seen.

Soon all was doused and the elements mauling Cape Point sent me scurrying up the steps to the control tower, a UFO-like 'saucer' with an eerie red light. Duty keeper Deon de Jager showed me on screen the telemetry system which monitors all the lighthouses in the Western Cape. The tower seemed like the bridge of a ship with its log books and weather divining apparatuses. From there shipping is closely watched and meteorological data gathered every three hours, to be relayed to Cape Town International Airport.

Drenched and shivering, I finally retreated to the keeper's cottage. After a hot shower I settled down to read about the passenger liner Lusitania which struck Bellows Rock just south of the point in 1911. It was the sinking of the liner in particular that prompted the construction of the lower light at Cape Point. On the fateful night the keeper ran down the cliff to Maclear Beach where his waving of a lantern warned the lifeboats carrying 774 passengers and crew away from the broiling surf. Notwithstanding his efforts to direct them round the point into the calmer waters of False Bay, two boats attempted to make the landing and capsized, resulting in the loss of many lives.

Next morning I drove up the Peninsula to Slangkop (1919) near Kommetjie. It's constructed of cast-iron segments and at 33 metres it's the tallest lighthouse in the country.

'I'm getting amazing readings from a wave-recorder buoy six nautical miles south-west of here,' said keeper Peter Dennett. 'The swell is currently 10 metres!'

But there wasn't time to dawdle as I could scent the end of my quest. Arriving at Green Point in the late afternoon, my lighthouse route was complete. The building's red-and-white diagonal stripes (which make it stand out as a day mark from the surrounding buildings) glowed in the soft light that shone like a benediction after the storm.

I stood on the lawn in front of the Egyptian-style structure with the Atlantic crashing below and thought of the early days of navigation in these waters. As far back as 1656 Jan van Riebeeck established signal fires to warn ships of dangers in Table Bay, but it was not until 1824 that a solidly constructed lighthouse was erected at Green Point. Today it's considered the 'home' of lighthouses, a fitting place to end my tour of Africa's southern lights.

Travelling the trails of !Xam
Don Pinnock – December 1999

In hundreds of caves and overhangs in the Drakensberg are paintings by the !Xam – the mysterious Southern San. But as Don Pinnock discovered, it takes a 4x4 and a good deal of shoe rubber to find them.

❧

It was a matter which could have been cleared up by a single conversation. But few settlers realise they owe it to history not to shoot first and ask questions afterwards ....

I sat gnawing at the problems caused by the short-sightedness of my ancestors, staring rather sadly at an extraordinary scene. A charging lion, about half a metre long, its whiskers bristling and its teeth bared, was painted on the cave wall with the definite strokes of a master artist.

Ahead of the beast, seeming to flee with great leaping steps, was a row of San hunters. Above them floated little red boxes which resolved, Escher style, into flying figures with antelope heads. These spiralled up the domed roof and into a circular indentation at its highest point.

The small cave I'd ducked into was an almost perfect dome, some two metres at its highest point and maybe five in diameter at its base. We'd found it atop a boulder-strewn hill behind a gracious stone farmhouse in a valley named Balloch, part of an area in the Southern Drakensberg known, rather oddly, as Wartrail.

The tableaux before us was dream-like, vivid, teasing cognition but inexplicable. The cave itself had a strange, alien presence and I found myself glancing out of the opening expecting someone else to arrive. But no one did – the !Xam had long gone: hunted down, shot, starved or frozen to death in their mountain hideaways.

At the turn of the century the historian George McCall Theal, with typical Victorian arrogance, had put the matter quite plainly. Bushmen, he said – using a name which was to be much contested later – "were of no benefit to any other section of the human family. They were incapable of improvement, and as it was impossible for civilised men to live on the same soil with them, it was for the world's good that they should make room for a higher race" ... (presumably his own).

More recent historians would call the events which Theal supported by a more uncomfortable name: genocide. The San were forced to make way, and sitting there

I realised there was nobody on earth who could now tell me with certainty what the painting on the cave wall meant. There are theories – books full of them – but San rock art still awaits its Rosetta Stone.

Some months earlier I'd phoned Susan Tonkin of Wild Cape Ventures in Ugie to ask if she could suggest a route that would take in San art sites of the Southern Drakensberg.

'It's possible,' she chuckled. 'But you'll need a 4x4 and some good hiking boots. They can be wild mountains.'

So September found me thrumming my way through Queenstown and Dordrecht to Ugie in a beefy Colt Rodeo double cab, wondering if I was in for baking heat or ice: these bergs can lay down ski-depth snow on Christmas day and fry you in July.

Ugie was balmy, with little white clouds giving no hint of snowstorms. I picked up Susan (we'd soon rename her Su San) and her forester friend Gordon McKenzie and headed up to Woodcliffe where Phill Sephton owns a farm so outrageously beautiful it hardly seemed real. Beyond the lawns of her self-catering cottage massive, muscular sandstone cliffs rose almost vertically out of the river and continued doing so up the valley until they lost themselves in the purple stickleback of towering Drakensberg basalt.

Next morning we followed the river upstream, past fields where rare crowned cranes gathered, then skirted valleys of indigenous riverine forest boasting Outeniqua and real yellowwoods (*Podocarpus* spp.), white stinkwoods (*Celtis* spp.), cheesewoods (*Pittosporum viridiflorum*), horsewoods (*Clausena anisata*) and Cape quince trees (*Cryptocarya woodii*) among many others.

The first cave offered a beautifully drawn cheetah, the second a single baboon. Then we trekked out of the river bed and onto a ridge overlooking Wide Valley with a splendid view of the high Berg. In a most unexpected place Phyll pointed out a rain-animal painting that looked to me like a nasty tempered moray eel. Near it was the first of many 'therianthropic' figures we were to see – humans in the process of transforming themselves into animals. Around it were masses of dots and lines known as entoptics: patterns seen in a trance state.

It doesn't take much stamping round San caves to realise their paintings weren't 'art in the park'. Frankly, they're weird. In the absence of a San shaman to explain them, the next best interpreter is Professor David Lewis-Williams of Wits University's Rock Art Unit.

In 1990 he published a useful little book entitled Discovering Southern African Rock Art, which was followed by the much more weighty Images of Power then

Fragile Heritage. Most of the images, he suggests, were painted by shamans recreating their own spiritual experiences, and he has collected a mountain of evidence to support this view.

For the San, it appears, there were two worlds, that of the camp and surrounding wild creatures, and that of the world associated with the supernatural and with strange creatures – a place of the gods from which power could be drawn. Between them were what could best be described as portals: certain shimmering water holes and cracks, or special surfaces in quartzitic rock – doorways between the two worlds.

The intermediaries between these worlds were shamans who, through trance-inducing dance rituals, could 'die' in this world and travel through portals into the spirit realm, seeking the power to heal, make predictions or bring rain.

From dances witnessed among living Bushmen, and from the perilously few records available, it seems that entering a trance could be painful, causing the shaman to double over and bleed from the nose. Often they would take on a therianthropic form, 'becoming' an animal, generally an eland. Often these creatures would be bleeding from their noses. What they experienced they painted: trail maps to other worlds.

All that's an educated guess, of course. We can't know for sure.

By the time we returned to Woodcliffe cottage we'd covered some 13 steep kilometres – a tough start to a week in the mountains.

Next morning we pointed the Colt's nose towards the picturesque village of Rhodes. First, though, we dropped in on !Kaggen's Cave and its fading herd of eland, then round the contour to Outlook Cave. Sitting there, doing what the name implied, a deep, healing stillness seemed to enfold us as we stared across at the emerald foothills of the ever-present Drakensberg. The next site, Storybook Cave, had two metre-high therianthropes – one pointing authoritatively at a crack in the rock from which an eland emerged – and a two-tailed cat.

It was about that time I realised that San rock art was not so much about pictures but about place. The caves and overhangs were rather like theatre proscenium arches marked 'entry', surrounded by elaborate scripts on how to enter and about what to do beyond the portals.

This trip was becoming a tour of the doorways to San heaven. But where on earth were the keys?

The drive which followed up Naude's Nek Pass was one of those which people buy 4x4s to experience, though we got up with only the back wheels churning. One false move and we'd have become a panelbeater's nightmare. Once over the top the vehicle was invaded by the delicious aroma of blossoming thickets of ouhoud (*Leucosidia sericia*) which seemed to grow everywhere.

Rhodes is one of those villages which time forgot before newness became a fashion. Nestled in a valley of the Drakensberg foothills, its houses have deep verandas, steep corrugated-iron roofs and sagging wire fences.

We zigzagged down the wide dirt streets, bemused by the almost overabundance of rustic charm, then pulled into Walkerbouts Inn. It's owned by Dave Walker – self-proclaimed mayor and Mr Trout – and isn't short of rustic or charm.

The bar counter was made of solid cedar and the fish tank had recently been vacated by some trout because it had sprung a leak. They languished with a platanna in the rather cramped quarters of a cooler bag with a bubble machine attached.

Dave's a large, easy going host who came to Rhodes because of trout. He organises fly fishing trips, runs the inn and fires up a mean pizza. Up the road is the ski lodge Tiffindell, but he's quite glad the favoured road to it bypasses the village.

'The yuppies go up there in their fancy 4x4s. Here we get interesting travellers and sheep farmers. Good people.'

Just outside Rhodes the next day Vasie Murray – farm owner and some-time film-set animal handler – took us up a valley which loomed in on the road and made each corner seem sinister. Desolate beauty might be a bit of a cliché but it's the only phrase which seemed to fit.

Martin's Dell Cave, high up one of the valley sides, had eland paintings so highly coloured they looked as if their long-gone painters touched them up annually. Above one was a white bird doing a high-speed dive into the back of a staggering grey eland.

In another cave, once filled with art, a farmer, who had used it as a shearing shed, painted the walls with whitewash to improve the light. In cultural terms it simply extended the gloom.

Nearby Willem Naude of Buttermead Farm – a man with a passion for rock art – showed us a cave with a painting of what has come to be called the lightning bird. It was connected to the bleeding nose of an eland by a zigzag line, possibly representing supernatural potency. If these little artists were primitive they certainly used sophisticated metaphors.

A mountain buttress and many kilometres later we followed the directions of Alan Isted to Bidstone Guest Farm which is run by his parents. His mum, Di, cooked up a fine meal and we sat clutching beers and discussing the idiot weather.

Alan's a snowboarding man and was chafing at the bit. It was hot when it ought to be snowing: global warming, undoubtedly, we agreed. In a few months time he'd be off to the Himalayas for the real stuff.

Alan's knowledge of rock-art sites is considerable – he's been hunting them down much of his life. The first place he took us to was Warwick's Cave at Balloch – the domed cave of the lion chase. The second required some serious walking through high-mountain canyons to Brummer Cave.

By this stage it might have been the daily hiking, the bizarre paintings or continuously hunkering down in places of power, but the trip was getting increasingly surreal. Brummer's Cave would blow me away completely.

The place was as large as a big concert hall, with a view over the Kraai River Valley, and was simply full of polychrome elands. They were drawn with such clarity and understanding of tone they seemed three-dimensional. Between them were busy human forms, curled snakes and other, odder creatures.

The paintings were perfectly preserved, possibly because they're so deep inside and far from weather and water erosion, but also because they were on two levels, both protected from cattle and sheep which obviously use the cave. And they're certainly way off the tourist map.

The looming buttresses beyond the vast cave mouth and the valley far below offered no hint of human life, but behind me the walls vibrated with evidence that this was once a San equivalent of France's Lascaux, and possibly far older. The presence of the little hunters was so strong, the silence which enveloped us seemed a gossamer portal away from their clicking chatter.

These Drakensberg foothills had been home to the San for countless centuries, some moving with the seasons and others settling permanently in great caves such as this one.

When the Nguni cattle herders appeared a thousand or so years ago the San simply moved to higher ground and – because they were so few, had no cattle and posed no threat – they were left in peace.

But from 1837 Dutch farmers, moving away from the British rule, trekked into Natal and before long were in conflict with black pastoralists.

After the defeat of the Zulus at the Battle of Blood River, settlement in the region increased. Wild game was quickly depleted and the San, deprived of their food source, raided livestock. Farmers retaliated with a vengeance, shooting San 'pests' on sight. (When Britain took over Natal, English settlers simply kept up the tradition.)

While the Natal Volksraad hadn't exactly specified extermination, the instructions were so broadly worded that discretion in that matter was left to the local kommandant. Thousands of San died. With a total estimated population of around 20 000 for the whole of South Africa, the effect of the virtual open hunting season on the San was devastating.

The final demise of the southern San is chillingly depicted by historian Nigel Penn: 'In the desolate obscurity of the 19th-century agterveld, the San were overcome by a piece-meal process of betrayal and defeat. By the 1870s the last remnants of the Cape San were being hunted to extinction. Those who were not shot were starved to death in the dusty margins of South Africa's most marginal land ….'

That sad history seemed oddly out of step with the elegant images behind me and the breathless beauty rolling in from the yawning cave mouth. I guess a conscience is what hurts when everything else feels so good ….

We left the cave reluctantly, and as we crested the valley a howling gale stopped us in our tracks. Driving wind saps the spirit, which may have explained why we arrived back at our vehicle feeling rather flat and disgruntled. Or had we disturbed something ancient?

From Wartrail we drove through the historic but unattractive town of Aliwal North and decided to push on to overnight at its aesthetic opposite: Burgersdorp.

After a fine meal and a comfortable night's rest at The Nook B&B in the care of Anita Joubert, I took a dawn stroll to investigate the Anglo-Boer War blockhouse. Along the way I had the unusual pleasure of being simultaneously crowed at by a rooster and barked at by a crow in someone's garden. When a tough-looking Staffy came up, yapping to get in on the act, the obviously tame crow beat him up and sent him packing.

The rock art trail would end some days later at Greenvale Cave in Dordrecht, a thousand kilometres from where it began. The cave has a strangely lyrical 'flute player' and some freakish nightmare creatures. But, in a sense, my personal quest for the spirit of the San ended in a canyon near Burgersdorp so remote that even the Colt seemed nervous – and so full of exquisite paintings it should immediately be declared a national monument and a World Heritage Site.

Known locally as the Valley of Art, it spans the farms of AC de Klerk and Ouboet Coetzee. They're well aware of its importance and are dedicated to its preservation. But sheep farming has fallen on hard times and there's no guarantee their properties will remain in sympathetic hands. Many farms in the area have been abandoned to weather – and probably the Land Bank – and are sliding into ruin.

Even at the dry end of a particularly dry season, golden-hued streams ran through reed beds and slid into deep pools cradled between towering cliffs of orange and black sandstone.

Almost every overhang seemed to be an art gallery teeming with images of profound sophistication. In one a group of hippos clustered in near-photographic perfection. In the Cave of Birth, amid a welter of polychrome antelope, therianthropes and unintelligible symbols and dots, was the drawing of a woman which was so graphic it must rate as one of humankind's earliest pornographic works. In Rainmaker's Cave strange, bloated creatures loomed while busy little figures towed them magically to bring an end to the dry months of winter.

But it was in the Cave of Dogs that I stared, dumbstruck, into the joyous soul of a departed people. Possibly because it's south facing and on less-friable rock, the images have been preserved down to the feather-strokes in the head-dress of a dancing shaman.

The wall was alive with hundreds of figures – here a hunting group with dogs, there a family group on the move, the men with bows and spears, the women cloaked with karosses, supply sacks thrown across their shoulders and digging sticks in their hands. Tall figures with antelope heads strode beside bent, old people leaning heavily on sticks. Marching with the throng were sheep (the San kept sheep?), prancing elands and packs of loping hounds. Three of the dogs were no longer than a centimetre each, but so perfectly drawn that you could feel the joy of their gambolling.

This is how almost all the caves we'd seen must once have looked. What were they telling us? The figures were all walking, running, striding across the huge tableaux: all moving. But to where? Whatever destination they had in mind, the real answer was terrible: to oblivion.

As I stood, staring in wonder, my eyes filled with tears of shame at what had been done to their culture. When some kommandant pumped a bullet into the breast of the last San artist, he would not have known that he'd murdered Africa's equivalent of Leanardo da Vinci or Renoir. Would he have cared?

How much richer the world would have been if, instead, they had stood side by side before one of the great panels while the artist interpreted his images ….

But they didn't, and the meaning of San art remains tantalisingly just out of reach. That makes it so intriguing, but also ineffably sad, like a dream you knew would change your life but which you forgot on waking.

History documents so many misunderstandings, but so few meaningful conversations.

Into the sands of silence
Don Pinnock – October 2000

*In the silent sand ergs of Central Sahara is some rock
art which raises profound questions about African prehistory.
Don Pinnock took a long, hot road to find them.*

☙

No bird greeted the dawn. There was not a leaf to shimmer in the slanting rays,
no breeze to blow it, no insect to chirr, no sound at all. As the yellow light
probed between sun-blackened, time-sculpted rocks of the Akakus Mountains it
set the peach-pink sand aglow. When I adjusted my position a small rivulet of sand
skidded down the dune face, hissing loudly in my silence-shocked ears.

If you placed your finger on a map of Africa midway between the coasts of
Libya and Nigeria, Mauritania and Eritrea, you'd be pointing to the spot where I
awaited the sun: right in the middle of the Sahara. It was a very strange place to be.
It was an even stranger place to begin a hunt for giraffe, ibex and elephant. And
Bushmen. But the camels were well rested and when I returned to camp after my
dawn gawking, the Tuareg guides had breakfast simmering. It would soon be time
to travel and, hopefully, begin to unravel a thread in the history of Africa's most
mysterious people.

The Sahara had not always been this empty. Some 6000 years ago – a mere
yesterday in geological time – a growing body of research suggests that it was
savanna fed by long, meandering rivers. Petrified forest vegetation has been
unearthed. In the Murzuq Sand Sea of south-western Libya the bones of crocs,
hippos, elephants and antelope have been found.

Until the great desiccation of North Africa, caused by seasonal shifts still only
partly understood, giraffes munched on acacia trees along now long-dead rivers.
And in rock overhangs Neolithic artists ground pigments and painted trance
dances, ceremonies and the animals that they hunted and revered. The oldest
bones yet discovered in the Sahara belonged not to Negroid or Arab people but,
astoundingly, to the oldest of all African inhabitants, Bushmen.

You don't have to have a reason to travel to Central Sahara, just a touch of
madness. Simply to be there is reason enough. But the possibility that the art was
of Neolithic San origin was intriguing. Also, the months I had available to travel

coincided with the northern spring. As both rock art and spring in the Sahara seemed equally incongruous, the trip had been irresistible.

Three months earlier all this had seemed impossible. The United Nations embargo on flights to Libya had only recently been lifted and tourism in that country was embryonic. Visas weren't exactly a problem, they just took time and had to be okayed by officials in Tripoli.

The first plane booking had to be cancelled because the visas hadn't arrived. Finally we touched down in Libya, but being Ramadan all flights out were booked up for a month. To get out we'd have to trek to Tunisia and fly from Tunis. Colleague Robyn Daly and I had flown up the Nile to Istanbul, then over a snow-cloaked Mount Olympus to Tripoli. The omens appeared auspicious.

Tripoli, Libya's capital, was founded by the Phoenicians, fell to the Nubians, was built to magnificence by the Romans (who named it Oea), sacked by the Vandals, invaded by Arabs, fell to the Turks and then the Italians – well, you get the picture.

Leaving it was a relief. It has an atmospheric old quarter, some really tasteless newer effigies and insane traffic. It's hectically urban. Less than 100 kilometres south, though, was the unsettling, but exciting, presence of the desert.

We set the odometer of the Kia minibus to zero and headed for Gadames. The air was sharp and the shimmering dome of the sky matched the blue of my backpack. Some 70 kilometres south of the coast the terrain changed to flat scrub desert, relieved occasionally by hardy fig and gum trees.

'Camel grazing,' commented our guide, Sherif Shebani of Coast and Desert Tours. 'Nothing much else out here.'

At first the mountains seemed unreal, a mirage balancing on the arrow point of the road ahead. But they gradually resolved into the Western Mountains, Jabal Nafusah, a chain which begins as the Atlas Mountains in Morocco and stretches clear across Algeria, ending in the sea as the ancient Roman city of Leptis Magna, east of Tripoli.

These craggy, mesa-like massifs, rising nearly a kilometre into the sky, are an escarpment which seems to dam the great sand sea. Along this range – forced there by Arab invasions which spread westwards from Egypt some 1300 years ago and hedged in by the southern desert – are the Berber people.

We hair-pinned up Jabal Nafusah below the town of Nalut and under the glowering stare of what seemed to be a castle. It turned out to be a 14th-century grain warehouse and olive press. Looking like the life works of a giant mud wasp, the place was a bewildering warren of grain 'cells' stacked all atop each other and accessed by now-crumbling stairs and ledges. Holes and ducts kept the bins cool.

Nalut is a Berber town, perched on the lip of the crumbling escarpment like cubist flotsam on the shore of a gravel sea. Some 30 kilometres south of the town the first dunes appeared – innocent mounds of rilled orange sand. As we rolled ever southwards wraiths of sand began to drift across the road, like fingers testing the hot tarmac surface. They were fed by peach-coloured dunes which had munched up the last of the scrub.

The camels, when they appeared, seemed entirely appropriate. We stopped, spellbound, as about 150 of the strange, complaining creatures streamed past, the slanting sun flaring silvery auras off their shaggy coats.

Their Tuareg herdsman shook my hand then touched his chest.

'Salaam aleikom.'

'Alaekum salaam,' I replied.

His face was the colour of the dunes and his eyes seemed to bore through mine to some ancient part of my brain. I sat, watching his departing back, not a little shaken by the contact.

Instead of the anticipated dunes, though, we rolled out onto a great gravel desert, varnished to an eerie sheen by wind-blown sand and stretching as far as the eye could see. To the west lay Tunisia and Algeria, to the east the trackless nothing of Tarabulus.

We are so accustomed to human ownership and use of the planet's surface that hundreds upon hundreds of kilometres of virtually untouched emptiness evokes a strange lightness of heart. Like the Antarctic, the Sahara is one of the greatest wilderness areas on earth. Its sheer hostility has preserved it for the very few who know and respect its ways.

Beyond a tatty little oasis, named Derje, darkness wrapped us in introspection. We'd been travelling almost dead straight for hundreds of kilometres.

'There are huge dunes here,' Sherif commented. But all we saw along the tunnel of headlights was the occasional moth and a fleet-footed white jeboa, reminding us that even out here life still maintained a tenuous hold.

After the desolation of the desert the guesthouse in Gadames, Villa Otman Hashaishe, was a delight – a small restaurant nearby provided a fine meal, the shower was hot and the beds comfortable. I got a sense of what an oasis must feel like to a traveller after weeks on caravan.

Gadames is described as the Jewel of the Desert and its heart is an artesian well which has provided water for thousands of years. The old part of the town – recently vacated, and being restored by Unesco – is an ingenious system of cool tunnels through a warren of multiple-storied houses and mosques.

Our guide, Mohamed Ali Kredn, was born in the old quarter and led us round unerringly. Without him we'd have been hopelessly lost inside a minute.

We left Gadames before sunrise under a full orange moon. The lights of the town soon disappeared and the dunes, rising and falling in the moonlight, looked like mid-ocean rollers. Dawn arrived quite suddenly in the moisture-leeched air. A glow on the horizon, then a ripple of bright gold which jiggled and formed into an enormous ball of fire dead ahead. The moon, like a pale lady afraid of the heat, slipped below the opposite horizon and was gone.

The day offered a sight both bleak and thrilling. The dunes had receded and we were crossing the Al Hamadah, a gravel desert so featureless that a molehill would have been an object worth studying. In every direction was a sort of biological and zoological nihilism, with the horizon as a near-straight line marked only by a colour change between earth and sky.

The arrow-straight road, silvered by the rising sun, seemed to leak the sky into a widening flow around us and swallowed it back up behind our humming vehicle. The day's goal: 1100 kilometres of absolute nothing. The boredom which this kind of road induces is an almost tangible thing. Your mind goes numb before the great emptiness, recoils upon itself and very soon begins to work in dream mode.

At an oasis named Ash Shwayti the road veered south towards Sabha, the largest town in southern Libya. Brave bushes – strung like green pearls along dry wadis – were a welcome relief from the smashed-rock landscape and occasional black, volcanic hill. Future colonists destined for Mars could spend time in these wastelands getting themselves acclimatised.

I first noticed the trucks when one sped past us loaded with onions and smelling delicious. Others followed carrying wheat, maize and watermelons, all heading out of the wasteland towards the coast. Then came the fields of Sabha and the out-of-place zik-zik of water sprinklers. The town wasn't the dusty desert place I'd expected: the streets were lined with trees and hedges, prosperity was obvious and we pulled in to a smart restaurant for hamburgers, kebabs and fruit nectar.

From Sabha the road snaked along a wide valley with a harsh, high range of mesas to the south and the edge of the massive Azzallaf Erg (sand sea) to the north. But, for more than 200 kilometres, the valley floor was covered with gardens and dotted with water towers, pines, palm and casuarinas. There was no place for this green abundance in my Sahara stereotype.

We turned into Africa Camp at Ubari 13 hours after leaving Gadames. It's an attractive little tented camp with a restaurant at the foot of pink dunes which stretched from east to west as far as I could see.

As night fell I trekked over a dune at least 100 metres high and settled on the powder-soft sand to await the moon. A large owl glided past. The silence was profound, and if I had any travel tension it soon leaked away into the sand. Perhaps I sat there an hour, maybe two. Forty days and 40 nights would have been just fine.

106

From Ubari we headed west along the foot of mesak (mesa) mountains. The dunes receded and we were once again on a sand sea. As we neared Al Awaynat the desert turned from lemon to slate. Dunes occasionally appeared on the horizon then drifted out of sight. In all that expanse there was nothing but pebbles, gravel and sand. When your eyes beg for variation it's surprising how many colours you can pick out of this stark geography.

We swapped the Kia for a Toyota Land Cruiser in Al Awaynat and headed dead south, following tracks towards the Akakus Mountains. The sun was low and when the foothills appeared they seemed forest covered. But it was an illusion – out there was nothing but black rock and yellow sand.

Without road signs, obvious features or even tracks, the only way I can explain how we found the Tuareg camel men is to say that our Toyota driver was also Targui. The desert men were camped in a sandy depression among crazy-shaped boulders. Their camels were hob-tied but looked placid and – if a camel has the capacity – happy.

Raia Abdul Alrhman Embarak greeted us courteously, shaking hands and touching his breast with the proffered hand. He was a desert-wizened man with clear, smiling eyes above his ever-present litham veil. But under his cloak you sensed steel. A fire was going and we were soon eating sand-baked bread and delicious Tuareg soup.

'Camels,' said Raia between mouthfuls, 'are my life.' His people have dominated Central Sahara for centuries as raiders and caravan riders and they are still the desert's greatest fighters – true knights of the great sand ergs. As a youngster Raia had crossed from Ghat in Libya to Niger with a caravan of dates. These days he does camel business in the Akakus, carrying archaeologists and occasional tourists.

Next morning he brought the camels down on their chests ready to ride. I swung my leg over the camel's back, nearly impaling my calf on the spiked saddle. Raia yelled something at me and Sherif translated: 'He says grab the hair on the camel's hump behind you or you'll break your teeth on the pommel when it gets up.'

I made a grab as the beast came up, backside first, and then gave a shove with its front knees. This threw me backwards as the camel came aloft. The saddle spikes, I figured, must be a way of getting rid of non-Targui.

We set off for the deep crags and valleys of Akakus. After several hours of travelling we turned up a wide wadi which led directly into the mountains. High walls of sandstone closed in as we lumbered up a virtual sand highway. The surrounding crags had the look of hammered sea cliffs. Wind-driven sand and time had transformed cracks and fissures into yawning caves, arches and canyons.

We finally dismounted near an overhang and gaped in wonder. The wall was covered in rock art. Here were giraffes, elephants, antelopes and people. In some scenes men with bows and arrows with hunting dogs pursued walah ibex, in others women braided hair or clapped their hands. Further up the valley was a trance dance conducted by foot-stamping and Bushman-like half-human half-animal therianthropes. On the floor were tiny arrow heads. Had they once carried poison? At another site was a huge, perfectly-proportioned elephant, and at still another were more recent drawings of camels and even Garamantine chariots.

Who had painted these pictures? And when? The questions hung in the silence of the desert unanswered. We do not yet know for sure. Their style, though, was recognisable. I'd seen it in many caves and overhangs at the southern end of the continent.

It would be incorrect to say that the trip back to the coast was an anticlimax. We went by a different route and saw other places: the desolate oasis of Brak, the flower-filled Berber town of Ghariyan, the ancient Roman city of Sabratah ….

By degrees the healing silences of the sand ergs was replaced by the bump and chatter of life. But back in the silent valleys of Akakus questions remained. Had the Bushmen once been masters of all Africa? Was it they who had crossed the land bridge into Europe? Are we all their descendants? The evidence would need more work to be conclusive. But it was compelling.

One thing is for sure, if some of the rock art in those mountain galleries is San, they were certainly great travellers.

Paddling back in time
Don Pinnock – December 2000

The Kowie River has a mouth full of many smart houses, wrecked ships and some wistful dreams. But, as Don Pinnock discovered, there are older and wilder things up around the bend.

For some reason the word DANGER surrounded by a red triangle seemed to mark the boundary between the bonhomie of the boets and swaers of Port Alfred and the heart of darkness. The rain-bruised clouds added to the impression.

Maybe the mid-river sign was merely marking a hidden reef. But its presence had the same unsettling effect that 'Here There Be Monsters' must have had on ancient mariners studying their hard-won maps. Some 180 years ago, when an ancestor of mine set sail for these shores, there were still maps carrying that warning. I eyed the danger sign, wondering about its portent, and paddled on.

Until that morning there had been others happy to kayak up the Kowie River with me. But the day had dawned wet and blustery. They quickly reversed their offers: 'No way! Not in this weather …' and went back to bed. So my trip up the river and into my own history would be alone.

In a sense, it was a trip with two beginnings. One had to do with a large motorbike, the other with a sailing ship on a far distant shore.

When I picked up the Kawasaki Vulcan from Yaron Wizman at Mitaka Motorcycles he looked worried. 'Spray lube on the chain at every petrol stop,' he advised. 'Check the oil and water. Watch out, it's fast.' Maybe I didn't look the motorcycling type.

He was right about fast. But, snaking along the foot of the Overberg in a light drizzle, the rain hammering on my helmet screen with a sound like chips frying, speed wasn't an advantage. The weather was probably only marginally better than in Wiltshire.

Wiltshire, an English county, was the site of the other beginning. Probably in just such a drizzle, a man with my surname sat in a village in the English county and decided he'd had enough of the gloom, lousy pay and a declining demand for swineherds. So he packed his family into a crowded immigrant ship in 1820 and headed for Africa.

Maybe he didn't read the small print – maybe there wasn't any – but conditions in the Eastern Cape, where they landed, were less than hospitable. The veld was bitter, there were animals which ate you, and the Xhosa were understandably angry at the sudden invasion of pale, plough-toting abelungus.

It didn't rain for two years. Then a flood took out the crops. My forebear gave up farming and moved to Grahamstown, where he bought an oxwagon and did transport riding. Every year, for generations – right up until my father's childhood – the family would trundle down to the Kowie in the wagon and outspan along the river banks. From time to time the men would brave the monsters upriver at Waters Meeting where they'd hunt for the pot.

These days Waters Meeting is a nature reserve and the best way to get there is by kayak. Conditions there are still, well, settler simple. There's a hut, a water tank and some bunk beds. All about are wild hills where afromontane forest meets subtropical valley bushveld amid symphonies of birdsong. Going there would have all the elements of pilgrimage.

In Port Alfred, when it finally appeared from under the clouds, I found Bev Young, a larger-than-life, Harley biker, Hells-Angel mama who works in the town's information office and organises everything.

'Hey, Don, you arrived in one piece?' she yelled as I staggered through the door after countless hours in the saddle. 'I must show you the crayfish. Did you know Port Alfred was ringed with game farms? This place will soon be the new Mpumalanga. And there's no malaria. I love this place. Would you like some tea?'

Half an hour later I'd been on a head-spinning verbal tour of the little port: historic houses, fishing, the endless beaches, great surfing, some juicy gossip, 43 Air School, the new marina, freshwater crayfish … and cold tea (she forgot to switch on the kettle).

'Oh gosh, I'm sorry,' she chuckled, 'perhaps you'd better check in to the Halyards and have a bath or something.'

I did, then went to explore.

Port Alfred has two elemental features which stand out above all the rest: its beaches and the estuary. I hitched a ride with environmental officer Anton Gouws doing beach patrol up to Three Sisters rocks. The beach must have been half a kilometre wide and the only tracks on the sand belonged to seagulls. The sounds that curled around us as we switched off the engine were their cries and the endless growl of waves. The rocks, sculpted by the hammering sea, looked like three giant chocolate layer cakes at the wrong end of a toddler's party.

The tidal estuary has another kind of beauty but has been the victim of men's dreams of fame and fortune. The dreaming began with William Cock, who arrived there from Britain in 1836. He built a house on the west bank (it's still there and known as Cock's Castle). Two years later he began diverting flow at the river mouth in an attempt to make it accessible to sailing ships. He managed this task and had a pier built, then went into denial as ship after ship was wrecked crossing the treacherous sand bar at the river mouth.

The port eventually attracted sailing craft – as old photos in the museum attest – but when steam replaced sail the harbour proved too shallow to take the iron ships. It now serves only ski boats and doughty surfers who leap off the pier into the raging surf.

More recently a marina was built on Cock's reclaimed land. It's an elegant place with fine houses, but I couldn't help feeling the river would one day spit out the constriction in its mouth and turn the estuary back into the delta it once was. It'd make a mess of all those beautiful gardens.

The upriver reaches, when I went exploring on the bike, were compelling, even though the weather map showed 40 per cent chance of rain with snow on the mountains. Anyway, venturing out in lousy weather ensures you have the world mostly to yourself. As long as you stay warm and dry, it's a traveller's bonus. Waters Meeting – where I'd spend the night – and the spirit of my ancestors were calling.

Spirits of another sort had called a man named Derek who I met on the way back into town. He was pushing a huge, box-like contraption on bicycle wheels. It had a propeller on front and messages from Jesus all over it. He'd just bullied it all the way from East London a few hundred kilometres away.

'We are a forgotten people,' he told me happily, 'but I preach and the Lord keeps the propeller turning.'

Back at the Halyards I consulted Andrew Hutchinson of Hutch's Boats. He took pity on me and offered to tow my kayak up to the caravan park. It wasn't something I was about to refuse, especially as the rain was pelting down just then. I took the hopeful view – by the time the tide began its upriver push, all 40 per cent of the rain should have fallen. I thought some dark thoughts about my sleeping ex-fellow kayakers and hopped aboard.

Along the way we picked up a food basket from Butler's Riverside Restaurant. It looked way over the top, but I was in a hurry and stashed the boxes into the kayak's storage compartments.

We puttered past the wreck of an old paddle steamer and through the Bay of Biscay (so named because the wind howls across it). At the caravan park Hutch cast me loose. Soon there was nothing but the lapping of water and the liquid piping of a black-headed oriole.

With some help from the paddles, the kayak rode the tidal surge past Cob Hole and I was soon at the ruin of an old mill.

'Would you like some frogs?' asked a man who was standing near it with a face to match the crumbling stonework.

'No thanks.'

'But you need frogs,' he insisted.

'Why?' I yelled back.

'Because fish love to eat them ….'

'But I'm not fishing!'

'Well you should,' he threw back, and then disappeared into the forest.

Soon after that rather surreal exchange the red danger triangle came into view. At a place named Fairy Glen the river turned westwards, narrowed suddenly, and became more confidential. Riverine forest dominated by tree euphorbias covered the enclosing hills and, as I turned the bend, a pied kingfisher hovered invitingly. 'Kwik kwik' it insisted.

Beyond a sharp northward bend the river straightened. Several kilometres ahead was a towering wall of forested hillside. The valley rang with the cry of fish eagles.

At a spectacular 360-degree oxbow named Horseshoe Bend was a jetty and a sign which read 'Waters Meeting Overnight Hut.' Joseph Conrad would have loved its mysterious invitation into the looming forest. Soon after hauling my gear and food boxes inside, the rest of the predicted 40 per cent of rain descended. I dragged a rough table onto the stoep and unpacked the food.

The contents were so outrageous it was comical: lobster, prawns, meat balls, samoosas, Portuguese rolls with sausages buried inside, fish fingers, cheese, biscuits, apples, bananas, a chocolate cake, a flask of carrot soup, another of hot chocolate, and a bottle of Guardian Peak Cabernet Sauvignon with corkscrew, wine glass and checked table cloth.

Among the goodies was a note which read: 'Learn to pause or nothing worthwhile will catch up to you.' Was I being spoilt or was this regular Butler's fare? I spread the packages on the cloth, uncorked the wine and tucked in.

A jackal nickered then yipped, fireflies sparkled in the bush and the silence was made somehow deeper by the admonitions of a purple-crested lourie. A small, brown form glided down the path: could it have been the rare barred owl?

Raising my glass, I peered through the ruby wine at the gathering dusk. Just what was the spirit of my ancestors? Would I feel it? Would it manifest? Should I invoke it? It seemed a bit childish to call out: 'Hey, spirits of my ancestors, I'm here.' But there was nobody around so I did it anyway.

Moments later a strange moaning began and I felt the hairs on the back of my neck bristling. What happened next nearly undid me. Round the corner, at speed, came a large male chacma baboon. On seeing me a few metres away he let loose a deafening 'baa-hooo' and skidded to a halt. At that moment all the hadedas roosting around about went 'haa-dee-da' together and I found myself standing on the table with the only weapon available – the corkscrew.

The baboon bounded off, the birds quietened down and in the absolute silence that followed I could hear my heart thumping like a tom-tom.

The rest of the night was quiet and the only visitor was a wily, large-spotted civet, which arrived to polish off the rest of my prawns. Dawn was glorious, with rays of golden sunlight levering the remains of yesterday's clouds out of the way. I packed up and set off downriver on a falling tide.

With three hours of paddling ahead, I had time for reflection. It struck me that I should, at least, consign to print this message to my descendants and anyone else who may be interested: Beware of invoking the spirit of your ancestors. You never know in what form it may appear.

Jonathan Livingston Gannet
Justin Fox – September 2001

An ageing Cape gannet living on Bird Island in Lambert's Bay on the West Coast looks back on a lifetime of flying, fishing ... and broken dreams. This is the story of Jonathan Livingston Gannet, as told to Justin Fox.

M y name is Jonathan, but my friends call me Jonnie Witvlerk. I've lived on Bird Island all my life. There are thousands of us here, living lekker close to each other. Nice and cosy. Sure there are fights, but mostly we get along like a nest on fire. The other birds keep clear of us gannets. We don't believe in apartheid or anything. It's just that birds of a feather they ... you know what I mean. The penguins are total poephols and stick to themselves over by the dolosse. The gulls are just wannabe gannets and the cormorants are shit scared of us.

I'm getting a bit long in the bill now ... not many flying years left in these old bones. I'm a widower, and last year I lost my only son, so I've had my share. But, hell, we've had some jols here on the island and the other gannets have been good to me.

Ja, I've seen a lot in my day. I remember the oil spills, the incredible red tide when the crayfish crawled onto the beaches, the attacks by cats and water mongooses. I remember how my cousin gannets in Namibia suffered when fishermen cleaned out the pilchard stocks. Why can't people stick to crayfish and diamonds? Ag humans, don't get me started on humans. They're worse than seals.

I was born in January 1976 here in Lambert's Bay. My parents told me I was a ravenous little klong (youngster), constantly demanding more anchovies, eating them out of nest and home. But I was a quick learner. As a fledgling I fell in love with flying. I used to waddle off to the edge of the colony to try out my hop-flying.

At first I was scared of the runways where the adults galloped into flight, so I'd walk to the shore and practice in the water. But when my fledgling friends started getting taken by those blerrie fur seals, I quickly sorted out my running takeoff. It goes like this: first you've got to let the other birds know you're heading for the runway, not trying to mess with their nests. So you point your bill into the air, you know, to show that you're going 'up'. It's called sky-pointing, for obvious reasons. Then you make your way through the colony. Some of the birds still give you kak, peck at you and stuff, so it's best to move quickly.

Once I'd sorted out my running takeoff, I worked on the tricky, stall-and-plop-down landing. Before long I was teaching myself how to fish. There's nothing that gives me greater pleasure than the hunt. I used to hang a little sign on my nest saying 'gone fishing' and disappear for weeks at a time.

This is how it works. I fly along at about 20 metres above the sea, scanning the dark water below. When I spot a fish that looks fat and juicy I hover, my whole body quivering with anticipation. Hey, excuse me if I wax a bit poetical … fishing gives me such a rush. Then I dive! A split second before crashing into the sea I stretch, swing my wings back and enter the water like an arrow. I take my prey either on my way down or up, swallowing it even before I resurface. Sometimes I plunge 10 metres down into that icy depth to spear a saury.

As a youth I used to hunt alone, but these days I love to fish with the others. It's so lekker when we spot a shoal and the whole flock rains down in a shower of splashing and feasting. It's like a dance, like all the birds are langvlerking together.

Once I'd mastered fishing I grew restless, wanting to learn more. The other birds said I was bedonderd (crazy), that our purpose in life was only to fish and bear offspring. But I became obsessed with flying – higher, faster, further.

I began practicing on my own and the others turned their backs on me, would have nothing to do with me. But I was on a mission: suiping the witblits of pure speed. From 300 metres, flapping my wings as hard as I could, I'd power into a steep dive towards the ocean, and soon learned why gannets don't make such dives. In just six seconds I'd be moving at 120 kilometres an hour and my wings grew unstable on the upstroke. Each time I tried to go faster a strange, hollow voice sounded in me: 'Jonnie Witvlerk, you are a gannet. If you were meant to fly like that, you'd have falcon's short wings and live on mice instead of fish. You must fly home to the colony and be content as you are. Get a wife, have an egg, settle down.'

Eventually I gave up. I won't say there haven't been regrets. Maybe if I'd climbed higher, maybe if I'd folded in most of my wing and flown on just the tips alone … maybe I'd have reached 200 kays an hour, possibly even terminal velocity! It doesn't bear thinking about. I came back to the flock and that's that. I'm just a Weskus (West Coast) klong anyway, not some pretentious seagull from Sea Point pumped on energy food filched from the Virgin Active health club or something. Who was I trying to kid?

So I returned, apologised to the groot gannet for my waywardness, and was accepted back. It was about that time that I first set eyes on Gasiena. Ag, her plumage was so silky, her snow-white lyfie (body) so attractive, the prettiest pair of wings you ever did see and a head as gold as the setting sun. Ooh, I was so lus, I could have, you know, had her, right there and then.

She used to stroll round the edge of the colony with the other meide, so I knew she was available. But of course I had to go through the whole elaborate courting process. First I had to woo her with endless calling, head shaking and bowing (tiresome). 'Liewe Gasiena, sal jy vanaand met my kom doedoe?' (Lovely Gasiena, will you sleep with me tonight) I brayed.

Eventually she responded, approaching with her head tilted upwards, for all the world as if she didn't notice me. Soon we were into furious courting (bill fencing) – twining our necks and clapping our beaks together.

In no time we were building a home together, a comfy cone-shaped nest we could call our own, made from guano, feathers and bones. Gasiena laid in August. It was a lovely egg, as blue as the shallows in the harbour.

Despite being from the Weskus, I'm quite an enlightened bird and got involved in the nest-husband thing. I even helped incubate, wrapping my warm foot webs gently round the little one. You know, keep the missus happy.

Gatiep hatched in October. The feisty little bugger was already shouting for food while still in the egg. He was black, naked and blind, but Gasiena said he was adorable and who was I to argue?

I had no idea bringing up a chick was such hard work. Gatiep constantly demanded sustenance. One of us stayed with him while the other went foraging, returning to throw up anchovies directly into his mouth. At one point I was so overwhelmed by my insatiable son, that I fled to one of the bachelor clubs on the fringe of the colony where I could talk fishing and roost a bit in peace.

Then Gatiep began to fledge. Man, I was proud of his first flight. We were a happy family and had one blissful season together.

But then tragedy struck. While in the water trying to clean guano off her body, Gasiena was taken by an ugly brute of a seal. I didn't know how to cope without her. Then last year Gatiep, who inherited my roaming genes, ventured too far south, beyond even our sister colony on Malgas Island near Saldanha. He was fishing near the sinking Treasure, and landed on the oil slick. I never saw him again. Ag, humans. We heard of his fate from a Robben Island penguin, who told one of our penguins – seaweed telegraph, you know.

I've never really recovered from that double blow. I'll live out my days here on the island, fishing, flying, shooting the breeze with the older gannets. But I don't have many seasons left and these winters get so cold.

Hey, there's a man with a camera and a cap with 'Getaway' written on it. Maybe he should bloody get away, bloody human. I think I'll go kak on his head – a lekker, big, wet, fishy one.

Splat!

Dhow dreaming
Justin Fox – December 2001

*What better way to reach the ancient Swahili port of
Lamu than sailing there with the monsoon by
dhow? Justin Fox flew to Mombasa, Kenya, to see if it could be done.*

The tangerine moon has gone behind a bank of clouds. There's the feeble beam of the lighthouse, but without chart or compass it's not much help. Errant fishermen have stolen the solar panels from the leading lights that once marked this treacherous entrance. Low spring tide and less than a fathom's depth over the sandbanks. We've been soaked all day and I'm shivering uncontrollably. Surf roars on both port and starboard bows. My five Swahili sailing companions are silent. The lateen sail flogs as they try to spill wind and get their bearings.

I look astern and see a dark shadow which, to my horror, suddenly turns white with a crash. Next thing the dhow is in the white water and we're surfing. If we broach now, Fayswal will capsize. The dhow slews hard over to starboard as we come off the wave, taking a torrent of water over the leeward rail.

Next thing we're into the calm of Lamu Channel and the lads break lustily into a Swahili shanty that lifts the hair on the back of my neck. Ahead of us we can make out the lights of the ancient port that has been our grail. By the grace of Allah we've done it.

Mr Hussain rocked back on his chair and looked out of the window to where a freighter and two sahala dhows were moored against the quay.

'So, Mr Justin, you want to sail to Lamu … on a dhow,' he said thoughtfully.

Mr Hussain is Mombasa's dhow registrar and was my last hope. For years I'd had the dream of sailing Africa's east coast on a traditional jahazi dhow. I would visit the ports and islands that marked the millennium-old route used by Persian, Swahili, Arab and Indian sailors – links in the chain of the slave, gold, ivory and spice trade. Phone calls from South Africa had produced no leads.

And here was Mr Hussain shaking his head. 'The great dhow trade across the Indian Ocean died out 25 years ago. These days there are very few coastal dhows operating out of Mombasa. But let me see what I can do.'

A man with kofia cap and walking stick was dispatched to snoop around the harbour and see whether anyone was prepared, for a small fee, to take the nostalgic mzungu to Lamu.

There was a model of a big jahazi on the shelf in Mr Hussain's office – he too had a soft spot for the age of Indian Ocean sail. From his bottom drawer he hauled out photographs of a Mombasa packed with trading booms from the Gulf. The stench of dried shark being off-loaded from the Somali freighter was a vestige of that complex network of commerce that encompassed most of the Indian Ocean rim. It had spawned a great maritime culture in Africa (the Swahili) and spread a religion (Islam) southward through its waters as far as Mozambique.

Eventually the old man returned with news. Mr Hussain looked angry and spoke fast in Swahili. Then he turned to me: 'The verdict is not good. There are no sailing boats available, only motor dhows, and no one wants to go as far as Lamu, or even Malindi. We found one fisherman who is prepared to take you to Kilifi, where you could try to find another boat.'

'But Kilifi is only three hours north of here,' I complained. 'Oh well, I guess it's my only option. How much does he want? I've budgeted US$200 for the whole voyage and this is only a quarter of the distance.'

'Actually, he wants US$500,' said Mr Hussain apologetically.

'But that's ridiculous!' I spluttered. 'I could fly to London and back for that. It's daylight robbery.'

I felt miserable as I dribbled a stone up the street towards the old dhow anchorage, past Vasco da Gama kiosk and Schmuck Laden Curios (no doubt heavily patronised by American tourists). A red banner was strung across the street: 'Liverpool FC'. I passed the redoubtable Fort Jesus where Islam and Christianity had butted heads over the centuries.

I reached the anchorage down crumbling steps. Piles of burning plastic issued acrid smoke. Cats and crows picked through the filth on the beach. A load of rubbish was tipped from the bluff above and avalanched past me. A man in his underpants stepped from a hori (sailing dinghy) bearing a few undersize fish. I imagined a fleet of ghost ships packing the anchorage, an offing studded with sails, and felt the loss acutely. All that was now shrunk to a few leaky ngalawas (outrigger canoes) and horis with sails made from plastic bags and sack cloth. It was a sad place. My dream of a dhow to Lamu looked about ready for the rubbish heap.

By my reckoning the matatu (mini-bus taxi) was full. It would be a three-hour drive to Malindi and, what with 12 passengers and all our luggage, the thing was bursting. Wrong. By the time we left Malindi there were 21 people on board. I think that bears repeating: 21. It was survival-of-the-fittest seating arrangements and I just hoped the driver's inscription to Allah would see us safely to our destination. I had a portly gentleman on my lap … and my luggage on top of him. In front of me sat a woman in buibui with only her eyes showing. Her daughter – a beautiful Swahili baby – stared at me transfixed. I blinked and she blinked. I stuck out my tongue and she stuck out her tongue. This was splendid entertainment. I was just starting to imagine … you know … sort of having one of those one day, when I pulled a face that was obviously not to her liking. The screaming started, then the vomiting, then the smell.

Let's just say I've seldom craved a destination so wholeheartedly. However the arrival, when I was eventually ejected onto Malindi beachfront, did not bring immediate salvation. I'd been given the name of a Mr Yussuf, who might be able to help. Six hours later he appeared with a fisherman in tow. 'Mr Justin, this is Yunus,' said Mr Yussuf while shaking my hand. 'For US$120 he will take you all the way to Lamu.'

Yunus Aboud was squint and carried a foot-long dagger. His band of sailors in khanzus (white robes) – straight from mosque – made four threatening figures in the shadows. To be quite honest I'd been worried about this moment all along. I thought of slavers, pirates, the quick throat slit and plop of a body overboard.

'Meet us on the beach at sunrise tomorrow,' said Yunus. We shook hands. I could not see his eyes.

I woke long before dawn in a flea-bag doss house beside the mosque. The call to Mecca broke into my sleep like a wave. At first I cursed the tinny voice, but then those words without meaning began to course over me. I found myself listening eagerly for the incantation of 'Allahu Akbar' (God is most great), even mouthing the pantheistic dogma myself. Indian Ocean matins.

I was down on the beach before the sun. My bags were stowed in smelly fish drums amidships. The yard was hoisted and lateen sail unfurled to much bravado and whooping. Fayswal was a sleek-looking thoroughbred and we were soon creaming along, sailing tingi (wind on the beam) northward. 'Ours is the number one dhow,' said Yunus. 'We win the Malindi dhow races every year.'

Past the sandbanks we were into a big, rolling swell and taking water over the bows. Shekh, our deck hand, was set to work bailing between the ribs. I looked astern and saw the Vasco da Gama pillar on a headland marking the entrance to the bay. Suddenly I remembered that it was in Malindi that the Portuguese mariner had found a willing pilot to show him the way across the ocean to India, marking the start of round-Africa trade with Asia. and half a millennium of European colonialism. The Portuguese cross had gained ascendancy over the Muslim sickle moon. I too had found my Malindi pilot.

The day wore on and, once the ice had broken, we were chatting amiably. Talk turned to politics and I found their opinions to be perceptive, their support for America's actions in the wake of 9/11 qualified.

The helmsman steered with his foot, the crew trimmed the lateen and Yunus set his lures. Soon he'd fought, and hauled in, two barracudas which where bludgeoned with a belaying pin as they came aboard. Kijoka sharpened two big-bladed knives – scrape-scrape – and I chuckled at my earlier throat-slitting imaginings. The barracuda was gutted and a make-shift stove erected on the deck in the shape of a wheel rim filled with sand and piled with sticks doused in paraffin and lit. A pot was placed precariously on the flames and soon we had barracuda on the boil. Kijoka butchered a pawpaw with a few quick strokes and handed me a piece. I rinsed off the fish blood and ate.

Surf crumbled over coral on our port side as we raced past Ras Ngomeni and the mouth of the Tana River. At sunset Fayswal passed Ziwayu Rocks, a haunt where fishermen often lie to for the night, but I cajoled Yunus into pushing on for our destination in the dark.

After a nerve-jangling entry into the Lamu roadstead we sailed up the calm waters of the channel on a dead run. Yunus and I leant on the bowsprit and regarded the moon. 'They say people have landed there,' he ventured.

I concurred.

'Americans,' he said disapprovingly.

'Yes,' I said, laughing. 'Bloody Americans.'

He wanted to know details: how long it takes, what sort of rockets, and do they aim straight at the moon (given that the earth is moving) or do they fly parabolically, like we did to beat the current on our way to Lamu? My knowledge was sketchy and I was unable to offer much. Bloody Americans.

Ensconced in a waterfront B&B I spent the ensuing days exploring Lamu town: fine, 18th-century Swahili houses with intricately carved doors; the old Omani-style fort; a museum crammed with models of dhows (including the mtepe, or sewn boat, which plied the Indian Ocean before the advent of nails); and narrow back streets where fat men rode donkeys with John Wayne panache, their feet only centimetres from the ground. It's an enchanting town with boats tied up to cannons, children leaping into the water from the jetty and men playing bao or mending sails and nets.

I also made other, shorter voyages on local dhows. There was a cruise round Lamu to the village of Matondoni where vessels are still built and repaired in the traditional manner. As we left port my captain lit up a huge bhangy (joint) and passed it round to his crew. I took the helm and within minutes my shipmates were reduced to giggling wrecks. They sang and drummed on the deck and seemed

120

incapable of even the most basic sail trimming. It was a wonderful few hours at the helm – sheeting in for the lulls, freeing off in the puffs, skirting the sandbanks and hugging the mangroves to avoid the meat of the tide. My companions laughed themselves to sleep on the thwarts and ballast sandbags.

On another occasion I joined a group of Dutch travellers for a voyage to Takwa ruins on nearby Manda Island. This dhow's crew were infected by the rasta spirit. They sprouted dreadlocks, sported reggae T-shirts and spoke in lyrics from Bob Marley songs … 'one love' and 'Jah will provide'.

Takwa is an ancient Swahili town tucked at the head of a mangrove creek. It's one of the many ruins that bear testimony to the phases of civilization – spawned largely by transoceanic trade – that have thrived in this archipelago. By the time we'd done the ruins we were all chanting down Babylon.

One morning, coming down to breakfast at Kijani House, my home on Lamu, we heard of the first strikes on Afghanistan. There was tension around the American guests, as though one of them had peed in their bed. Outside on the wall the graffiti read: 'USA is big terrorism'.

But the atmosphere on the streets was decidedly benign. In the evenings I sat in a side street with a crowd, just out of mosque, watching CNN at a hole-in-the-wall kiosk. Owner Ali plonked me in a sofa up front and their hospitality could not have been warmer. Once a youth spotted the infidel and chanted, 'Osama, Osama', a few times, but the others laughed at him. That was the full extent of the animosity. I felt privileged to be at Ali's alley kiosk, in the heart of Muslim Africa, during such momentous times. How simple it was on screen and how complicated in this corner of the Indian Ocean.

Back on the waterfront on the brink of departure, I came upon Fayswal at anchor. Yunus and the lads were back from a fishing expedition to Paté Island, and making ready for the return leg to Malindi.

'Jambo, Justin, habari!' they shouted across the water, as though I were a prodigal shipmate. My heart went out to them and I suddenly felt very alone. When we'd stepped ashore a week earlier, I'd been one of the unsavoury Malindi louts reeking of fish oil and making too much noise in the anchorage. Now I was just another mzungu tourist, showered and shaved and bound for a distant home. Part of me – a very real and aching part – wanted to ditch my luggage, swim out to where my dhow was already tugging at the tide and make sail, make African sail, and fly south with the monsoon.

Paddling wild
Don Pinnock – December 2001

As kayaking spots go, the mid-Atlantic has to be one of the most remote. Given the chance, Don Pinnock and Neil Rusch just had to try – and go for a few obscure records.

～

The idea had been irresistible: to kayak Tristan da Cunha, the most remote inhabited island on earth. It had been a good cocktail party conversation but … why not? So next day I phoned the St Helena shipping line. Would they take kayaks? Sure, they said, no problem.

'You're mad, of course,' insisted Captain David Roberts of RMS St Helena when I called him up to confirm. 'The weather down there's unpredictable. It's just off the Roaring Forties and slap in the middle of the Atlantic. You'll probably die but, well, that's your business.'

So, one sunny Cape Town morning saw me hoisting a sea kayak over the deck rail of the RMS and stowing it in the ship's cavernous foreward hold.

Not many ships sail west from Cape Town into the setting sun. Soon the seagulls fell behind and around us was nothing but empty sea.

The RMS has excellent anti-roll stabilisers but is somehow too short for the long Atlantic troughs. So, for five days of total decadence, and far too much good food, we rocking-horsed our way towards the tiny island. After a while I got used to the motion and, after the trip, found it difficult to sleep in a bed that didn't move like a cradle.

Tristan slipped into view early one morning, a brooding volcano with near-vertical walls of black lava disappearing into a surprisingly calm sea. It is, indeed, the most remote permanently inhabited island on the planet, St Helena being 1200 nautical miles up the Greenwich meridian and Cape Town 1500 miles to the east.

'You're lucky with the weather,' said Captain Roberts, seeming a little disappointed. Perhaps he missed his Royal Navy days of wild seas when men were men. Having been awed by tales of the island's legendary nine-metre swells, I was delighted.

From its base on the Mid-Atlantic Ridge to its occasionally snow-capped crater, Tristan is around 6000 metres high with some 2000 metres sticking out of the water. Its steep sides provide little space for the village of Edinburgh and near-impossible conditions for a harbour. So the RMS dropped anchor offshore and we were ferried in by friendly, weather-beaten Tristinians. Being fishermen and boat people, the two kayaks – the other one belonging to journalist Neil Rusch – attracted a good deal of interest. The locals make beautiful, canvas-covered longboats, but they'd never seen such strange craft as ours before.

'Watcha goin ta do wif em?' a burly fellow enquired.

'Go to sea,' said Neil.

'Naah! You're not serious.' He shook his head worriedly. 'But the weather be good today ….'

The kayaks were hauled onto the quay from the longboat ferry, bright splashes of colour amid the oily cranes and fibre-glass fishing boats. Tristan has a nasty reputation for sudden weather changes and right then the weather was good. So we decided to get the kayaks in the water as soon as possible.

This posed a problem. The little harbour was purpose-built for fishing boats which are dropped into the water by crane, not run from a slipway. The water was a good metre and a half from the quay top. There were the remains of an old slipway, but it was broken, kelp covered and looked decidedly dangerous.

However a great splodge of kelp had built up in a corner of the harbor and took my weight when I stepped onto its ooze. I dragged my Skua onto it and seal-dived it into the water – paddling frantically to avoid being chucked back onto the kelp by a surge.

Neil was fussing about somewhere, so I powered out of the harbour before an audience of dozens and into the open water – savouring the idea of being the first kayaker ever to do so in Tristan. After about half an hour – time enough for me to paddle round the RMS – Neil scooted up and we set off westwards along a spectacular coastline.

Tristan comes in three intense colours: Night-black lava, emerald-green grass and turquoise sea. The effect is psychedelic. While the top of the volcano was clothed in cloud, the sunlit laval platforms were littered with vents and the sides of the 600-metre base scarred by deep 'gulches'. Round one corner the rocks fluoresced with slashes of bright fire orange.

I was staring so hard at the weird island that I didn't see the yellow-nosed albatross until it had nearly scalped me. They're strangely inquisitive birds, completely unafraid of humans and were quite prepared to buzz us at close range, skimming the waves. They never seemed to flap.

One finally plunked itself onto the water beside us and powered round the kayaks to within paddle distance to see what we were about. Close up we could really appreciate the size of these beautiful birds. Wandering albatrosses have up to four-metre wingspans and their yellow-nosed cousins are not much smaller.

We paddled past the potato patches – little lava-walled gardens where Tristinians grow their famous 'taters – and alongside sharp rocky fangs to Anchorstock Point.

'I think we should go right round,' Neil said.

'You're nuts,' I protested. 'It's late, this is one damn big island and nobody knows we're going to attempt it.'

Neil sat looking south for a good long time, then reluctantly followed me back towards Edinburgh.

Back in the harbour, as I beached the kayak, trying to avoid getting dumped face first into the smelly kelp mush, Neil slipped quietly out to sea again. I figured he wanted to take a trip round the RMS, as I had done earlier, and stowed my Skua beside a rotting yacht which had been dismasted and washed ashore.

When Neil wasn't back by six o'clock that evening I began to worry. When he wasn't back by eight the island administrator had notified the chief inspector who had mobilised a rescue crew. They were preparing to launch two fast boats when, at nine o'clock, the RMS radioed that they'd spotted Neil coming round Anchorstock Point. He'd made the circumnavigation.

When he arrived, cold, shivering and exhausted, he was treated to a severe dressing down by the inspector, who said he'd never used his handcuffs before nor the prison cell, but he had a damn good mind to use 'em right then. The administrator looked stern, the rescue crew were mightily irritated. Neil had broken almost every rule in the kayaking book.

Back on the RMS as it set sail for Cape Town a fews days later Neil looked a lot less contrite.

'When the fuss blows over what have we got?' he asked with a wicked gleam.

'A record?' I suggested.

'Yeah, right.'

In search of the strange
Don Pinnock – December 2001

There are those mountains you climb to reach the top. Then there are other mountains, and other reasons to climb them. Don Pinnock found two of them in northern Madagascar.

૨૦

' The way to cook a tenrec,' Zakamisy explained as we stomped up through the dripping mist forest, 'is to first boil it, then peel it to remove the prickles. After that you grill it.'

Tastes a bit like pork, evidently.

The conversation about tenrecs had begun back in Antsiranana where Zak said he thought he could root one out from the underbrush. Not to eat, you understand, just to regard. Tenrecs are mammals best described by what they're not: they aren't shrews, platypuses, hedgehogs or moles, but have something in common with all of these. I couldn't wait to see one.

Right then, though, we were heading up a trail to Amber Mountain. The forest was dark, dense and full of things with names like dragon trees, flaming katys, polka dot plants and outrageous, balletic orchids with tongue twister titles like *aerangis*, *jumellea*, *bulbophyllum* and *phaius*. It all seemed to belong to some remote epoch. In this landscape it wouldn't entirely surprise you to see pterosaurs gliding through the trees and velociraptors sprinting across the trail ahead. But the more we hunted for tenrecs, the more they weren't there.

'They're not fady,' Zak explained, after another fruitless forage in the soggy leaf litter. 'Lemurs are fady, so are chameleons, but not tenrecs. So they get eaten.'

We had time on our hands, maybe another 10 hours of hard climbing, so it seemed okay to begin yet another conversation about the complexities of Malagasy customs.

'What's fady?' I asked.

Zak, you must understand, is not your common sort of guide. His father was a musician fairly famous in northern Madagascar, but he died when Zak was quite young. Zak and his six sisters were brought up in a peasant village by his mother and beloved grandfather, who was both a champion bare-knuckle boxer and a storyteller.

In his youth the old man had been press-ganged by the French into building the road to the top of Amber Mountain upon which we were walking – though after 50 years of neglect it was a mere precipice-hugging, tangle-foot path.

Zak learned French, then English, then Italian, and decided growing rice and mangoes wasn't for him. His ambition led him, eventually, to York Pareik who runs a travel outfit named King de la Piste. A piste, in case your French is as lousy as mine, is a dirt road, or a track, or a ski run ….

Zak soon learned the Latin names of almost every Madagascan plant and creature. So now – in his late 20s, with a head full of tribal customs, hundreds (maybe thousands) of traditional stories and a fine grasp of modern ecology – he's a sort of Renaissance man. You ask him a question and you invariably get a very full answer plus peripheral anecdotes.

To radically paraphrase his answer, fady is a taboo system so complex that neighbouring villages and even close neighbours don't necessarily share it. Taboos can vary from community to community or family to family, even person to person.

Perhaps eating pork is fady, or digging a grave with a spade which does not have a loose handle is fady (not too much contact between the living and the dead). In Imerina area it's fady to hand an egg to someone; it must first be put on the ground. In many areas it's fady to work in the rice fields on Thursdays, or work at all on Tuesdays.

Places are also fady, and all over Madagascar you will see trees or rocks lovingly cloaked in bright cloth, or bowls full of money beside certain objects. We even came across a skeleton in a cave with a platter of coins beside its grinning skull.

A close relative of fady is vintana, which cuts up time into good times and bad times to do things, which means people might suddenly stop what they're doing and sit down for an hour or two.

Some things, though, are generally agreed to be fady, like chameleons and lemurs. Chameleons, from tiny scraps of rainbow to huge, near-metre-long dragons, are everywhere and, in the forests, lemurs hurtle all over the place, or sit and stare at you. Some will even steal your lunch.

It's just a pity there's no taboo on slaughtering rain forests – only about 10 per cent of them are left and vast areas of the island are either eroded ruination or rice paddies. Well, there you are.

Now to the purpose of my trip: I'd come to Madagascar with Sabine Bultemeier of Animaltracks to explore two mountains, one entirely cloaked by some of the surviving rainforests, the other ripped to shreds by water. I was filled, like Kipling, with a 'satiable curiosity about an island where almost everything was endemic, volcanic or just plain odd.'

Any trip necessarily begins in Antananarivo because that's where international flights land. It didn't take me long to realise it wasn't Africa. Antananarivo is a traffic jam clamped round a curious, pointy roofed city surrounded by endless rice paddies. It takes a while to get anywhere, but the people along the roads are charming and mostly beautiful Indo-Malayan, or Malayo-Polynesian so it's not a chore to grind along in first gear. Coming in from the airport, I just sat and gawped at all the delightful strangeness.

But my mountains – Ankarana and Amber Mountain – were in northern Madagascar, so I flew out next day to Antsiranana and King's Lodge. York, who owns the lodge, is seriously laid back. He has a fleet of elderly but serviceable Range Rovers plus some year-old twins who keep him and his wife, Lydia, awake at night. There was a time, he confessed as we clutched cold Three Horses beers and watched the afternoon sun get swallowed by a volcano, when he wore his hair long, sampled interesting substances and travelled the world in dangerous public transport. Then he found Antsiranana and decided he'd arrived at his Shangri-La.

I couldn't argue with him about that.

Next day Zak packed up our kit and victuals, picked up a shy cook named Bridget and we set off on the grimiest journey I have ever experienced – and I work in Africa.

Madagascar's not dubbed the red island for nothing. When forests are slashed and burned the oxidised laterite soil beneath them is singularly infertile and soon erodes, spreading fine ruddy powder over the whole island. In the rainy season roads are a quagmire; when they're dry each bump produces an effect not unlike hitting a fat bag of bright red flour.

When we arrived at the spiky buttresses of Ankarana we were astonishingly red, with our personal colour showing only where dark glasses had been. Each rivulet of sweat made the mess even more surreal and sticky.

Well, never mind all that. Let me tell you about Ankarana. On an island of strange things it has to be near the top of the strangeness list. It's a limestone massif sticking abruptly out of the plain and covered in razor-sharp limestone karst spikes known locally as tsingy. Instead of going round it, rivers chose to run through it, forming caves, canyons and eerie underground tunnels. You can walk through several hundred kilometres of these things. In places huge caves have collapsed, forming isolated pockets of river-fed forest with sunlight streaming down from above. Creatures live in there that you'll find nowhere else on the planet.

We hiked through the inky black caves, some with stalactites and stalagmites twinkling in our torchlight, then climbed up the mountain to view the forests and rivers from above. A troop of rare crowned lemurs came to investigate. I bent

127

down to photograph one, and three others jumped on my back to see what I was doing. Fady works wonders in the trust department.

We camped at the foot of the tsingy mountain, watched the setting sun turn them orange, and Zak produced some local rum. It was spittingly awful. When I refused to sip more Zak told me a story which seemed to justify getting motherless on bad booze and opened up a later discussion about why the Malagasy are a nation of grave diggers.

There was once a mamalava (rum drunkard) who nobody respected. He was around during a famadihana, a time of year when, for some reason or other, corpses are exhumed, their bones dusted off, danced with and carried to some other place (I saw empty graves all over the place).

When the skull of the skeleton being exhumed was exposed it began to move this way and that. Everyone ran away in fright. But the mamalava took a closer look and saw it was being moved by a little tenrec in the brain cavity. He called everyone back and after that they all approved of his rum habits.

'And that,' said Zak triumphantly, 'is why it's good to drink Malagasy rum!'

Well, maybe.

Next day we headed through more red dust to Amber Mountain. It's a thing apart, a great volcanic massif covered in ancient mist forest with its own wet microclimate. Manokan Ambre, as it's called, towers over the northern tip of Madagascar with, more often than not, a soggy cloud frown across its lofty peak.

We overnighted in a very neat, clean hut at Roussettes Forestry Station and hit the trail in a light drizzle at an ungodly 05h00 the next morning. Half an hour after passing an atmospheric little waterfall (sacred, of course) near the hut, we were gazing down into the forest-cloaked mouth of a crater lake named Mahasarika.

The forest was ... weird. A glance at the statistics will tell you why. Madagascar has around 10 000 plant species of which about 80 per cent are endemic. It has eight species of baobab whereas the whole of Africa has only one. Of the 258 species of birds, 107 are endemic. Then there are lemurs – 30 species. They're primates which look like monkeys with foxy faces and cat eyes. And tenrecs, which Zak promised ....

We hiked past huge panda trees (*Pandanus* sp.), fluffy topped *Araliaceae* literally dripping with epiphytes, many of them orchids, huge manaries (*Dalbergia* sp.), massive tree ferns (*Cyathea* sp.) and spooky dragon trees (*Dracaena* sp.).

A turkey-sized Madagascar crested ibis, the bane of tenrecs and chameleons, scratched in the under storey, a monticole played hide and seek in the upper branches of a manary, and Madagascar bee-eaters buzzed through the mist-edged glades. Lurid lichens sprouted from the rotting trunks of trees thrown down by the area's violent cyclones and in the stream beds boophis frogs muttered contentedly.

The place was simply glorious and, as far as humans go, we had it all to ourselves.

Around five hours deep we came upon a moody crater lake which appeared suddenly as we stepped out of the forest onto its grassy apron. From there it was a slippery, tough climb out of the crater and up to the summit, marked by a neat concrete pillar and a plaque with the words Pic D'Ambre. My GPS registered an elevation of 1488 metres and, in case you like exact locations, it read S12°35.778, E43°09.188. In the swirling mist we couldn't see more than a few metres.

Nearly an hour later, after we'd munched the scrambled-egg sandwiches and fruit that Bridget had prepared, the murk suddenly lifted. Below us was a great crater – I suspect it was the one named Renard but we weren't sure – and beyond that the Mozambique Channel. There's something about the view from the highest point of anywhere that makes it worth the pain.

Twelve hours after starting we were back in the hut. My feet hurt and I was suffering from the strange emptiness I often feel after climbing a mountain. Maybe I looked glum.

Zak, ever perceptive, handed me a glass of rum and said: 'Would you like me to tell you a story?' He gave me no time to reply.

'There were once three friends, bon? A duck, a chicken and a dog. They lived together in a village. Once every week they'd take the taxi-brousse to the market in Antsiranana. But one week, when they were half way to market, the taxi driver he told them that because of the cost of gaz-oelie, the fare had gone up from 300 francs to 500 francs each.

'The duck he had the extra cash, the dog was rich anyway, but the chicken he had only 300 francs. So when they arrived in the market the duck got off and paid 500 francs. The chicken paid 300 and told the driver that his friend, the dog, would pay the rest. The dog had a 1000-frank note. The driver took it, got in the taxi-brousse and just drove off.'

'That is why, today, when you see a duck in the road it's not worried about the car, the chicken always runs away shouting and flapping, and the dog he chases the car going 'woa, woa woa'....'

'Are you feeling okay now?' Zak asked, looking at me with his wise, serious eyes all etched about with smile wrinkles.

'Yes, sure. Fierce rum, though. Do you think if I drank it I could spot a tenrec?'

'Well, we could try ….'

Valley of the dolls
Robyn Daly – January 2002

A 250-kilometre horse trail across the foothills of Kilimanjaro and Meru craters can take its toll – unless you're a super fit rider, or a pair of hypochondriacs with their bag of tricks comes along for the ride.

ॐ

At Kilimanjaro Airport Air Tanzania's flight from Johannesburg has rattled down the runway – and about time too, since the beer ran out somewhere over Malawi. There is the customary confusion at customs which has no significance other than to remind visitors that this is an African country and officials are to be respected. Just who the officials are, is a matter of further confusion: everybody wears flip-flops and shirts with sweat stains; perhaps it is the size of the patches that denotes how important an official is – big stains, big stress, big importance.

More confusion follows around the conveyer belt which soon gives up conveying. It can be forgiven: there are few flights in Africa which generate the amount of luggage as the one to Kilimanjaro, and no other mountain with the same appetite for Gore-Tex.

The masses file out, wrestling trolleys laden with poles, packs, boots and thermal undies. They stop at the doorway, each and every one, to catch their first sight: Mount Kilimanjaro, holy grail. Coated in icing, pink from a fading afternoon, it looks as benign as a birthday cake. Over the next five days the masses will be shuffled up and down again. Their hands will be held, their luggage carried, their noses wiped, their temperatures taken and the most frequent words they'll hear will be: 'How're you doin'?'

One of these sturdy mountaineers approaches a handful of people smoking outside: 'Who are you climbing with?'

'Oh, we're not, we're going on a horse safari.' It's the wrong answer. The offer of friendship, conspiracy and camaraderie is withdrawn; the sturdy mountaineer lopes away to watch his luggage being loaded.

The huddle of horse riders (easily confused with the mountaineers as they also have someone attending to their luggage) climb into a rap-trap Land Rover to drive away – in the opposite direction to the holy grail.

The scene is now a stable at the foot of another large mountain. Without the fluff of snow and pink sunset, this one is severe and imposing: Mount Meru, Tanzania's second highest mountain. A group of nine horse riders are fussing over their mounts. With seven days' riding ahead some vital decisions have to be made. Which horse, in particular. Will I be able to control this one at a gallop, or should I stick to an old sloucher? Does the saddle feel comfortable? Are my stirrups too short? It goes on and on, but before tedium sets in the train of riders mounts up and the ride begins.

Head of the queue is unmistakably Danish Lisa Schovsbo, trail leader. She and her family left Denmark in the '70s to find their farm in Africa. At 60-something she's not quite Meryl Streep, but she's tough as leather, rides upright with one hand on the reins, the other holding her whip which she tucks under her arm – dare I say, straight out the Schutztruppe? Fortunately the whip is to keep the horse in line, not the riders … or is it? Nobody feels up to testing the theory.

Behind Lisa is French lawyer Ann, on a strong thoroughbred. Half way through the trail, and once her arms have been pulled nearly from their sockets, she'll swap him for a sloucher and enjoy the rest of the ride. Next come three South Africans: Sharon, who ends up riding four different horses on the trail (for no apparent reason other than she likes variety), her 18-year-old daughter, Nicole, who finishes the trail in a Land Rover (but more of that later), and Debbie, matched to a tee to laid-back Castle who is just about the only castle in a country where Kilimanjaro is the name of the local fortifier.

Next come the lads from America: Dana and Jeff. They've been planted on two horses that couldn't be further from their own characters. Fantasia and Straight One, two complete bitches, must have surely inspired the quip that horses are dangerous at both ends …. And when it comes to Dana and Straight One, well, you can't ignore a little irony: for bitchy Dana isn't and straight he certainly ain't.

Other characters include a groom, Albie the trail helper, and a journalist who gets up everybody's nose with a long-lensed camera. But enough of that, for here's a pretty picture: our riders, under the stern gaze of Meru and Lisa, plodding through sun-baked savanna.

By the close of the first day, the horses have shrugged off their riders and paraphernalia and are munching quietly. The riders, too, are munching on three courses more appetising than oats. They have showered from a bucket hanging from a flat-topped umbrella thorn (*Acacia tortillis*) which tore the knickers of a novice in the art of bush ablutions. These pantie-wreckers, dotted all over the veld, are still a novelty on day one, by day four or five, they're monotonous. That's East African savanna for you: flat tops, flat tops and flat tops. A few fever trees add variety but the scenic draw is three extinct volcanoes which dominate the plains:

Kilimanjaro, Meru and Longido. They're too far apart to be seen in unison, but always, in the distance, there's one hulk (sometimes two) of blue-grey volcanic rock, almost timeless in their multi-million-year histories.

The first rider yawns at the enormity of all this and waddles stiff-legged off to bed.

'I wonder where the climbers are?' says Sharon.

'They'll be heading to Kibo today, then summiting tonight,' Debbie reckons. 'No doubt a few are already experiencing altitude sickness.'

'Aren't there drugs for that?' someone asks.

'Oh ja,' replies Debbie. 'You can take a diuretic, Diamox, and Decadron, which is a steroid ....' The Q and A continues for a while, then is forgotten as the mountain appears.

It is the riders' first full sight of Kilimanjaro. Wind, dust and clouds have conspired to keep Uhuru concealed. Briefly, for one afternoon, the atmospheric curtain lifts and the riders stand in the full magnificence of this trail setting. Here are fever trees and plains with barely a blade of grass. A bachelor group of elephants, a great tusker among them, strips trees some 50 metres away. The horses stand, they've seen it all and are unimpressed by the backdrop of one of the world's tallest free-standing mountains. Somewhere on its slopes and thankfully too small and far away for the riders to see, the masses are willing their brains to put one foot in front of the other.

But for the riders, smug in the knowledge that all it takes to go forward is to kick the horse in the ribs, drama is not far off.

First they startle a spotted hyena sleeping in the shade, then they gallop across the dust plains in the wake of a yodelling herd of zebras not quite sure if the horsy snorts and hoof beats they hear are friend or foe. Then Nicole's horse trips, she pulls up and doubles over. Floods of tears.

A twittering of panic: 'What is it?' 'Are you okay?' Nicole's face is white, her eyes red. A quick inspection confirms all limbs intact, ten fingers ... (these things have been known to go missing in the reins). Her injury is a common one among those who venture to stretch their legs over a horse's back. The pressure of muscles gripping to stay on has a way of hammering the groin. In short, Nicole has pulled a ligament – in a place where no one but she is going to massage with Deep Heat.

Her sweet pony (one of a herd of Brumbies donated to Tanzania by Australia when the population of feral horses there was exploding) plods along to the evening's camp under thorn trees. Once there another interesting twist in the plot occurs.

Ever true to American travellers abroad, Dana and Jeff have brought along an impressive cooler bag filled with pills. Jeff takes charge. Out come the pain killers and muscle relaxants, fished from the melee of malaria tablets, tranquillisers, sleeping pills ….

'I have a friend who's a pharmacist,' Jeff explains shyly.

Dana adds. 'Yeah, we've been popping pills since we got here.'

'I took an anxiety pill for the first day,' Jeff admits.

'What's that?'

'Oh, it's like Valium.'

Jeff and Dana's bag of 'dolls' marks a turning point in the horse safari, and forever afterwards events in the first half of the ride are referred to as 'before the pills' and those afterwards as 'after the pills'. You see, Nicole's groin injury, which sadly means she keeps her legs closed and on terra firma for the rest of her holiday, is simply a catalyst. With proof that riding isn't for sissies, it's not so bad to complain of tender thighs, aching knees, sore arms, shoulders and, most common of all, a devilishly sore bum (talk of blisters on the nether regions is entering into too much detail though and considered poor form).

In the final scenes, the character of the train of riders trotting across the plains is much changed. Where before there were gritted teeth at every bump and jolt of the horses' bodies, now each rider is in a state of drug-assisted bliss. The gruel of spending six hours in an English saddle which was never designed for anything longer than a fox hunt on the neighbouring squire's estate, is long forgotten.

The riders are now able to sit back, relax and enjoy the variety of birds and animals that generally dull vegetation can produce. This is, after all gerenuk country, and the strangeness of a gerenuk with its giraffe-like neck attached to an antelope's body holds its own absurdities.

Back at Kilimanjaro Airport, and almost in one piece, the riders wait for Air Tanzania to rattle them off Tanzanian soil. The mountaineers, looking a little thinner for wear, are there too. Debbie calls to one of the climbers: 'Did you make it?'

The man replies: 'Yeah, we all got to the top, but it was really tough. Did you climb?'

Debbie gives him the now standard answer, then enquires: 'Did you take any drugs?'

'Na, didn't need to.'

The man wouldn't have thought to ask that question of a bunch of horse riders.

In the footsteps of David Livingstone – Missionary road to the interior
Don Pinnock – February 2002

He loaded an oxwagon with the few provisions his meagre missionary salary would allow and set off, walking beside the jolting vehicle for a thousand kilometres into the African interior. Thirty three years later he would be buried in Westminster Abbey, a national hero.

Since then no missionary or explorer has been more reconstructed, deconstructed, psychoanalysed, or turned into a stained-glass saint. Almost to the day, 160 years after David Livingstone stepped ashore in Africa, Getaway deputy editor Don Pinnock and his wife, Patricia, headed north in a 4x4 to follow where Livingstone's footsteps led. And they would lead extraordinarily far ....

Likeability is not a characteristic normally associated with explorers. Burton, although undoubtedly brilliant, was considered a haughty bastard. Captain Cook flogged sailors and cut off the ears of thieving Polynesians. Stanley was bumptious. Cortez killed, looted and pillaged. Out beyond the boundaries of their civilization, it seems, Europeans had to be steely and singularly bloody minded.

So I didn't expect to like David Livingstone. Behind the screen of public adulation, he was a man of questionable character. He spent only six years with his subjugated wife, Mary, left her in absolute poverty while he travelled, and failed miserably as a father.

Yet Livingstone was to become the hero of England and the darling of Queen Victoria. As a child labourer in the cotton mills of Blantyre, Scotland, the tenacious Scot had studied Latin by propping a book on the spinning jenny. He was seen as a man of simple, honest origins who had made good. But he considered himself a failure. And, in many respects, he was. Not only missionaries or traders followed his trails, but gunrunners and slavers as well. Many young missionaries who answered his call to open Africa to trade and Christianity died of malaria.

Livingstone sponged shamelessly off his father-in-law, the saintly Robert Moffat, badmouthed other missionaries, condemned Africans who couldn't abide by his narrow Christianity as backsliding fools and made life hell for Europeans travelling with him, fearing they would steal the glory of his discoveries. While he is characterised by some as everything a Christian should be – noble and spiritual with the common touch – there are others who consider him a mean-spirited clod. If psychotherapy had been available in the mid-19th century, he would have been a prime candidate.

But the man walked, by rough estimate, 42 000 kilometres through uncharted areas of a continent believed by Europe of the 19th century to contain monsters, cannibals, or worse. He traversed pitiless deserts; followed great rivers still wild and unpredictable today; stood, amazed, beside shimmering lakes and waterfalls of the Great Rift Valley; and documented, meticulously, the customs of unheard-of peoples and the strange flora and fauna of a then Dark Continent.

He charmed warlike tribes with a mirror and a magnifying glass and was adored by powerful chiefs as well as men he had snatched from the hands of Arab slavers. And he wrote ripping travel diaries.

When he died, his faithful attendants buried his heart and entrails beside a tree, dried his body like a kapenta fish, carried it through dangerous savanna for 1500 kilometres – then followed it to Britain.

To describe Livingstone as enigmatic would be a gross understatement. More than a century after his death he remains mythical. The idea of setting off in a well-equipped 4x4 to see where he went – and to get a sense of how Africa had changed since he plodded through – was irresistible.

As we got beyond the borders of South Africa, however, the extraordinary respect for Livingstone shown by even simple peasants caused us to ask another question: just what did this man mean to Africa?

Drizzle from a grey winter sky followed us as we slipped out of Cape Town and over Du Toitskloof Pass. But it soon relented. By the time we were winding up Michell's Pass, bars of sunlight were picking out patches of bright fynbos.

Enticed by an old stone restaurant named Die Tolhuis in the mountain fastness, we stopped for an early lunch. It really had been a tollhouse: 3d a wheel, 2d a horse or ox and ha'penny for pigs, goats and sheep. In 1852 Livingstone, penniless after 11 years up north, would have driven his dishevelled wagon, and equally dishevelled family, past it on the way back to Cape Town. Had he paid the toll? His diaries do not mention it.

Ceres drifted by, neat and green, and then we began our long haul across the dusty roads of the Great Karoo. Hottentotskloof, Sutherland, Fraserburg and a great, flat emptiness – we were already way off the tourist route.

It was Sunday and Carnarvon, when we nosed into the dorp, seemed to have been evacuated. The hotel was closed, the restaurant was barred and a guesthouse dark. I banged on the door of the hotel, hoping someone could tell us where we could stay. After I'd given up and begun walking away, a man appeared.

'Hotel's closed,' he said, stating the obvious. Then he peered at the artwork on the door of our Mitsubishi Colt and asked: 'Who's David Livingstone?'

We drove round a bit, then found a deserted campsite, the grass dry and frostbitten. But it had hot water. The build-up to the trip and the bumpy driving had exhausted us. Dust had poured into the back, turning everything grimy brown. We flipped up the rooftop tent but couldn't find the portable neon light. We forgot where we'd packed the snacks – cooking supper seemed out of the question. Soon after sunset the temperature plunged to zero.

Patricia huddled in the cold, torch-lit tent, cold and miserable. 'Why are we doing this?' she asked. I thought of our children at home (rather better provided than Livingstone's) heating a pre-cooked, frozen meal and probably jostling for space with our labrador around a roaring fire and couldn't come up with an answer. All night the dogs of Carnarvon barked at each other and now and then a donkey brayed hideously. It was a miserable night.

Next morning we stuffed plastic bags in the canopy's leaky joints and nosed into town. There we found the Ou Kraal Kombuis. It had once been the Adelphi Café and Cinema and is now a shop, dance hall and restaurant run by Barbara van den Berg. Versatile building. Breakfast was generous and cheap and we left town with a rising sun, feeling guardedly excited. Deep in Africa we would remember that camp site as one of the best. Our learning curve was just coming off the baseline.

On the endless-seeming flat road between Carnarvon and Prieska we met Avi Morris, a karretjiemens with a tatty wagon, two ragged donkeys and a young foal tied up in a bag next to him. He said he was a woodcutter.

'There's no wood around here, just scrub bush,' I commented.

'Yes,' he sighed, 'that's why I'm going to Prieska.'

He had been on the road, all alone with his three asses, for two days. It would take another three, we estimated, for him to reach Prieska. He had no money and the road stretched away from him like an arrow. Time past, time future: Avi Morris and the great blue sky, still plying the old missionary road to the north in a creaking wagon.

'Wagon-travelling in Africa is a prolonged system of picnicking,' Livingstone had written. 'Excellent for the health and agreeable to those who are not over fastidious about trifles, and who delight in the open air.' Looking doubtfully at the old man and the bleak, winter-crisped Karoo, we wondered about that.

The Mary Moffat Museum in Griekwastad is an interesting place, with pictures of the sad-eyed Victorian lady and a fine old pulpit. There was also an old photograph of her grave, somewhere in the Zambezi floodplain, but there was no caption to tell us where. We visited and pushed on further, overnighting at the moody and delightful Witsand Nature Reserve with its generous cottages and strange, growling dunes.

We arrived in Kuruman three days after leaving the Cape – it had taken Livingstone two months. In Britain, when the young Livingstone was looking for a cause, Robert Moffat had lured him to Kuruman. There was a vast plain to the north, he told the eager young man, over which the sun rose on 'the smoke of a thousand villages where no missionary has ever been.'

When the weary oxen pulled Livingstone's wagon into Kuruman in July 1841, it was the northernmost Christian mission in Africa, built near the eye of an eternal spring. As it was then, the Moffat Misson is today a place of peace and tranquillity, a truly spiritual centre where we spent two happy days researching in the mission's excellent library, making friends and holding hands in the Memorial Garden. Its gentle director, Richard Aitken, and his wife, Jane, made us welcome, in the old missionary tradition.

Holy ground, it seemed to me as I listened to the morning prayers in the church Moffat built, is a simple thing. It's a place where generations have laboured at soul work. It creates harmony: simple as that.

Kuruman was the most important outpost of the London Missionary Society, but the young Livingstone was soon disillusioned with the place. He chafed to head north. With another missionary, Rogers Edwards, and his wife, he got his way, and together they established a mission station at Mabotsa, near present-day Zeerust in 1843.

Livingstone nearly lost his life there. He was encouraged by the local people to shoot a troublesome lion, but he merely wounded it and it leapt at him, shaking him 'like a terrier dog does a rat' and fracturing his right arm. He felt, he said, a sort of dreaminess in which there was no sense of pain. His assistant shot the lion and saved his life. His arm, however, set badly and was ever after weakened.

Back at Kuruman, Moffat's eldest daughter, Mary, nursed him back to health. Under an almond tree in the Kuruman garden the young David went down on one knee and proposed marriage to her. She was, he wrote to friends, 'a matter-of-fact lady, a little thick black-haired girl, sturdy and all I want.' Still today there are debates about whether the union was based on love or the expectation, current at the time, that every missionary needed a wife to look after him.

Today, under giant syringa trees sprinkling yellow winter leaves over the mission, there is a broad wooden arrow pointing north with the words 'Missionary Road to the Interior'. Livingstone had named the way north God's Highway. We took the sign as our cue and hit the missionary's trail once more, a little sad to leave the peaceful mission.

By a remarkable set of coincidences we made contact with a resident in the Zeerust area, Arto Toivonen, who had located the mission site of Mabotsa. It's on the edge of a village named Gopane and was on no modern map we could find and in no guidebook. It was there that the missionary first met his only convert, Chief Sechele of the Bakwena. All that's left now are foundation stones quarried by Livingstone and a sign under a tree marking it as his first mission: 1843–1846. But the rains failed, the Bakwena moved on, and Livingstone returned to Kuruman.

In Zeerust, where we went for diesel, was another sign pointing north and an indication of the Aids crisis we would encounter throughout our trip: 'Monty's Tombstones. Deposit only R25. Lay-byes accepted.' Wherever we travelled, the undertakers were doing a stiff trade.

The Livingstones' honeymoon was a 12-day trip to their new home, not Mabotsa but a second station Livingstone had begun at Tshongwane. During the two difficult years they spent there, Livingstone indulged in his passion for exploration, travelling east to the Magaliesberg. But he had heard tales of a great lake to the north and began making plans – in defiance of the wishes of the London Missionary Society.

Drought forced the people, and the missionary couple, to move again and they settled on the Kolobeng River further west.

For us, crossing the border into Botswana was like moving from the Third World into the First. The place is prosperous, the people seemed well educated and polite and the main roads are in good condition. These were the descendents of the people among whom Livingstone laboured. Wise chiefs, good policies plus diamonds and cattle have transformed them into one of the wealthiest nations in Africa. We overnighted with friends in Gaborone – a modern, booming city – then set off west to search for Kolobeng, until then a small red star in a Map Studio atlas.

At this new site Livingstone built the only real home his family would enjoy with him. There he and the community erected a small church and dug a canal to bring river water to the mission's croplands. The challenge exhilarated him. In a letter he criticised missionaries languishing 'down in the Colony.' They should be 'right up here, riding on the world's backbone and snuffing like zebras the free, pure, delightful air of the great western desert!'

At Kolobeng Livingstone built, farmed, healed the sick, and preached to Sechele's people. Mary taught in the school they'd built, cooked, and tended her children, Robert and Agnes. (Mary was to bear six children, two of whom died in Africa. Robert died as a young soldier in the American Civil War). In 1841, against the wishes of the worried tribe who feared the wrath of their dead ancestors, Livingstone baptised Sechele.

We rolled across the Kolobeng River and turned through a gate. After a while Alfred Piet came trotting up. He's warden to almost nothing: Livingstone's house is now just a ring of foundation stones, the church even less obvious. The most noticeable remnants are a stone seat upon which Livingstone's patients sat and a circle of stones marking the grave of the couple's fourth child, Elizabeth.

Mary would produce five children in six years and come close to death after two of the births. Childbearing would ruin her health (she suffered a mild stroke with each of the last two) and curtail any sense of achievement in mission work. In Victorian tradition, she would have no choice in the matter.

Livingstone would later boast of his self-sufficiency at Kolobeng, but his letters to Moffat told a different story. Requests were endless: 'I may as well tell you some more of our wants,' he penned, 'a trowel; large and small beads; a ladle and bullet mould; heifers if you can get them at any price; she goats; a musket if you have one to spare; vine cuttings; fruit stones for seed; pictures; the large vice mentioned ....'

Livingstone, who had banned Chief Sechele – who was also the tribe's chief rainmaker – from invoking rain (and from polygamy) as a price for salvation, was blamed for the droughts at Tshongwane and Kolobeng. Rain fell all round, people noticed, but not on the mission. His own children were half starved. Livingstone dealt with his growing problems in his typical manner: he planned an exploration trip.

Teaming up with a wealthy hunter, William Cotton Oswell, Livingstone set off across the trackless Kalahari in June, 1849, to find the 'great lake' he had heard of. They passed through what is now Lephepe and Serowe, then northwest through the thirstlands to Letlhakane to the Botete River. They nearly died from lack of water and some oxen perished from being bitten by tsetse fly. On the first day of August they stood on the shores of Lake Ngami.

We took a more easterly route, overnighting at a comfortable camp site beside the Marang Hotel in Francistown, then travelling west through the Makgadigadi Pans to Maun. After a laid-back evening of beers and travel chatter at Audi Camp and a well-earned sleep, we tracked down the Nhabe River to search for the fabled Lake Ngami. It had disappeared.

By GPS reckoning we were in the dead centre of the lake, but all that surrounded us was flat yellow grass with a watchful patrol of vultures overhead. Later enquiries established that it had dried up 20 years before, victim of the curious cyclical tilting of the Okavango basin. We rolled out the canopy, broke out the table and chairs and sipped Earl Grey tea, thinking about the terrible hardships that had befallen the missionary there on his second trip to the lake.

When reports of the lake's discovery reached London, Livingstone was awarded a gold medal by the Royal Geographical Society. Oswell took a back seat.

A year after his first visit, however, Livingstone returned to Ngami, this time with Mary and two small children in tow. It took them four months and 10 days. It was an awful journey.

'In some parts we had to travel both day and night continuously for want of water,' he diarised, 'and then tie up the oxen to prevent them running away 'till we had dug wells. I lost four in pitfalls made for game, two from drought, one by a lion ....'

The two children went down with malaria first; soon all his men were sick. The mosquito was not suspected as the vector for malaria, and one winces to read Livingstone's complaint that he 'could not touch a square half inch of the bodies of the children unbitten after a single night's exposure.' Using a mixture of jalap resin, calomel, rhubarb and quinine – a remedy hit on by trial and error which was to become known as the Livingstone Pill – he cured them.

Mary, weakened by fever, gave birth to Elizabeth after her return to Kolobeng and, in childbirth, had a stroke which was to leave her face temporarily paralysed. Two weeks later the child died. As she succumbed she gave a piercing cry, a sound, Livingstone wrote, which would haunt him to the end of eternity.

Almost a year later, in 1851, (to the horror of Livingstone's mother-in-law, Mary Moffat) the family was back in a wagon heading north once again. This time they took a more easterly route across the dead-flat plains of Makgadigadi. Like a recurrent nightmare, thirst again overtook them, this time in the terrible Mababe Depression.

Eventually, miraculously, they reached the territory of Chief Sebetwane of the Makololo tribe and, after some hacking, the Linyati River. When they reached Sebetwane's capital, named after the river, the party was given a tumultuous welcome. Within weeks, however, the chief died from pneumonia. As luck goes, Livingstone was a veritable Jonah to the Africans he befriended.

After a few nights in Maun, back at Audi Camp gathering our strength to follow the spectre of Livingstone's wagons northwards, we teamed up with two solo travellers, German Roland and South African Justin, and headed for Chobe National Park. Our goal was Kudumane village, just south of the park entrance, where we hoped to spend the night. It was a mere 130 kilometres away. How deceptive distance can be off the main roads in Africa.

The road to Chobe was in reality a maze of tracks, none signposted and many just thick sand. We ended up at the gate of Moremi Wildlife Reserve in error, tracked back to a village named Shukumukwa and eventually hung onto the GPS for dear life through wild places in fading light until we ended up, almost by accident, in Kudumane.

Being lost in the wilderness didn't feel good. For Livingstone it would have been far more testing: most of the time he had only the vaguest idea of where he was or what perils lay ahead. We felt a creeping respect for the man.

Kudumane is a Tsegu-San village with mud-walled, thatched-roof huts, goats, donkeys and beautiful, petite, naked children everywhere. For 10 pula each we were given a camp site, then we whiled away our time discussing Tsegu traditions and the San name of stars with the locals.

As the sky deepened to purple-black the Milky Way sparkled to life from horizon to horizon. In the woodland a hyena whooped as we prepared for bed. As he took his leave, one of the San, Mandwar Sebinelo, turned and said, almost as an afterthought: 'Our gods will stay with you.' It felt strangely reassuring.

We rolled out of the village before the sun rose and headed up yet another frightful sandy track. If this was the main road to a large national park they were catering for nothing but intrepid and well-equipped travellers.

Inside the park, though, the roads were better. We soon met wise-looking elephants, batty-eyed giraffes, skittish zebras and wildebeest, a tawny eagle on every other dead tree, lilac-breasted rollers, huge flocks of guinea fowl, pale chanting goshawks and a lone kori bustard.

Despite the claim at the park offices in Maun that the camping sites in Chobe were full, we drove up to the Savuti Gate and were offered a fine site behind a bombproof blockhouse, which turned out to be the elephant-proof ablution building. The reason for the structure's solidity soon became clear. As we sat round preparing lunch, a jumbo with serviceable tusks wandered up to investigate. We suddenly figured that inside the vehicles would be a good place to eat.

That evening, Justin nearly had his steak snatched from the tailgate of his vehicle – centimetres away from his ear – by a huge spotted hyena and we were confined to the ablutions for a bit while an elephant patrolled the gate. Everyone retired to the safety of their rooftop tents except Justin – who had a ground tent. Patricia lay awake for quite a while worrying about him, expecting more customers for his delicious camp cooking.

Chobe is an extraordinarily wild-feeling place, with minimal roads (tracks, really), few people and vast areas of mopane woodland and combretum. At times you gaze across rippling grass to the horizon; in other places the trees restrict your view to a few metres.

Elephants and tawny eagles ruled, raucously attended by yellow-billed, red-billed and grey hornbills. Every now and then a Swainson's francolin would sprint ahead of the Colt, kicking up sand as it dived into the verge grass.

Travelling up the Savuti Channel, dead on Livingstone's trail, we found the plain broken by several hills with complicated San names such as Gobatsaa (leopard), Damagosera (kudu), Qumxhwaa (cave) and some stark pans. Livingstone, too, would have marvelled at huge baobabs on the slopes and listened with satisfaction to the soft calls of green pigeons. Mere emptiness can be frightening, but wilderness is somehow comforting and confidential.

From Savuti we headed northwest towards Linyati, Sebetwane's capital, but elephants had pushed trees over the track and deep sand had built up from floods. So we headed northwards instead, past the Gcoha Hills and through the Chobe Forest Reserve to Katchekabwe and the Chobe River.

When Sebetwane died, Livingstone and Oswell, who was again travelling with him, left Mary and the wagons and rode north to visit a river people, the Sesheke or Borotse. They were amazed to find a river which was nearly half a kilometre wide with huge floodplains. They had found the Chobe, and Livingstone rightly concluded it to be a main feeder of the Zambezi. He now knew where that great African waterway was, and he began to dream.

When Livingstone returned from the Chobe his missionary skin had split like a chrysalis and a full-blown explorer had emerged. Africa beckoned irresistibly. The man who had caught the world's attention with Lake Ngami now had to overcome his greatest obstacle – the burden of his family.

He wrote to the London Missionary Society that he needed three years' freedom from family responsibilities. Instead of leaving Mary and the children in Kuruman, he trekked with them to Cape Town. They presented a strange spectacle: people stared. After 11 years in trackless Africa it was evident that the world had passed them by. Even Livingstone found he had lost the knack of stairs, and turned round to go down as if on a ladder.

With no-doubt mixed feelings, Livingstone booked his family on a ship to England with virtually no plan for their support. He simply assumed the Missionary Society would care for them. As it turned out, this didn't happen. The LMS was unhappy with Livingstone's non-missionary adventures and felt little responsibility towards his uninvited family, who became paupers dependent on handouts from distant family and friends. Mary, under impossible stress and far from the Africa she understood, began drinking heavily.

It has been suggested by several biographers that Livingstone's main reason for exiling his family from Africa was that if Mary had remained anywhere on the continent they would live together from time to time and more children would be conceived. An explorer simply could not afford an endless procession of children. More probably, Mary didn't get on well with her fussy mother and couldn't bear the thought of Kuruman without David.

While in Cape Town, Livingstone had taken instruction in mapping and navigation from the Astronomer Royal, Thomas Maclear, who was soon confident that his pupil had navigation sussed. The men talked about the possibility of a trip from the west coast of Africa to the east, clear across the continent, and the chance of finding great lakes rumoured to be in the centre of the continent.

When Livingstone arrived back at Kolobeng, he found his house smashed and looted by Boers, who had accused him of gun running. This simply hardened his resolve to head north again. He was not without fears, however.

'Am I on the way to die in Sebetuane's country?' he wrote in his diary. 'Have I seen the last of my wife and children? My soul, wither wilt thou emigrate? Where will thou lodge the first night after leaving the body?'

In May 1853 Livingstone was back at Linyati. Shortly afterwards, he was staring in wonder at the great moving waters of the Zambezi River. One of the greatest expeditions of the 19th century was about to begin.

We were acutely conscious at having abandoned our own family as we watched the sun fall over Buffalo Ridge Camp, where we overnighted above the Chobe floodplain. It was wild and we were rather lonely and far from home. Each time, before entering a new country, the feeling would return. We sat, tapping e-mail messages home, fretting over the absence of anything in the inbox. Had they forgotten about us?

At sunrise we headed through eastern Chobe to fill up with our last gulp of cheap Botswana diesel before joining the queue of long-haul trucks at the Kazungula Ferry across the flooding Zambezi. Money changers flapped wads of notes at us hopefully, and one offered us diamonds 'cheap, cheap'.

Our destination was Zambia, and we were finally wedged ahead of a huge road hauler on the shuddering ferry deck. The precarious craft fought its way across the surging waters and deposited us safely into the hands of easygoing border officials on the far shore.

'Where are you going?' a smart-looking officer asked.

'We're in transit.'

'Where to?'

'Ujiji and Zanzibar.'

'Eh, eh, eh, big journey!' Thump, stamp.

'Is that a picture of David Livingstone on your truck?'

'Yes, sure ….'

'Good man, that one. Have a safe journey.'

We limped into Livingstone over impossibly potholed tar, tired and hungry, and discovered the green lawns of Fawlty Towers Backpackers and the mixed delights of the Funky Monkey Restaurant.

That night we turned in to the dull roar of Mosi-oa-Tunya, the smoke that thunders. Next day, we agreed, we'd visit the falls, replenish our supplies, then get ready to follow the brown, flooding Zambezi, the river which would fire, then utterly destroy Livingstone's greatest African dream.

Trekking ancient sands
Robyn Daly – August 2002

Following in the tracks of old-time explorers and German Schutztruppe, Robyn Daly saddled up a camel and trekked through the Namib from the Tsondab Valley to the edge of the Kuiseb River.

☙

S an hunters called their desert 'the land God made in anger', early Portuguese mariners dubbed it the 'sands of hell' and sailed on past. With such a reputation, the Namib escaped human scrutiny and was written off as a wasteland hardly worthy of notice. Then in 1965 the first American astronauts, Gordon Cooper and Charles Conrad, relayed photographs of the desert as they orbited the earth in their space shuttle Gemini V.

Photographs from space showed a rippled sand sea extending 900 kilometres along the edge of the Atlantic Coast and some 120 kilometres inland. They revealed giant dunes – some as high as 350 metres – marching north in near-perfect formation from Lüderitz to the Kuiseb River canyon where the sheer size of the fissure in the Damara sediments is enough to stop a desert in its tracks. Suddenly, with a zoom lens, the Namib became a place of beauty.

The desert is still being photographed from space, nowadays by orbiting satellites not spaceships. The lenses are stronger, sharper, the images of wind-sculpted sand sweeping towards the filigreed Kuiseb are works of art in their own right, but still they show no signs of life, or that life is possible. It remains a vacant world, beautiful, fascinating, and desperately lonely.

Now supposing Landsat took a picture of the Namib on just the right sunny day in March, and someone with fancy computer equipment zoomed in very close on the Tsondab Valley, then on one red dune in particular with a view of the puckered Naukluft Mountains.

The picture would show a group of eight camels kneeling in the sand. Standing in front of an especially wide-mouthed and obstreperous individual you would see a little man with a grey-white beard. If the shutter clicked at the right time, you'd see the man's hands in the air, sheer exasperation on his face. That would be Lumpi.

'JOU BLIKSEM SE KAMEEL!' yelled Lumpi as Maria jumped up on all fours for the umpteenth time that morning. Packing camels for safari was patently a task that demanded the patience of a saint, and Lumpi, as his language suggested, was running thin on saintliness. He tapped the sjambok on Maria's front legs, 'Koes! Koes!' (sit, sit) he growled at her. Maria shrugged her hump and begrudgingly koessed.

It took upwards of two hours for the pack camels to be packed and the riding camels to be saddled on the first morning of our camel journey into the Namib. For four days we wouldn't see anything mechanical – it would be just us and the camels. Everything had to be carried: clothes, food, water, toilet paper and all the rubbish we would produce along the way (including the used loo paper).

We'd slept the first night on the lee of a sand dune – somewhat fitfully as Leonie, terrified of creepy crawlies, had flicked her torch on and off through the night to check for scorpions. To no avail. The red sand next morning was embroidered with tracks of sting-wielding visitors, beetles and corn crickets which came out unseen by her in the light of the Milky Way.

Making up the trail party were three Americans, Leonie, the scorpion scout from Windhoek, Don Pinnock and myself. We helped lug the canvas bags with provisions and heavy water containers; Lumpi did most of the fastening and checking. Once the make-shift camp had disappeared into saddle bags, all that remained was to take a camel by the nose-rein and lead it deeper into the desert.

Standard practice each day was to walk the first hour, giving the camels time to adjust to their loads and to ensure that tables, chairs and water containers sat comfortably on these curious creatures which didn't look at all as though they were designed to be furniture removers. As we walked, sand trickled into our boots as unstoppably as the contents of an hour glass, filling them to the brim and rubbing blisters at the tips of our toes. Walking was part of trekking and there seemed to be something ancient and right about putting one foot in front of another in this isolated part of the continent. There was also something very welcoming about Lumpi's command, when it came, to halt, koes the camel train and climb aboard.

Walking is for romantics I decided, swinging my leg over a big camel stallion called Jimmy. He had a saddle made for two and taking turns with me at sitting in front or back was Amy, one of the Americans. It took a short while to get the hang of steering with one rein (Jimmy was not too pleased at having his nose pulled about) and then the day and the desert stretched before us. There was ample time for reflection.

Husband and wife, Lumpi and Waldi Fritzsche of Reitsafari, walked the whole day, occasionally chasing a reluctant walker from behind. They seemed to have the stamina of their camels and were tough as camelthorn acacias. 'My family came out to Namibia with the German Schutztruppe,' said Waldi, walking at Jimmy's nose for a while just in case he got other ideas about where we were headed.

Camels had been in the Namib for a few years before Waldi's family arrived. Curt von Francois brought in the first camel in 1889. It's not known what purpose the camel served, only that von Francois bought it in Tenerife before he left with his troops. The story goes that the camel used to go wandering (possibly searching for a herd to join) and one day it escaped and drowned in Sandwich Harbour. A few years later a recruitment of camels arrived to transport luggage and carry mail between Windhoek and Walvis Bay.

More camels were imported until, by 1906, there were about 2000 in the country. They were part of the great expeditions into and across the desert. In 1909 Hauptmann von Rappard crossed from Chamis to Spencer Bay and along the coast to Lüderitz Bay. Some expeditions failed, such as that of Major Maercker. He had to turn round because he could climb only seven or eight dunes a day and could not reach the sea before his provisions would run out. But Georg Stillger succeeded, crossing from Sesriem to Tsauchab. Just 40 kilometres into his journey, a 200-metre high dune blocked his way. But he and his trained camels climbed for eight hours and finally reached the top.

We climbed dune after dune, sometimes getting off to lead the camels, at other times picking our way up slip faces and over crests on camelback. The dunes changed colour with the passing of the hours, bleached and pale in the heat of the day, warming to peach then rust as the sun keeled over westwards, then burgundy, purple and lilac by the time Venus twinkled above the horizon.

Our second night was in the bowl of a great red barchan dune plumed with grass tufts shedding seeds into the breeze. Beneath a sky strewn with stars we tucked into stew while Leonie kept watch over the creepy crawlies.

She had chosen a tough part of the world to confront her fears. The Namib has upwards of 200 species of beetle, 11 species of ant, which come out after sunset to sip the evening dew, not to mention the geckos, lizards, moles and snakes which swim in the sand.

Peering at a toktokkie beetle whizzing down a dune face the next morning, I wondered what the desert would look like from a beetle's perspective; each grain of sand would be magnified at such close range. All the quartzite grains and their rusty colours tinged by oxides must combine to make a kaleidoscope of the beetle's world. And we'd made the mistake of thinking the Namib denuded ....

It seemed the closer we looked, the more populated and colourful it became. In just two days the bleak big picture had been filled with small life which struggled ingeniously to survive.

Don broke my reverie, rushing over the crest of a dune, a roll of white toilet paper flapping in his wake like a peace flag. 'Come quick, I found a sidewinder.' It seemed the adder and Don had designs on the same patch of dune. The sidewinder's tracks, sweeping brushstrokes on a minimalist canvas, led us to it. S, S, S it spelled over and over again as it slipped away to find a peaceful place to lick the dew from its scales.

With the second day's trekking we reached the Kuiseb River, a vast canyon winding east to west and separating the golden dunes on our side from the bleakest looking landscape imaginable. The 19th-century Swedish naturalist-explorer Charles Anderson took one look at the desert and wrote: 'A shudder, amounting almost to fear, overcame me when its frightful desolation suddenly broke upon my view. Death would be preferable to banishment in such a country.'

This barrenness and the hazy grey-green light which reflected off the sedimentary rock of Damaraland across the Kuiseb canyon were enigmatic. It looked as though someone had clawed the landscape with a giant impressionist rake.

The valley, separating dune sea from stone desert, is an oasis where wild figs grow and camelthorns, tamarisks and tsamma melons thrive along the river bed. We passed nara melons, a strange fruit which looks like a melon but is actually a member of the pumpkin family. It sends a deep taproot into the sand and that way siphons water into the fruit.

That night we camped up high on the crest of a star dune, so named because changing winds have whipped and pulled the sand into arms stretching out in different directions like the points of a star.

Dinner was lentil stew for the humans, a feast of bushman grass for the camels, which were let loose to graze until just before dark. Much to Leonie's horror, we were joined for supper by a dancing white lady spider. Pure white and highly sensitive to light (even moonlight is too harsh) this member of the huntsman spider family is indigenous to the Namib. They're highly territorial and will eat any spider (even of the same species) that ventures near its burrow in the sand. To calm arachnophobic nerves (and here Leonie wasn't alone) we shooed the lady to a more respectable part of the camp, but she had her revenge, setting up a new home in the dead of night, unknown to me, under my sleeping bag. I found her again next morning and breathed a sigh of relief that there had been no need for territorial eating rituals in the night.

The camels set out on the last day at a cracking pace, carrying light loads with just enough water to get us to the trail's end, across the Kuiseb, by sunset. The sun seemed to climb higher than usual that day, perhaps it was the heat from the dark rocks glowering from across the valley. Jimmy's hump began to dig into my nether regions and no matter how many pillows I piled on the saddle I couldn't escape it.

We crossed gravel plains along the edge of the canyon and thudded through a sea of dunes on foot. Then it was on across great spaces that surely inspired the Nama people to call the desert Namib, 'plain without end'. A herd of Hartmann's zebras spied the camels. They stood their ground until they felt we were getting too close, then turned, a tight pack of striped bodies, and fled, moving with symmetry, their camouflage shimmering like a shoal of fish as they finally streamed behind the reptilian tail of a dune.

Beyond the zebras we turned north to negotiate on foot the steep slip faces of powder-white dunes into the valley. It took some zigzagging to find a safe route for the camels to descend. Then we were down, weaving through camelthorn thickets, the smell of the Kuiseb River fresh in the camels' nostrils, taunting and agitating them.

Finally we arrived at the river's edge. The camels koessed for the last time so we could unstrap their loads, then were set free to drink for the first time in four days. As human celebrations went, there was sparkling wine, cold beer and sandwiches.

The sun set on the land that had lost its emptiness. Stars came out and high above a satellite flew over the once-bleak smudge of the living Namib.

Back when the earth was a pear
Cathy Lanz – November 2002

Around 250 years ago, astronomers were still undecided about the shape of the earth. A survey at the tip of Africa provided an answer which nobody liked. Cathy Lanz peeped into the past and found a strange tale.

֍

I t all started – as so much else in history has – with a disagreement between England and France. Newton, in the English corner, said the earth was oblate – a kind of squashed sphere. Quite the opposite, said the French, the earth was clearly elongated.

To prove their case the French sent survey missions to Lapland (Arctic) and Peru (equator) to measure the shape of the northern hemisphere. Their results suggested Newton may be correct – but the French weren't capitulating without a fight.

The missing proof, either way, was an accurate measurement of the radius of the earth in the southern hemisphere. Back then, in the 1600s and 1700s, that was not a measurement freely available from the nearest satellite. While the northern heavens had been well catalogued, the southern hemisphere was, astronomically speaking, still a blank.

Some dedicated astronomer was needed to exile themselves for a few years at a godforsaken spot well south of the equator.

The Abbé Nicolas de la Caille, a young French astronomer-geodesist, was just the man, decided the French Académie des Sciences. The year was 1751; his destination – the fledgling colony at the Cape of Good Hope. De la Caille set up his little observatory at 'the second house in Strand Street, counting westward from the Heerengracht' (Adderley Street). Today, it's the site of Edgars.

In just over seven months he catalogued nearly 10 000 stars (on a clear night you can see about 3000 with the naked eye) and graded them according to brightness. He also added some new constellations, including Mons Mensae (Table Mountain). This was next to the Magellanic Cloud – so Table Mountain had its table cloth. In 1920 the name was shortened to just Mensa, but it remains the only constellation named after a mountain.

De la Caille also endeared himself to his hosts, the Dutch, by determining the exact longitude of the Cape – which was essential for navigation – and surveying Hout Bay.

Those tasks done, he set about measuring an arc of the meridian, which would, in turn, yield the important measurement of the earth's radius. In lay terms, this involved measuring the distance between two points along a north–south line (or meridian), coupled with an accurate reading of the latitudes of the two points. And it was all done with triangles.

After several recce trips into the unmapped country north of Cape Town, De la Caille selected the northern point of his arc. 'This,' he wrote in his journal, 'was a habitation called Klipfontein, situated at the foot of a mountain which abutted on another very long and steep, called Piketberg.' The southern point of the arc would be his observatory in Strand Street – and therein lay his mistake.

From an eight-mile baseline, painstakingly laid out by hand on the Darling Flats, De la Caille built up a series of triangles connecting his Cape observatory with high points on Kapokberg (south of Darling), Kasteelberg (at Riebeek Kasteel) and Klipfontein (near Aurora). The history of geodetic surveying in South Africa had begun.

In 1753, after a year of meticulous observations and calculations, De la Caille released his results on a stunned world – the southern half of the earth was less curved than the northern half. The earth was a pear.

No fault could be found with De la Caille's meticulous work but astronomers were, if not sceptical, then highly perturbed by his findings. De la Caille himself admitted: 'I had not expected the result to be so large, but an observer can only stick by the precision of his measurements and not by their result.'

Without any contradictory proof, and given the abbé's eminent standing as an astronomer, his measurements stood – and the earth remained a pear for the next 100 years.

In 1820 the famous surveyor Sir George Everest (after whom the earth's highest peak is named) stopped off at the Cape en route to India. After inspecting the country in which De la Caille's arc had been measured, Sir George – borrowing from his experiences in the Himalayas – was convinced that any discordances arose from the gravitational effect of mountains at both ends of the arc.

He suggested that the arc be resurveyed and extended to nullify the influence of Table Mountain and Piketberg. This was finally done by Sir Thomas Maclear, astronomer royal at the Cape from 1833 to 1870. Incidentally, Maclear's batman was Thomas Bowler, who became a greater success as an artist than he ever was as a serving man.

After archival research to locate the exact position of De la Caille's observatory in Strand Street, Maclear and his two assistants, Charles Piazzi Smyth and William Mann, embarked on the exhaustive field work, which took them from 1838 to 1847.

Much of the exploratory work involved finding the exact sites of De la Caille's beacons. This is what Maclear found atop Kasteelberg: 'The summit forms an oblong undulating ridge of sandstone rocks and brushwood. On top of the second [peak] there is a heap of stones piled on three rocks …. About 12 feet NW of this heap are a few handfuls of charcoal … which inclines me to think the spot may have been part of the area of De la Caille's signal fire. I brought away some of the charcoal' (which is still preserved in a bottle at the South African Astronomical Observatory).

The survey involved climbing several high mountains, each time lugging up the heavy and ungainly theodolites and solar reflectors. One particular instrument used to make very accurate latitude measurements was the 12-foot long and very fragile Bradley's Sector, which Maclear had borrowed from its reluctant owner in England.

Much of the manual work was done by a party of sappers from the Royal Engineers at the Castle. This account, written by their commanding officer, Sergeant John Hemming, indicates just how chaotic conditions sometimes were during the survey: 'A few casualties occurred to the men of the service. One man was unfortunately drowned while bathing, and another was lost while in a state of intoxication, by a fall into a deep gully. I got a broken head with a bludgeon from a drunken fellow, but providentially soon recovered.'

Despite the goings-on of the sappers, and toiling over inhospitable terrain with delicate instruments, Maclear finally repeated the measurement of De la Caille's arc of the meridian. He then extended the system of triangulation north into Namaqualand and south to Cape Agulhas (where he proposed the site for the Agulhas lighthouse).

Maclear's results came as a relief to the astronomical world. Newton had been correct – the earth was the same shape at both ends – an oblate or orange shape, slightly flattened at the poles. Everest too had been correct. Mountain masses at both ends of the arc had indeed been responsible for De la Caille's discordances.

More than just a verification of De la Caille's arc, Maclear's work provided the first modern survey of the Cape Colony and laid the foundations for all further trigonometrical surveys in South Africa.

Visiting the Western Cape dorpies of Darling, Riebeek Kasteel and Aurora today, it's hard to imagine they were once apexes in the pursuit of the shape of the earth.

Only Aurora carries any visible reminder of its famous geodetic past. The name is Latin for 'dawn' and is appropriately stellar, but seems to have been bestowed quite incidentally. It's a blink-of-an-eye-sized place dwarfed by the Piketberg behind. Though the castle-like Dutch Reformed church suggests they are still waiting for the dawn of a large congregation of devotees.

The church, a general dealer, a café and a few blocks of well-kept cottages, peopled mostly by retirees or weekend visitors – and that's Aurora.

One semi-retiree who's put the place on the map is Helmut Wokalek, previously of De Kelder in Stellenbosch. At his L'Aurore restaurant he prepares hearty German cuisine which has diners driving from as far as Cape Town for lunch.

There was no eisbein and chunky chips cut from local potatoes in De la Caille or Maclear's day. But the farm Klipfontein existed then, and is still there today, straddling the Redelinghuys dirt road.

An archaeological team from the University of Stellenbosch located the exact spot of Maclear's observations – on the farm's old threshing floor. Digging about a metre down, they found a flat stone chiselled with the letters BySR (abbreviation of Bradley Sector).

Last year, to mark the 250th anniversary of De la Caille's arrival in the Cape, a monument, incorporating the chiselled stone, was erected on Klipfontein, on the exact site of the archaeological dig.

It was a strange sensation – to stand on the spot, more than 150 years on, and look out on the same mountains, same dam and, unless I'm mistaken, the same trees which appear in sketches by Piazzi Smyth of the Klipfontein station.

For the extension of the arc, Maclear placed a beacon on top of the mountain – modern maps denote it as Engelsman se Baken. It was obviously a strategic spot because the defence ministry subsequently located a radar tower up there too.

On a clear day, the views from here extend as far as Table Mountain and westwards over St Helena Bay. Making the most of this lofty viewpoint, is Mountain Mist, a rustic collection of self-catering cabins. The resort is a big hit with hikers, nature lovers and, particularly, bird watchers. Twitchers come from all over the world to spot the rare, but rather uninspiring protea canary here.

Heading southeast from Aurora, Riebeek Kasteel (or Kasteelberg) rises from the Swartland vineyards and wheat fields as an isolated ridge of several peaks.

It's almost as high as Table Mountain and De la Caille found it rather daunting: 'I ascended Riebeek Kasteel to make a signal. This mountain is rather high and long ... I placed a signal at the second peak, reckoning from the north, and had all the trees near it cut down.'

Allesverloren Wine Estate now resides at the base of this peak. Glass of fortified nectar in hand, it's a good place to picture the conscientious abbé, sitting up there all night, staring through a telescope.

In this scenic enclave of vineyards and olive groves, Nicolas de la Caille has not been forgotten entirely. The area's newest wine cellar, Meerhof, has named its flagship range in honour of the French astronomer.

It was while sipping on a maiden vintage Meerhof Cabernet, and contemplating the views from the cellar restaurant, that I reached my own conclusion concerning the shape of the earth. It's neither a pear nor an orange. It's a grape. A fruity Cabernet Sauvignon grape, squashed, fermented and aged a little in French oak.

Great White
Cameron Ewart-Smith – March 2003

Long feared as crazed, cold-blooded killers, white sharks are proving our first impressions very wrong. Cameron Ewart-Smith looked behind the hoopla, while cage-diving in the unlikely boom town of Gansbaai on the southern Cape coast, and discovered a majestic animal in critical need of some good press.

~

Y ou are a thousand times more likely to die hanging your Christmas lights than to be attacked by a great white shark. Even dogs – our best friends – killed more people worldwide last year than have been killed by all species of sharks in the past hundred. With approximately 150 scalps a year, coconuts are positively bloodthirsty by comparison.

Even so, as a journalist entering the shark-infested waters off Dyer Island, near Gansbaai at the south-eastern point of Walker Bay (close to where the Birkenhead went down), I was particularly anxious. If there's one group of people sharks should be peeved at, it's us. No other group has spread more falsehoods and hyperbole than the media … with the possible exception of Hollywood directors, that is. If sharks were Americans, they'd sue … and if I were a movie director I'd be safely ensconced somewhere high and dry in the Sahara.

Anxiety soon fled, however, as Brian McFarlane helped me and underwater photographer Geoff Spiby into the metal cage bobbing on the surface next to Predator II, the 12-metre catamaran he uses to take tourists shark-cage diving. He asked us to leave the scuba rigs on board and breathe using only our snorkels, as the mechanical sounds made by demand valves tend to scare the sharks – that's right, I said scare the sharks.

Unfortunately it was summer, not the best season for cage diving, but as we slipped into the cage the signs that we'd have a good encounter were promising – a five-and-a-half metre female was mooching around. Let me say it again in case you glossed over that statistic – FIVE-AND-A-HALF METRES – bigger and heavier than a long-wheelbase bakkie.

As we submerged, peeping out from the bars and holding our breaths, the shark appeared out of the gloom. Passing within touching distance, she glided by effortlessly, propelled by imperceptible movements of her tail. It looked almost artificial … as if she were a model toy driven by a little engine. The eyes were not those of a puppet, however. They were alive, assessing us, unfamiliar visitors to her aquatic realm.

Rice cake or rump steak?

Sharks are attracted to dive boats by chum: the evil-smelling concoction of fish blood and oil that Brian had been ladling into the water since we anchored. This forms an oily slick behind the boat. Supreme opportunists that they are, whites follow the feint trail, hoping for a windfall – a dead whale, seal or big fish. All they find at these boats, however, is a tuna head tied to a rope. And, what's more, the operators usually drag this toward the boats preventing the sharks from getting it.

This chumming and baiting has concerned other coastal users since cage-diving operations began. It's banned in the USA and many people in South Africa would feel happier if this were the case here too.

'There is no clear evidence that shark-cage operators are responsible for the perceived increase in shark activity and shark attacks in recent years,' affirmed shark expert Dr Len Compagno. I caught up with him in his cluttered office – festooned with remnants of old wetsuits, pictures and other shark paraphernalia – at the South African Museum where he is curator of fishes.

'Chumming is not a new activity – fishermen have disposed of fish guts and blood into the water round their boats since fishing began, so to suddenly get hot under the collar about 10 or so licensed operators using chum, is unfortunate.'

Not surprisingly, the shark-diving operators agree. 'It's ridiculous,' said JP Botha, co-owner of Marine Dynamics, one of the licensed operators working out of Gansbaai.

'We've been blamed for attacks that happened over a thousand kilometres away, involving different species of sharks. Luckily, with the scarcity of evidence, all the hoo-ha is beginning to subside.'

Chumming for sharks isn't the Lotto. Certain areas tend to be good for sharks – Dyer Island off-shore of Gansbaai is arguably the best place to dive with white sharks anywhere in the world. But if you drop chum into the water at random, you could wait a really long time before any whites pop by for a visit.

Of course that's not to say that whites have a limited distribution. They occur in temperate coastal waters worldwide, yet have a penchant for turning up where they're not expected. Debbie Smith, who runs the Rocktail Bay Dive Centre in Maputaland, has seen two whites while out with dive groups: one in Ponta do Ouro in Mozambique, the other off Rocktail Bay, south of Kosi Bay.

'I had drifted over the reef to check on a hole where we normally find turtles and came face to face with a three-metre female white shark. Keeping the group close, we watched as she circled us serenely. She then passed roughly a metre from us, before disappearing into the deep blue. It was magic, she was not aggressive at all, probably just curious.'

Unfortunately, this curiosity is probably the root cause of most negative interactions between sharks and humans. Let's not call them attacks, because that has sinister connotations.

'White sharks are curious, intelligent, apex predators,' said Len Compagno. 'They actively investigate new items in their surroundings and it isn't uncommon for them to investigate floating objects. Some of these behaviours, and I am hesitant to say this, may even be playful. We've seen sharks pick up floating planks and toss them, once twice and more – without a rational explanation. It's kinda like they're bored and kicking a can about.'

'But, and herein lies the problem with their human interactions, their major manipulatory organ is their mouth. So when they investigate you in the water, they can do excessive damage, even if to the shark it was only gently mouthing you to see what you are. To be sure, if it was a full-blown predatory attack they'd easily cut you in half – big sharks have been known to slice 200-kilogram bull-seals in two.'

Apex predators are those at the very top of the food web – very simply: they eat everything and fear nothing. Yet they face the same problems all predators do – every predatory interaction has to be seen as a cost–benefit decision involving the amount of effort exerted in the 'chase,' for the amount of energy returned by eating the prey item. Basically, do you chow the stationary rice cake or the galloping rump steak? In this scenario humans are, luckily for us, rice cakes.

Sharks make split-second decisions on the energy content of a prey item as soon as they bite into it. If they bite you they immediately assess you as something not worth eating and so are unlikely to finish you off. If you were a seal with a high percentage of energy-rich blubber, however ….

There have, of course, been instances of sharks eating people; such as the white captured in the Mediterranean with the bodies of two adults and a child in it. But these are relatively rare and probably have lots to do with the nutritional state of the shark in question. If the shark is half-starved, then rice cakes make a welcome snack until something blubberier comes along.

Back off – that girl's mine!
Scientists are also beginning to understand more about the behavioural interactions between white sharks. However, research in this direction is slow and frustrating

according to Ryan Jordan, a PhD student from the University of Pretoria currently studying white shark biology.

'There are just so many unknowns – we are really just discovering aspects of the very complex lifestyles these animals lead. A little bit here, a little bit there.'

Some of the interesting trends scientists such as Ryan are beginning to notice, however, is that sharks definitely interact with each other and communicate using body language. For instance, stiff, arched bodies and gaping mouths (underwater) seem to be threat displays, warning off other sharks.

These same behaviours interest Andre Hartman, another co-owner of Marine Dynamics. Andre, it must be said, is God's gift to the media – a real old man of the sea and seemingly fearless shark man. He has been featured in numerous documentaries and was one of the central characters in the National Geographic cover story of April 2000. He has lived and worked with whites his whole life and now regularly dives with white sharks outside of protective cages.

In this very high-risk activity, understanding what the whites are trying to communicate is the difference between a nice dive and Davey Jones's locker.

Andre was also the first person known to have placed his hand on a white shark's snout, by accident originally, and notice that the shark went into a kind of trance. With his hand on their snouts, sharks stand on their tails in the water between the engines of his boat, heads out, motionless. Why and how this works no one is quite sure. But possibly it has something to do with the over-stimulation of the organs of Lorenzini – or the complex sensory array in their snouts capable of detecting miniscule electrical pulses, which aid the shark in hunting. Whatever the reason, it's still dramatic to see two and a half tons tamed by this Daniel of the ocean.

In summer, however, Andre has noticed the sharks are much more skittish and weary. 'Everybody down there seems to get a little stressed out and so I tend to be far more cautious. Even the snout trick doesn't usually work,' he told me.

I asked Len Compagno about this, who said he wasn't sure of the exact causes, but did mention that many sharks have a definite mating season. During this time males assert their dominance. This is especially true when receptive females are in the vicinity. For ragged-tooth sharks at least, this seems to happen in the southern summer.

Is this also a factor in white shark behaviour? It's hard to tell as mating white sharks have never been documented. However, the pattern fits. What this means of course, is that white sharks kicking round Southern Africa during the summer holiday are not only more likely to encounter people, but could be feeling a little aggro when they do.

Could this explain the recent spate of interactions between surf-skiers in the

Western Cape and great whites? No one can say for sure, but think of it this way: surf-skis are six-odd-metre intruders. If there were females in the vicinity, males could easily be saying: 'Hey dude back off, that girl's mine.'

This aggressive, dominance behaviour could also help explain the attack on Craig Bovim off Scarborough on the Cape Peninsula, Christmas Eve.

He was in the water diving for lobsters, when he noticed a four-metre shark, initially thought to be a raggie but more likely a great white. The shark did not attack immediately but hung around – possibly issuing threats Craig didn't understand. Keeping it in sight, he tried to head into the relative safety of the kelp, but too late. The shark 'investigated' him and in the process, unfortunately, Craig stuffed his arms down the shark's throat.

He pummelled it with his knees and the shark, realising its error, released him and departed. His arms, however, were already badly lacerated and he was losing blood fast. Craig headed for the beach, from where he was rushed to hospital by air ambulance. I am glad to report that Craig is recovering.

The rapid response of medical-rescue services has been the number one factor in decreasing the percentage of fatal interactions – attacks if you must – between sharks and humans. 'The best way to deal with the shark issue is to remain calm and emotionless. It is far too easy to shout: "bring in shark nets" or "kill all sharks" – both of which amount to an environmental disaster,' according to Compagno. 'The reality is, we are in their world and in some ways we have to accept the consequences. That doesn't mean we should stand idle. Rescue services should be trained and prepared to deal with the trauma of shark "attacks"'.

Sharks are not killers but, rather, they have killed. And therein lies a subtle difference. Killer implies ruthless, cold-blooded and malicious. None of which apply to whites. They kill to survive, as do we.

Worldwide shark populations are in alarming decline. White sharks, in particular, seem to be threatened, even though they are protected in large parts of their range. This is due to the price on their heads. Shark-fin soup made from whites' fins fetches top-dollar; a set of jaws could bring in a couple of thousand dollars. With that sort of reward an active black-market exists.

As Ryan Jordan pointed out: 'That is only the direct mortality. It's hard to quantify the effects of over-fishing, which reduces available prey and by-catch, or sharks caught incidentally while fishing for other species. These are probably even more detrimental to population numbers.'

That there should be any doubt of the survival of white sharks is a tragedy. After my experiences diving in the shark cages, it's hard to think that such a majestic creature could be heading towards its end.

Possibly, just possibly, we journalists can help prevent this. We now have a different story to tell. Whites don't target people deliberately and, all things considered, would probably be mortified to know we hold them up in such fear. As Joseph Conrad said: 'The belief in a supernatural source of evil is not necessary; [humans] alone are quite capable of every wickedness.'

Rummaging through Africa's attic
Justin Fox – March 2003

Justin Fox joined Mike Copeland and the Getaway Land Rover in Nairobi for the third Cape-to-Cairo leg. They embarked on a long trek across the desert wastes of northern Kenya, into Ethiopia to Addis Ababa. From there they traced a northern circle through the mystical highlands.

❧

I stood in the hot rain outside Nairobi's Jomo Kenyatta International Airport, surrounded by badgering touts, waiting for Mike. The Land Rover emerged from behind a row of palms, mud-spattered and looking the part.

'Hey, hop in Justin, let's hit it,' said a bestubbled Mike Copeland, driver and guide for the Cape-to-Cairo expedition. I tossed my luggage in the back and we were off, squeezing into the confusion of downtown traffic. We drove between brutal glass highrises with marabou storks stalking among the traffic like businessmen and then out of town into the countryside.

Kenya: blowouts and bandits

The road led north through coffee and banana plantations. The landscape became drier towards Isiola and police roadblocks more haphazard affairs, almost indistinguishable from the bandit hold-ups we feared. Acacia savanna petered into desert. Billowing cattle trucks, stacked with Turkana tribesman riding shotgun on the roof, eased out of their grooves and slid across the road towards us. We'd head for the ditch to be enveloped in their dust.

We reached Laisamis Mission Station at sunset where Father Fernando let us pitch our tents in his compound. Kiswahili choir voices issued from the church. I asked a group of girls if I could photograph them, but two louts chewing miraa (a narcotic leaf) had other ideas.

'Why you taking picture?' said one aggressively, green twigs sticking to his teeth like salad. 'You exploiting the children. You give me money.'

It was not the last of the hostility. In the coming days, driving north through desert, there were a number of tense encounters. The Turkana, Samburu and Borena live in a near-lawless wilderness with stock theft and raids from Somali shiftas (bandits) a constant threat. Even the herd boys carried AK47s, which added a certain compliance on our parts.

Hours of desert driving, then a tank piled with troops, or a camel train, centipedal and ghosting in a horizon mirage. The lonely track to Lake Turkana entailed a two-day detour, but we wanted to see the Jade Sea's stark beauty. The road, however, was jagged-stone-and-boulder madness. Somewhere in the flatlands we heard a pop and hiss. Blow out.

There we were, in the midday sun, toiling at the change. Jack and grease, sweat and swearing. And the question of what to do? The road to Turkana was diabolical and known bandit territory. With the tyre a virtual write-off we had only one spare. A week in the Chalbi waiting for a recovery truck held little allure, so we turned the Land Rover round and headed for the safer option of Marsabit. Later we'd hear that an overland vehicle ahead of us was stopped and stripped by shiftas.

The dripping forests of Marsabit National Park came as cool relief. Studded with volcanic craters, it's home to a surprisingly large number of bigger game, such as elephant, buffalo and reticulated giraffe.

We made camp on a grass lawn beside Lake Paradise, a perfect volcanic sphere. A dozen red elephants stepped from the wall of hardwoods opposite us, their ivory glowing yellow in the last rays of the sun.

Darkness seeped from the shadows. A chorus of night sounds took over, echoing round the bowl. I woke off and on during the night, listening; the most complex, complete sound I'd ever heard. There were so many varied instruments which grew in intensity as dawn approached: the staccato clucking of guinea fowl, tree castanets, the hiss of high leaves. Horns, wind instruments, strings, and always the oboe frogs.

At a police checkpoint we were offered an armed guard to ride the Ngaso Plain with us. Mike declined. So, foot flat, we hurtled across unforgiving stone. It was a scary, bone-jangling run, but we reached the border in one piece and, after two hours of polite bureaucracy and an exhaustive vehicle search, eased over onto the right-hand side of the road and into Ethiopia. Goats lay in our path chewing chat (another version of miraa), stoned off their floppy heads. The Landy weaved between them.

Ethiopia: nothing quite prepares you for it. The Christianity, heavily influenced by Judaism, is more Old Testament than New, the calendar seven years, and the clock six hours, behind ours. The food – injera (a staple pancake-like bread), wat (spicy sauce), kitfo (raw minced meat) – was unlike anything we'd tasted. The language is ancient and written in elegant, swirling script; and the architecture is magnificent: pre-Christian citadels, rock-hewn churches and fairytale palaces seemingly out of the pages of medieval romance.

Into Africa's attic

Straight blacktop spooled towards Addis, red termite mounds lining the route like a colonnade. The land grew lush again with enset (false bananas) towering over rondavel hamlets and pastoral commonages where cattle grazed and boys played soccer.

Tourists were a rarity in these parts and, as we slowed through villages, children ran beside the car shouting 'farangi, farangi' (foreigner) or, more irritatingly 'you, you, you' sung in a continuous chorus that sounded like a siren.

We dodged Djibouti-bound trucks disgorging acrid smoke on the highway into Addis. A young woman with aquiline features lay asleep on a bed beside the road. 'Bier, not bed,' said Mike. 'And she isn't asleep.'

Addis held little allure as we were hungry for open road. The highlands beckoned and our Landy ate the kilometres skyward over mountain passes and Italian-made stone bridges. The earth opened in chasms; millet-and-wheat patchwork fields pimpled with haystacks filled the valleys. Little girls suspended in baskets on stilts acted as human scarecrows.

We climbed through 3000 metres into Drakensberg-like mountains of craggy basalt. At last Lalibela, home to the unofficial eighth wonder of the world: the rock-hewn churches. But these 800-year-old monoliths are not ancient relics preserved as museums; they are living places of devotion with pilgrims arriving every day to pray. On saints' days the churches are packed with worshippers in white robes, leaning on their prayer sticks or prostrating themselves before the altar, the priests resplendent in gold and red. Services last all night accompanied by drumming, chanting, incense and tolling bells.

We descended stairs into holes cut by countless masons, and followed tunnels leading to church precincts. Perhaps the most beautiful is Bet Maryam. We emerged into a courtyard and were met by beggars in rags: mumbled prayers, outstretched hands (many leprous and without fingers). A blind woman followed our footfall, moaning.

Inside the church it was cool and dark. A boy read from an illuminated bible while bearded priests stood over him. His voice, chanting in ancient Ge'ez, echoed through the space. The paintings and icons depicted biblical stories, and monks drew back curtains to reveal vellum books and the intricate silver fretwork of hand crosses.

Dangling from 20 metres of leather

The Land Rover traversed seemingly endless mountain passes into Tigray, Ethiopia's northern province and cradle of its ancient civilisation. Outside Mekele we passed a caravan of more than a hundred camels, loping out of the wheat fields like a fleet.

163

They carried salt bricks from the Danakil Depression – one of the lowest, and hottest, places on earth – bound for market.

In town the camel drivers told us they'd been trekking for three weeks. The camels' backs had salt-encrusted wounds where the bricks had chafed them. Man and beast rested in the shade while traders haggled over the precious commodity in a manner little changed in the last millennium.

The rock-hewn churches of Tigray make for fascinating off-the-beaten-track exploring. Had there been time we could easily have dedicated a fortnight to visiting the isolated monasteries, many of which have been visited by only a handful of farangis. Our route took in those that were easily accessible from the main road, but they still offered steep climbs to cliff-face cave churches or hilltop settlements set in olive groves. Most remarkable was Debre Damo. This 6th-century, male-only monastic enclave is perched on an impregnable flat-topped koppie. Surrounded by cliffs, the only way up is by a 20-metre rope.

It was early morning when we arrived at the base and shouted to be hauled up. After a protracted fee negotiation with unhelpful boys and a mongoloid teenager the rope was lowered. A goatherd tied a length of inexpertly laced cowhide as a 'safety harness' around my waist. Slipknot instead of a bowline, I noted ruefully. He thrust the plaited-leather rope into my hands and said. 'You climb mistah, ishee?' (okay?)

Using handholds in the rock and partially shimmying up the worn leather, I eventually hauled myself over the lip to find that the eight-year-old who'd been taking up the slack on my safety line, had not put a turn round the bollard provided. If I'd fallen it would have been tickets for both of us.

The settlement looked like a Tuscan village with dry-stone walls and herds of goats and sheep. 'Only boy animals, no girls,' said our priest guide. Getting an ox aloft meant inspanning a troop of monks to haul it up on the same rope I'd used.

Here too were hollows cut in the rock, where pilgrims found their final resting places. Peering into one of the caverns we saw a body, partly decomposed, flesh still hanging from the bones. Queasiness propelled us onward ....

We drove through inselberg country, destination Axum, the northernmost city of our highland circuit.

The town is layered with millennia of history, but most striking is the great stelae field. Hewn from single blocks of granite, the tallest of these monuments to the dead – erected by King Ezana in the third century – stands 23 metres high. Beside it, shattered into megaton blocks, is an even larger stele that toppled soon after erection.

You trip over the ancients wherever you go in Axum. Beside the stelae field is Queen of Sheba's Pool where women come to collect water (nearby ruins are said to be the remains of the legendary queen's palace). Just beyond the stelae field is the holiest precinct in all Ethiopia. The Arc of the Covenant purportedly resides in a humble building beside the ruins of a fourth-century church and is the spiritual home of the Ethiopian Orthodox Church. Only the keeper of the key is allowed in. Only he knows the truth.

Burnt-out tanks and fabled palaces

The road led south-west through a land in the golden glow of harvest; reapers moved like ants, gnawing at the crop with sickles while others winnowed and cattle threshed. There was no sign of the predicted famine to come. It struck me then that this had always been Africa's bread basket, one of the first places our nomadic ancestors took to the plough so many thousands of years ago.

Over a rise we came upon the remains of a battlefield. Hostilities with Eritrea had only ceased the previous year and border raids were still common. Mangled armoured cars, artillery pieces and burnt-out T-55 tanks punctuated the fields. Local farmers continued to plough, simply taking a detour round the military hardware.

Further down the road we came to a bridge which created a bottleneck, prefect for ambush. Lined up, as though in a shooting gallery, were rows of tanks, all shattered. We inched past, watched by farmers carrying semi-automatic weapons.

The Landy approached the Simien Mountains climbing into a landscape contorted into improbable shapes. Cones and squares, noses and fingers. Up through 3000 metres again, switchbacking through the basalt buttresses. We topped out into high alpine scenery: pine and juniper, cattle grazing in green meadows, waterfalls.

After sleeping a night in an unsavoury Simien establishment where sewage arrangements were still in an experimental phase, we descended to Gonder. Resembling Camelot, this lovely city was home to a string of 17th- and 18th-century kings who built fabulous palaces and churches and were great patrons of the arts, creating an African Florence.

We devoted two days to exploring. Debre Birhan Selassie Church houses some of the finest religious paintings in Ethiopia, its ceiling decorated with winged cherubic faces. The palace complex itself has recently been restored and boasts ramparts, turrets, banqueting halls and defensive walls. It's a place you can while away many hours marvelling at this strange Arcadian Africa.

Then a two-day drive back to Addis via the thundering Blue Nile Falls. Our last night on the road was spent in another insalubrious truckers' stop. No condoms next to the bed this time, I noted, but the girls were lined up at the bar and the Aids exchange system was in full swing. Later, there was the scream of wood on lino floor, and moaning. Down the line to death.

I woke early to find the trucks gone and a vulture perched outside my window. The run to Addis was a breeze on roads whose tar became smoother as we approached the capital.

It was almost midnight when Mike deposited me at Addis International. Don Pinnock and I would pass in the air, him flying in to join Mike on the last big push to Cairo, me heading for the softest of pillows and food I could recognise … and pronounce.

Putting a new spin on road trips
Robyn Daly – June 2003

*Let loose two blondes with too much time on
their hands in a topless sports car and all sorts of
things are uncovered. For a start, they invent a
new way of reading maps, which lands them in the western Free State.*

Freedom … a word that sings like a summer wind brewing up an electric storm over maize fields. It's being able to take the Oxford Dictionary and toss it in the bin. The surprise of sand between your toes and waves lapping at your ankles in a land-locked province. It's the unexpected. It's following the wind. A credit card without limit. A sports car with its top down. A holiday with no itinerary, no destination. A journey.

We had a bottle, a map and a convertible. The map was placed on the bonnet of the car, the bottle on top of the map – on the dot of Johannesburg. 'I'll spin first,' said Carmen, my travelling companion from those free and hedonistic days way back when at university. She gave the bottle a twist, it spun one and a half times and stopped. She traced a line with her finger from the bottle top to …

'Parys,' she said.

And we were off, roof down, the wind in our blonde hair – plus petrol fumes, road dust and insects. Even freedom comes at a price.

Parysian platteland

With one foot in the North West and the other across the Vaal River in the Free State and an island golf course between its legs, Parys is a phenomenal town – all the more so because it's the crash site of a meteor umpteen million years ago. True to form for city poppies let loose with a credit card, we ignored the things that fall out the sky (dimpled or not) and went shopping.

I'm not sure what it is about Parys, maybe it's still radio-active from the meteor, but there's a buzz about the place. It's a magnet for sculptors, painters, potters, you name it, and it seems to be one of those towns where outsiders are accepted on merit, not background, colour, gender, sexual preference or language.

For the shopaholic, there's culture and history by the trolley load. First stop was Die Blakermakers for some hand-wrought metalwork and the cutest little glass flower candle holders, 'darl', then on to Pine's Antiques which yielded a must-have umbrella stand, and to Berne's Diner – straight out of the '70s – for home-made ginger beer and a burger.

'We could stay,' said Carmen. 'Or we could go on.'

Out came the map and the little whisky bottle again, much to the consternation of a Parysian police officer patrolling the aisle to the loo.

'Heilbron, do you think there's life out there?'

There was and there wasn't, depending how you looked at it. We rolled in while it was just light enough to read the names on the marked gravestones. For the most part, there wasn't much reading necessary. During the Anglo-Boer War Heilbron was the site of one of the largest concentration camps, with more than 2000 women and children detained there. The graveyard is extensive, mostly unmarked graves, with a monument to the British soldiers on one side and a monument to the Boers on the other.

A cold shiver rippled the trees surrounding the graveyard. We left before any ghosts arrived.

The Commodore Hotel is about the only place to get a drink and a game of pool in the farming district of Heilbron, but it's a dingy, seedy joint with some dodgy-looking locals. Nevermind, it was nothing an extra layer of make-up and a squirt of perfume couldn't deal with. It was there that we met Wessel Hattingh junior from Francolin Creek Guest Lodge. A farmer chap of burly proportions doing stand-in duty while his tourist-minded parents were in Johannesburg, young Wessel was a little out of his depth at having to entertain two girlies with little more than shopping on their minds.

With the general dealer closed and nothing else about town that sold more than tractor parts, he took us to the Heilbron Golf Club for dinner. Still in city-slicker mode it was salads and starters all round. Wessel, not one to fly in the face of trendiness, ordered much the same.

'So what do you do in Heilbron?' we asked coyly.

Wessel shrugged. 'I farm mostly, and on free weekends I go away to visit my girlfriend.'

Heilbron, it seemed, was a place to escape from, not to. But Francolin Creek on Wessel's parents' farm was as quiet a country retreat as any. After eight hours 'on the road' (largely taken up with shopping, to be honest) smooth cotton sheets, en suite bathrooms and the sound of a Free State thunderstorm were better than any retail therapy.

'I can't believe there's wine tasting in the Free State,' Carmen nattered next morning as I tried to keep our ultra low-slung MG TF160 in one piece following Wessel's bakkie along a jeep track made for well-sprung ox wagons. Eventually we gave up and piled into the bakkie for the last leg to Goede Hoop Guest Lodge owned by Wessel's aunt and uncle.

The Hattingh family owns two of three farms on the Riemland Wine Route, an ingenious idea to bring the fine traditions of wine tasting and farm-hopping upcountry. It's also a clever marketing strategy for Boland wines, there for the tasting.

Aside from having a moody old basement cellar virtually overflowing with good wines and serving brunch fit for a Heilbron farmer, the genteel Goede Hoop Guest Lodge dates back to 1892 and is one of the few farmhouses in the area that wasn't burned down during the Anglo-Boer War. It also sells wine. And so, with appetites satiated and bottles clinking dangerously in the boot of the spiffing new 'Morris Garage' sports car, we laboured back along the jeep track to the tar to spin the bottle again and follow the freedom of the open road.

Kroonstad, said our Footprint guidebook, is 'a dull town on the Vals River. It is only worth stopping here for provisions.' After Heilbron's distinct lack, the Edgars, Truworths and Foschini on Kroonstad's main drag was the only excuse needed to spend the night.

We followed road signs into the 'burbs' where the trees are green and the gardens well tended, and found Arcadia B&B. The face-brick chalets are set in a profusion of roses and enough cement garden figures to make guests wonder whether PPC is a shareholder.

It was a Friday night and Valentine's to boot – no time to stay in. First stop: Arcadia's bar – a little too reserved, but cosy for starry-eyed couples. The Hacienda Hotel was more our style. From the outside it looks a place of dubious repute, inside it's all dark-wood panelling, dull lighting and old-style hotel friendliness, an overnight for sales reps or somewhere for an illicit affair.

The hotel was bought by mistake at an auction. 'My uncle and I went to buy chairs. We didn't realise the whole hotel was for sale,' said owner-cum-manager Claire Khoury. 'My uncle was talking during the bidding and, being Lebanese, he uses his hands a lot. Next minute we were the new owners of a hotel, at a bit more than what we'd budgeted for the chairs!' Proof enough that not all is dull in Kroonstad.

Deeper into the heartland
Next day, the spinning bottle led us on a merry zigzag route, first to Bothaville – an outpost town with almost more garages than there were cars in the street – then to Hoopstad, an utterly hopeless looking place ... for tourists, that is. Undeterred we stopped in at the Spar and asked the blonde cashier, 'What's there to do in town?'

She shrugged. 'Nothing really.' A few more questions from us and shrugs from our informant revealed absolutely no reason to hang around, so with music blaring, roof back and hair flying wildly in our faces, we roared out. This time the bottle had pointed to Bloemhof.

The town of Bloemhof's main attraction is its dam, the Free State version of a seaside holiday. It also has a generous – for what is basically a one-road town – selection of places to stay, and glorious sunflower fields 'to match our yellow convertible,' Carmen reasoned.

What really clinched the deal was the monument to Bles Bridges just outside the town – and the prospect of spending the next morning sunbathing beside the Bloemhof Dam. The Why Not Restaurant and Gastehuis seemed just the place to stay. To be fair to the likes of Bothaville and Hoopstad, Bloemhof is on the N12, so tourists are as common to this part of the Free State as Brahman cows in the fields. Elsewhere though, asking for a B&B recommendation was rather like asking for ET's phone number.

Much like Bloemhof, Christiana (to which our bottle pointed next) is no stranger to travellers. It too boasts water sports (on the Vaal River) and there's an Aventura Resort among the many places to stay. Beyond that, it doesn't have quite the same bright-eyed and bushy-tailed atmosphere of Bloemhof and instead has beggars and dirty pavements, though the Spar is very fancy.

Aventura Christiana was where we headed for the night following rumours that the place had a health spa. The resort must have been built with a special offer for face brick and is begging for more greenery. Aesthetics weren't going to mar an opportunity for self-pampering: a jet bath, facial, manicure, pedicure and credit-card load full of cosmetics later and we were ready to hit the road again, both bearing satisfied grins.

To Dealesville, pointed the bottle. But there was nothing there except a leiwater system wide enough to float a corpse.

Next stop was Bloemfontein. We found a sign for Glen Country Lodge a few kilometres outside the city and decided to follow that. It was a good choice, with the lodge's chalets set in profuse gardens on the edge of a willow-lined river. Our greeting – from ducks, black swans, dogs, an overweight cat and human hosts – was friendly. We were told that dinner of home-made spaghetti bolognaise was nearly ready and needed no further reasons to spend the night.

For two shopaholics to pass by Bloemfontein without stopping at a mall is like trying to stop the sun revolving around the Free State – it does, I promise. Mimosa Mall was just too close to the edge of town to be ignored. Thereafter – sporting new hairdos and a few other 'necessities' – we were back on the road, dodging thunderheads threatening to douse the newly ploughed fields.

'Philippolis,' said Carmen, pointing at the map. 'What's there?'

What's there indeed! Fouchinie is, for a start, but it's the local version of the department store, selling cheap plastic pumps and the height of domestic-worker fashion. There's also loads of Anglo-Boer War and Bushmen history, a friendly hotel pub for the evening's entertainment (together with the town magistrate, lawyer, hotelier and other tipple lovers), a museum to Sir Laurens van der Post (who grew up here) housing copies of 25 of his books, and the old jail that has been converted into a guesthouse.

Still bent on freedom, we declined the offer of the lockup for the night and cruised into Oppie Stoeppie B&B for the warmest Free State reception and definitely the best meal of the journey, home-cooked Free State mutton stew.

The colours of freedom

As fate would have it – or the polarity of the bottle or whatever it was guiding our travels – our direction the next morning was undeniably back to Jo'burg. With the boot of Mr Morris' yellow convertible bulging and our bank balances well and truly in the red, we put the roof up and gave our cheeky MG the chance to show its mettle on the Great North road.

Not far out of Philippolis we pulled over at a herd of horses grazing on the dun-coloured veld. There was the stallion, a golden palomino, and his honey-coloured mares with foals nearby. The stallion stood facing us, muscles in his neck quivering, his ears flicking back and forth.

Next minute he was off, his mares at his heels, the foals at their flanks. The herd of horses spread out across the veld, against a backdrop of koppies and a thunderous sky. Their tails streamed out behind them, wild and free.

Walking with demons:
four weeks in the Drakensberg
David Bristow – June 2003

The Drakensberg had long been editor
David Bristow's favourite haunt. However,
although he'd crisscrossed it numerous times, he
had yet to complete the ultimate Berg hike. He coerced
an unsuspecting ally and set off in search of a dream,
and found some demons.

T he basic idea was a simple one.

As concepts go, The Grand Traverse is rather basic: to walk the Drakensberg end to end. Simple. It's a largely uncharted and trail-less route, extending from more or less Mont-aux-Sources in the north to (depending on which source you consult) Sani Top or Bushman's Nek in the south.

Over the years various hardy mountaineers have done, or attempted a 'grand traverse', but the official record is held by an American ex-Peace Corps volunteer in Lesotho. In 1994 Tom Wimber walked alone from Mont-aux-Sources to Xalanga (Vulture) Peak in the north-eastern Cape, an amazing 549 lonely kilometres.

For a growing number of people the grand traverse has become a challenge much like the Argus, the Comrades or the Dusi – just another ultra feather to put in their competitive caps. For my companion, associate *Getaway* editor Adrian Bailey, it all started rather innocently when, during an idle conversation with his wife he had pondered: 'Wouldn't it be a cool thing to do ....'

Pity him for he knew not quite what he was letting himself in for when, on discovering that I was planning such a hike, he eagerly volunteered to accompany me. I was relieved to have the company, but my motivation came from a deeper, darker source. I was born with the mountaineer's curse – I have a compulsion to see what's over the next horizon, and the next.

I also had a certain reputation to uphold: I was the author of a hiking guide to the Drakensberg. I had an audience, I had critics, I had something to prove. Whether we achieved or failed in our task it is, ultimately, for you, dear reader, to decide. So settle into your comfy chair, and bear with us as we set out to conquer the spine of the dragon.

Witzieshoek to Organ Pipes

Rain, hail, sleet and snow.

I had decided April would be a wonderful time to do this walk, all green and singing streams. The morning we set off from the comforts of Witzieshoek Mountain Resort was full of promise.

The chain ladders to the top of the Amphitheatre were a lot harder than I recalled, but then I was carrying 10 kilograms more, and was 15 years older, than when last I'd done it. That evening a cold, rattling wind picked up, so we sought out the shelter of a stone kraal wall behind the Eastern Buttress.

As is my custom in the mountains, I lit my pipe; it was to be the last time, for reasons including a miserable cold and the freezing weather to come. As it turned out winter came early, and furiously so.

Over the next two days, overnighting behind Icidi and Rwanqa passes respectively, we were constantly worrying about two things. The first was getting too close to the edge of the 3000-metre-high escarpment and literally falling over the edge into the bottomless sea of mist. The second was meeting the escarpment edge on the wrong side of the Mnweni Cutback.

Following one of the pleated valleys too far inland into Lesotho, and having to backtrack around to the other side of the cutback, would mean getting to Ledger's Cave late. And that would almost certainly mean missing the two local guides who would be hauling fresh supplies for us up Mnweni Pass. It was to be the first of three scheduled food drops on this first leg of our traverse, and upon these drops rested the success of our pilgrimage. Our daily schedule became an ever-increasing burden.

Mist was billowing over the escarpment and we were stumbling round, the blind leading the blind in the land of the unseeable. Dustings of snow covered the high ground as far as we could see into Lesotho, when we could see anything between the torn sheets of dragon's breath steaming over the escarpment edge.

Everything in the Drakensberg is 'Very Big'

Ultimately, we found the toughest task of the hike to be choosing the correct route. Paths were scant, often confusing or patently going the wrong way, but mostly non-existent. When you are faced with row upon row of indistinguishable peaks and ridges, a map is only a partial aid to making the right choice. And as Adrian would say, everything in the Drakensberg is 'Very Big'.

The thing is, it's not flat up there. The ground slopes this way and that; valleys crisscross, intersect and seem to go round in great big arcs; every prominent point on the escarpment is in fact a truncated ridge, some running north–south and some east–west. If you assume the escarpment runs north–south and all ridges east–west, you're in for a 'Very Big' time.

173

Our first major blunder was round the Mnweni Cutback. When we saw green terraces and stone-and-grass huts far off in a valley below us, we knew we were lost. Sounds of a donkey train moving through the mist were ominous, for 'twas the season of the dagga harvest and the mountain passes all the way from Ifidi to Bushman's Nek rang merrily with the tinkling of smugglers' donkey bells.

We were so determined not to turn back too soon towards the escarpment edge, we ended up way inside Lesotho. This was also when we learned that wide paths with head-high cairns do not necessarily mark the watershed, although sometimes they do.

It was a mighty slog, but with weary hearts and legs we made it to Ledger's Cave and our appointed rendezvous with cheery Caiphus Mthabela and Mkhonjiswa Mtolo of the intrepid Mnweni Guides. That night the temperature plummeted, then it rained, then sleeted, and finally hailed through the rest of the night.

We awoke to a classic Berg morning: a clear sky, the Mnweni Cutback packed with candy-floss clouds and the land under an ice carpet. Amazingly, from then on, although we often suffered plummeting temperatures at night with rain, hail or snow, we never had more than drizzle and sleet during the days. But that infernal wind!

It hounded our every step, knocking us around every time we crested a ridge, and snuffling its way into our hoods, our sleeves and anywhere that was exposed. It never gave in and, ultimately, it was the wind that wore us down.

From Ledger's Cave, past Mponjwane and Rockeries, the Saddle and Ntonjelane Pass, we hugged an escarpment wrapped in thick mist, then ducked behind Cathedral Spur into the Kwakwatsi Valley. Camp was set near the head of Mlambonja Pass, and next day was a long haul skirting Xeni, the Elephant, Cockade and giant Cleft Peak (3281 m) to Windy Gap above the Organ Pipes. This was our next food rendezvous, but we very nearly missed guide Wiseman Mduli from Cathedral Peak Hotel, who we found huddling just inside the pass, sheltering from the howling wind.

Organ Pipes to Giant's Castle
Tears, sweat, toil and finally a lucky break.

The whole night at Windy Gap an icy gale raged. The valley was filled with the clanging and voices of dagga smugglers descending or returning up the pass.

The next day marked our halfway point on the first leg and was supposed to be a rest day. But thank goodness we decided to push on, for the worst was yet to come. Cleft Peak has a twin, Ndumeni Dome, on the south side of Windy Gap. We headed up the Rockeries skyline, making for the two small caves set in a deep gully near the head of Thuthumi Pass. We reached them worn out, but after nervously recce-ing the other side of the gully, found an easy traverse to the Tlangaku's headwaters.

Let me say in our defence that the new KwaZulu-Natal Wildlife maps were not yet available, and we had to rely on the old Slingsby series. Good as they are, they show very little of the Lesotho side of the watershed and so are of limited – and frustrating – use when attempting a summit traverse. The Tlangaku River followed by way of some wide S bends into Yoddler's Cascades on the Tlanyaku River, one of the treasures of the trip. But, after following the cascades for several kilometres, the ground became alarmingly steep. We cut out to the left in search of Didima Cave (formerly known as Ndedema).

Let it be recorded that, minute details aside, I can recall every step of that merciless zigzagging climb up the western slope of Didima Dome (3245 m), the depressing realisation that we'd topped out at a nek, and still had a two-kilometre grovel round two spurs to the cave. For me that was the low point, emotionally, of the hike. I daresay a tear or two of frustration were whipped away by buffeting gusts when we sank to our knees on the edge of Twin Peak.

Mercifully Didima Cave was among the finest of the Drakensberg and for once we enjoyed a spacious night, out of the elements and not having to cook and sleep under each other's armpits.

A cave to avoid; no one at home

The next day started off well, although the going round the headwaters of the Didima River was without path and over rocky, tussocked slopes. Soon we were onto a more-or-less path that lead for over four kilometres along some of the highest, yet unnamed prominences of the escarpment (one was subsequently identified as Pampiring, 3335 metres).

However, locating Nkosazana Cave (which I had used twice previously), proved to be a treasure hunt in deteriorating weather. When we found it, it was no jewel: it was cramped, damp and litter-strewn.

On the map it looks like a doddle, yet the three-kilometre trudge up Nkosa-zana Valley to the head of Ship's Prow Pass was a mission. When we reached the nek the icy wind hit us, so we scurried down to the wide river valley below us. The right decision in the circumstances, but there followed a labyrinthine route linking valleys ever deeper inland, with much scope for losing ourselves. That we missed the top of Leslie's Pass – our third food rendezvous – by just one ridge infuriated Adrian but was a relief to me.

The tale of how Champagne Valley resident Klaus Piprek and his weary band of make-shift carriers found us after the appointed guides chickened out, how their chopper lift back down missed them, and how they stumbled into Injisuthi

175

Camp very late that night, is a noble and sobering one. We were ever grateful they did make it.

Midday on the tenth day of our hike saw us buffeted by a wind that seemed laden with stinging icicles, sitting atop Mafadi Peak, although 'peak' is perhaps an inappropriate description for a basalt pimple on a wide, sweeping ridge some way back from the Injisuthi headland.

What gives it authority is the fact that it's 3446 metres high (or as more recently measured, 3451 metres, see Bush Notes January 2003). And that makes it the highest point in South Africa (the highest point in Southern Africa is a 3482-metre-high pimple on a ridge, not far from Sani Top). It was my birthday. I unwrapped my cellphone and tried to phone home for some TLC. I got myself on the answering machine.

Sleeping the sleep of the innocent

It was to be a long day, round the back of Injisuthi Dome, down down down into a deep, lovely unnamed valley with waterfalls and pools, and up up up a tussocked slope to finally plop out in a valley behind Popple Peak, at 3325 metres one of the 'kulus' (from the Zulu word for 'big') of the Giant's Castle area. It was just about sunset and the usual evening storm was approaching. There we pitched our faithful two-person Isodome, 15 linear, hard kilometres from our previous camp so our GPS told us. Funnily, although it was among the hardest days of our traverse, we were feeling strangely perky. It was still my birthday, so we cracked open a bottle of Jack Daniels and for the first time slept right through the 14-hour night.

By now we were starting to increase our daily distances to the point where we were an entire day ahead of schedule. From Popple Peak we reached Bannerman Pass, close to our proposed overnight stop, by mid-morning. We had two and a half days left: a hard push over the Bannerman Ridge to Bannerman Cave, followed by a much harder roller-coaster run to Giant's Pass, then the slog down Giant's Pass to Giant's Camp. I was bracing myself for the 300-metre climb over Bannerman Ridge when Adrian cut into my laboured thoughts.

'Our basic aim is to get to Giant's Camp, right?'

'That, indeed, is it.'

'Well,' he tapped irritatingly on the map, 'why not go straight down here?'

A radical thought, and one which offended my purist goal of traversing the entire Berg. But Adrian didn't know that.

'We can go virtually in a straight line down from here to the camp, or we can walk for another three days to get to the same spot.'

Hard logic to fault when you're sitting in the lee of Bannerman Ridge and your plan promises only heartache.

We hefted our packs, and turned sharp into the dark, gaping funnel of Bannerman Pass. By lunchtime we had reached the hiking hut on the contour path so, after a rest, kept right on going. At 17h00 and close on 22 kilometres from our previous camp site we staggered into the pub at Giant's Camp. Beer. Whiskey. Shower. Food. Wine. Beds, with duvets.

That night the heavens opened and we awoke to see the Berg etched in white. It looked lovely. But it would have been hell to be up there. We'd had enough for now, and turned for home to recharge our batteries.

In the kingdom of the Rain Queen
Robyn Daly – October 2003

There's much more to Tzaneen and its surrounds than fruit farmers under pressure from land redistribution. It is beautiful countryside with an ancient cycad forest, tumbling waterfalls – and plenty of rain. Robyn Daly went in search of the woman in charge of the clouds.

The pitter-patter of rain comes in the night like the footsteps of a child creeping into your room to snuggle under the bed covers. The raindrops possess a magical power to transform the world of fine-edged lines of tree plantations, hilltops and winding roads into a fuzzy place that is at once wet and cosy and warm and wonderful.

In the kingdom of the Rain Queen, even the least philosophical of us is compelled to pose the question: where does rain come from? Around Magoebaskloof, Duiwelskloof and Tzaneen in the Limpopo Province, where the newly crowned Queen Modjadji VI holds sway, rain seems omnipresent, hanging in the air, just waiting to fall. Even when there's not a cloud in the sky, the weather can change within an afternoon. It can get so persistent at times you might wonder if a rain queen isn't needed to keep precipitation in check rather than summon the annual crop drenching.

A cloak of mystery

On a continent where rulers run around beating their authority on their breasts, you'd be hard-pressed to name a leader who doesn't command from the limelight. The Rain Queen is an exception. She's closely guarded by a bevy of 'wives', the daughters of tribal headmen sent to live with her in the royal kraal. She doesn't get out much, except to attend the computer course she's studying, and spends most of her time a mystery to her people, who speak guardedly about her.

All the secrecy and mystery didn't make a royal visit easy. It involved long-haul negotiations with a prince of dubious authority and more than a few dead ends. Then along came a man who knew a man, who knew a man …. Lengthy cellular calls, SMSs and much promising not to ask the queen indiscreet questions, and it was arranged.

178

In the Royal Kraal

A strange kind of matriarchy exists in the kingdom of the Rain Queen. Tradition prevents her from marrying, but she can choose a lover (or lovers) to father her children. He is never named and can't claim paternity but must sneak into the royal kraal under cover of night to visit the queen and then disappear unseen before sunrise.

'We must first fetch the headman,' said Albert Muday, the man who knew a man etcetera. There was a hold-up at the headman's house before he emerged sheepishly and was introduced by Albert as Nelson Morwahleta. 'He overslept,' explained Albert. Nelson nodded and flashed a smile that was desperately in need of dental attention.

'This is a sensitive mission,' said Albert. 'We must be careful. And do not ask sensitive questions.'

It is customary to wait under the giant fig tree where the headmen gather to discuss matters of great importance with the queen. By comparison with the rest of GaModjadji, the Royal Kraal was very smart, with rondavels and a big house in the process of getting a new roof. The queen looked rather ordinary, wearing a Vodacom T-shirt, floral skirt, moccasins and a knitted beanie. The traditional leopard skin was hidden away for more important occasions.

Albert and Nelson began with the traditional greeting, which involved bowing and soft hand-clapping, then a lengthy ice-breaker.

A woman in control

You'd be forgiven for expecting to find a puppet queen tied by her wrists and ankles to ancient tradition and the will of her headmen. Instead Mokobo Modjadji is Africa's only woman ruler, a leader in her own right who has plans and ideas of her own which will inevitably come head to head with her traditional role.

She's been offered a scholarship by Nelson Mandela to study in England. But the headmen are not happy about her leaving.

'That is my decision,' she said, the gaze of her almond eyes unwavering.

What will she study?

'Social development. I want GaModjadji to have a lodge for tourists to visit. We have a lot to offer here.'

And what about tourists visiting her?

'It can be arranged,' she replied.

Out of the Royal Kraal after much bowing, soft hand-clapping and a monetary gift for the queen which had left my wallet much leaner, Albert and Nelson were in high spirits.

'The Queen was happy today,' Albert translated as Nelson rattled his teeth with all the agreeable nodding. 'It is a good thing we educated her.'

The sky was blue and the morning sun cast a merry glow over GaModjadji and the neighbouring cycad reserve near to where Nelson and Albert lived. There was no sign of the vaporous cloak that would cover the Rain Queen's kingdom by late afternoon.

The new queen, only just beginning her work, might well find it involves returning the favour and educating her headmen.

From the mists of time ...

Makobo Caroline Modjadji is the sixth Queen Modjadji, but her ancestry can be traced back a very long way – to Mwanamutapa dynasty at Great Zimbabwe. It is said that around 1600 a princess bore a child by her brother to found a new dynasty.

The story goes that the Princess, Dzugudini, fled south with her son, Makaphele, taking with them the sacred rain charms and royal insignia of the Rozwi Kingdom. One of Dzugudini's grandchildren was Mohale, who also entered into an incestuous relationship by having a child with his daughter, Maselegwane, promising her the rain-making charms if she complied. Thus, in 1800 she took the name of Modjadji.

Modjadji (meaning 'queen mother') was never seen and stories naturally began to spread. Many believed she was immortal and it was thought that Rider Haggard based his novel She on her (except that the dates don't match). Many of the traditions have remained over the generations, but the Rain Queen of the 21st Century will face some tough challenges. Traditionally she may not marry, but takes a secret lover to father her children. Will this queen follow tradition?

Previously, when rain queens became too old to rule they would end their lives by drinking from a cup of poison. When asked if she would follow suit, the Queen replied: 'It is not practical to do that anymore.'

Originally Modjadji, Queen of the BaLobedu people, was acknowledged as queen over a vast area, bounded by the Great and Little Letaba and Molototsi Rivers. In 1892 territorial boundaries were demarcated by Paul Kruger's government and her kingdom shrunk to 179 square kilometres in the Duiwelskloof area. Even today, chiefs and indunas from much further afield acknowledge her supremacy.

Zimbabwe's wild side
Justin Fox – March 2004

Jedsons is an isolated camp on the border of Chizarira, one of Zimbabwe's most remote national parks. It's an ideal place for walking safaris, but out in the bush Justin Fox's party got far more than it bargained for.

'Oh no, poachers,' hissed Steve Bolnick through his teeth. Smoke curled skyward from a narrow gorge 50 metres to our right. A fire this far inside the park could mean nothing other than poachers curing meat.

'You two find some cover,' said guide Steve. 'Leonard and I will go take a look.'

The two men moved stealthily into the gorge's thick bush. My walking companion, Des van Jaarsveld, had served as an army recce back in the 1970s and had seen plenty of action in that bush war. This 'contact' was triggering all sorts of memories. 'If only I had a weapon,' he muttered.

Just then Steve and Leonard emerged from the bush at a crouching run, motioning us firmly to fall back. We grabbed our packs and ran. Further down the valley we stopped in the cover of trees. 'Must be seven or eight of them,' said Steve. 'They're curing racks of meat. Got hunting dogs too – it's a wonder they didn't hear us.'

'Might be well armed,' said Leonard.

'I think we'd better call the police,' said Steve. 'Leonard, you run back to camp, get the Land Cruiser and go to Lusulu police post. Bring as many cops as you can.'

Our Tonga tracker set off at a run. It was better to bring in the law and not try anything on our own. Besides there was the 'tourist' issue (me). Poaching occurs in most African parks and guests are always steered away from any confrontation. This had happened to me the last time I was in the Kruger, but I hoped I wasn't going to miss out on the action again.

Into Zimbabwe's wilderness

I'd arrived in Zimbabwe two days earlier to visit Jedsons Safari Camp, a private lodge on the border of perhaps the country's most remote national park, Chizarira. In the weeks leading up to my visit the South African press had run a number of stories about rampant poaching and how safari operators were taking advantage of the country's turmoil to conduct illegal trophy hunts. Horror reports spoke of more than 50 per cent of game having been wiped out in some national parks. This was a chance to assess the situation on the ground.

The drive to Jedsons took five hours on a long rough road through rural Zimbabwe. The spectacular camp – four safari-style tents and a honeymoon suite – is on a sandstone ridge studded with mountain acacia (*Brachystegia msasa*) high above the plains. Meals are in a thatched lodge or on a deck beside the pool. I was accommodated in the honeymoon suite, a leopards' eyrie set on an outcrop of rock with its own spa bath and treetop deck. The four-poster bed offered views of a water hole and a sweep of wilderness beyond. That night I would wake to the sound of an elephant drinking in the moonlight just below me.

No sooner had I arrived than an electrical storm rolled in. We watched it coming from the pool-and-braai deck. Vanguard rainbows marched out front and an ethereal light bathed camp as we waited for the downpour. The thunder was so loud we flinched. 'The big boys are moving lots of furniture around up there,' said Des, co-owner of the lodge with Steve.

Dusk found us at Jedsons' lookout gazebo enjoying snacks and G&Ts as sheet lightning purpled the gathering gloom. It was spell-binding … and just a bit sinister. The country's past and present illicited divided feelings, even in the face of such sublime beauty.

Walking with the smaller fry

Next morning we were up at sunrise for a short bush walk. 'Just a cupl'a hours to acclimatise and get a feel for the area,' said Steve, leading the way with his .404 rifle, followed by Leonard Simunchembu, our tracker. Steve is particularly knowledgeable about bush minnows such as lizards, bugs and beetles. There were fascinating discussions on velvet mites and ant lions, edible caterpillars and the medicinal uses of the more unusual plants. It was an outdoor lecture of the highest calibre.

Scrambling down the side of a cliff, we entered a small cave which Steve said was probably used as a thief's lair. There were the remains of a drum, assegai, knobkerrie, a few pieces of broken pottery and a tin chest. Leonard suggested the drum might have been used to summon more thieves to trap returning migrants in the valley and rob or murder them. I thought it might be a poachers' hideout.

We'd been tracking a herd of buffalo for some time when we began to see vultures. Assuming a kill, Steve led us up a valley whose trees were adorned with the birds. Then we saw the tell-tale smoke.

Only shoot if they fire first

So there we were, waiting for the police. The talk was all about the old days: foot patrols, contacts, ambushes. We began walking towards the lodge to intercept the cops before their vehicle came within earshot of the poachers. Not having much faith in Zimbabwe's police force we feared they might be apathetic: maybe send one man with a rusty revolver. However, rounding a bend, we came upon our Land Cruiser with Leonard and a posse of eight policemen carrying FN rifles. This was more like it.

Des took command, drawing a map of the valley on the ground with a stick and using old bush-war terminology. The idea was to split into two groups, Steve leading one onto the ridge above the gorge, from where they'd initiate the arrest; the rest of us would fan out at the mouth of the gorge to intercept anyone who tried to flee.

'Hey Justin, you'd better go back to the lodge and have a cocktail by the pool,' suggested Steve.

'Not a chance,' I said. 'If there's a fire fight I'll stay at the back out of harm's way.'

Rifles were cocked in the still, sticky air. We marched out in single file. As we entered the valley watches were synchronised for an arrest in 15 minutes. Then we split into our two 'sticks'. I tailed at the back of the valley detail behind a clumsy young cop who kept tripping over stones, sending them bouncing over the rocks, clink-clink-clink. One stifled a cough. Stern looks from the inspector. After 10 minutes we were near the gorge and Des indicated we should close up and move into ambush positions. I set my Nikon's focus to infinity, speed to 500. My hands were shaking.

Next thing a line of seven poachers stepped from the bushes directly in front of us, and everyone froze. For a moment nothing happened. The cicadas screamed in the midday heat. Then all hell broke loose.

Des and the inspector shouted an order to stop. But the poachers had already ditched their bags of meat and were sprinting up the valley away from us. I found myself running in pursuit with a policeman on either side of me firing from the hip at fleeing figures, rifle cracks shattering the stillness. The cop behind us began shooting over our heads at a poacher scaling the ridge.

Then a .303 opened up on us and we ducked. Taking incoming fire, I suddenly felt utterly vulnerable. I'd never been shot at before, and guessed none of these young cops had either. 'Pull back Justin!' called Des. 'This is chaos. They're shooting at anything that moves. We'll hit our own guys.'

I needed no encouraging as we doubled back and ran into the gorge. There we found a butchered buffalo. We stood among entrails buzzing with green flies, the air filled with the stench of death. The curing fires still smouldered and hunting dogs circled us, barking. A cop dispatched one of them and the others took off.

Next thing the bushes on the ridge erupted with more rifle fire. We ducked and Des shouted, 'Cease firing, it's us!'

Then Steve emerged leading a cop handcuffed to a poacher whose left arm had a bullet wound. 'Thank God we got one,' said Steve, slightly shaken. 'Now we'll get the names of the rest.'

The poacher was just a teenager and explained haltingly in Ndebele that this was his first raid, that he'd been brought along to help carry the meat. Our adrenaline was draining and the heroic anti-poaching sting was taking on a different complexion. The lad was from a local village, hungry, unemployed and trying to make a few dollars. His clothing was torn and his sandals held together with string. He swayed on his feet, close to fainting. So much for the faceless, heavily armed poachers we'd bravely hunted in our heads.

Steve helped remove his shirt and found that the bullet had shattered his humerus. The arm hung limp, swaying, so we applied a tourniquet. His blood seemed unnaturally red against the lush green of Chizarira's bush. 'We'd better get him to hospital quickly,' said Des. 'He might lose the arm.'

When everyone was finally mustered, the police insisted on carrying back all the nyama (meat). I trailed behind the boy as we walked him out. Everyone was loaded with meat, the head carried by the horns between two men. Brushing through the long grass I glanced down and noticed my boots and legs were streaked with blood. I looked for a wound, then realised it came from grass flecked with the boy's blood.

Back at the lodge I said goodbye to the policemen who wanted their picture taken, for which they struck team poses. Here was I, a foreign journalist being asked to photograph ZANU-PF police. I felt snared in complicity and urged the cops to get him to a clinic as soon as possible.

At last the police Land Rover jounced away, blood from the buffalo spilling out of the tail gate.

Reporting to HQ

There were many other walks and drives, not nearly as exciting but infinitely more pleasurable. For instance, an evening game drive took us through an enchanting forest dotted with elephants and up onto a koppie for sundowners. At a natural spring the soft sandstone had been worn into a trunk-shaped keyhole by generations of thirsty elephants. European bee-eaters enjoyed in-flight meals of termite alates emerging from their mounds like dandelions against a low sun. On another occasion a surprise bush dinner was laid on by Des in a forested glade. We approached through the trees to a scene that looked like a mini, night-time Harari. The clearing was festooned with paraffin lamps which lined a path to our table.

On the last day we drove north to park headquarters to pay respects to the warden and discuss anti-poaching measures. It also gave me the chance to get a good overview of Chizarira. The main north–south route is hardly used and Leonard had to hack us through many sections. It transpired that I was the first guest in the park in the three months. The game viewing – elephants, zebras, buffaloes, kudus, waterbuck – was good and the miombo woodland beautiful.

The park's camps at Kasvivsi, Mucheni Gorge and Mucheni View are rustic (sleeping platforms and basic ablutions), but each has a spectacular location. The two Muchenis are particularly dramatic, set on basaltic cliffs with precipitous views down the escarpment into the Zambezi Valley.

The warden at headquarters was a dignified and soft-spoken young man full of praise for the 'Jedsons operation'. The warden lamented the fact that he couldn't be of more assistance in curbing the poaching scourge. Alas, he had limited manpower, no diesel, no phone and only one operational vehicle to patrol 192 000 hectares.

Steve and Des agreed that their camp would have to be responsible for the south, instituting foot patrols. National Parks would contribute two rangers to lend more authority. Jedsons would also seek sponsorship for tents, backpacks and equipment to allow long-range patrols from HQ.

So there were some positives to come from this episode. Poaching, even if it's at subsistence level, destroys a resource which will be one of the few cash cows when Zimbabwe emerges from this dark phase. To have white Zimbabweans from the private sector teaming up with parks board and regional police in anti-poaching initiatives has got to be good. Despite being ZANU-PF controlled – and contrary to much shrill reporting – parks and police are staffed with many concerned individuals wanting to preserve their national heritage.

The road back … and forward
'We really need to make the cops feel part of the process,' said Steve as we drove back to Vic Falls. 'Their morale is low, they're badly equipped. If we can get them involved in anti-poaching and secure private-sector funding, it'll help counterbalance the rot.'

He talked about the need to resurrect Campfire (Communal Areas Management Programme for Indigenous Resources). The project has fallen on hard times, but its aims are worthy: the sustainable use of natural resources in the interests of conservation and the relief of poverty. Money from ecotourism needed to be seen to be working to uplift communities, thereby lowering dependency on poaching.

Passing Lusulu, we stopped at the police post and were greeted like old comrades in arms. We learned that the boy was in Binga Hospital, but there was no word on his condition. Most of the gang had been arrested and the man who'd supplied them with the gun fined. So our police buddies were following through. Suddenly I had a surge of hope again. It's a dangerous thing to bank on, hope, but it's all the locals in this corner of Africa have. And at least there's a germ of it about in Chizarira. If they could just hang on until the madness passes, God's own country would surely blossom again?

Hock deep in the delta
Robyn Daly – March 2004

People who like walking say that the only way to experience the wilds is on foot. Obviously they don't ride horses, haven't galloped with giraffes or diced with zebras. Combine some wonderful horses and one of Africa's best wildlife destinations and an Okavango Horse Safari beats diesel fumes.

There was a methodical swoosh, swoosh, swoosh, swoosh not quite as deep as the sounds of an elephant making a channel crossing, nor as frivolous as the rustle of red lechwe feet fleeing through the floodwaters. Swooshing horses' legs in deep water was accompanied by the odd thwack as a wet tail flicked against a hindquarter to dislodge a fly. The steady rhythm of the walk was occasionally broken as horses paused to pluck a water lily or snatch at a tuft of reed grass. All around us the water was glassy still and the deep, dark colour of the horses' eyes.

The swoosh faded as the last horse emerged dripping from the water. Soft shkwick, shkwicks could be heard as hooves sucked on mud. The sound dissolved to faint thuds on firmer ground. Then silence. We stopped beside a herd of giraffes.

In the early morning before the cicadas strike up on their violins, the silence in the delta is so deep you can almost hear the water evaporate. The grind of giraffe molars on thorns was as loud as if it were happening in my own mouth. Gulliver wasn't smoking his socks on his travels: I swear I could hear my horse, Ebo, talking ....

Ebo: Hey Lamu, what do you call these giant Houyhnhnms* again?

Lamu turned his wise head towards the younger Ebo: Giraffes. But they're not Houyhnhnms, look at their feet. And they have four stomachs.

Ebo: They are tall as trees.

Mashushu (from where he was grazing a little way away): Hey Ebo, what sound does a falling giraffe make if there are no Houyhnhnms around to hear it?

Ebo blinked his long-lashed eyes and put his head down to graze. The stocky Mashushu could be quite insensitive.

Adventure at every turn

From the first sniff Ebo gave me, in the pink glow of a sun that's about to rise, it was clear that he was a kind, gentle horse. A five-year old bred in Zimbabwe as Indian Justice for racing, he was brought to Okavango Horse Safaris in 2002 for a career change and a new name. It is the story of most of the trail horses.

Looking round the selection, owners Barney and PJ Bestelink have an eye for a good horse. There is every shape, size and colour, and all sorts of temperaments to suit different guests' personalities, but the horses are sensible and obviously well-adjusted to their trail lives. They also seem to enjoy their jobs: they're always keen for a run with zebras and when it's time for the long water gallops that characterise riding in the delta, they plunge through the malapos (floodplains) with ears pricked.

This is not something PJ and Barney just stumbled upon; it's taken nearly 20 years since their first delta ride in 1986 to hone and perfect trail riding in a wilderness that has many pitfalls for horses. As the first people to bring horses into the Okavango, they were met with hoots of derision from locals and lodge staff.

'"They'll never survive," people would tell us,' said PJ one evening at Mokolwane Camp around a log fire spitting orange stars into the darkness. But this didn't stop them. PJ bought Barney a three-year-old Arab stallion and a bargain load of horses. Then they set out from Maun to ride north to their home at Guma Lagoon near the top of the delta's panhandle.

'We were so disorganised,' laughed Barney. 'We didn't have a night watchman and none of the horses were trained. PJ had aerial maps of the delta and we used them to find our way.'

Madness. You'd say. But PJ has had a history of running expeditions off the seat of his pants. He's explored the delta from top to bottom and back to the top again. When he arrived from Namibia in the early 1970s he ran expeditions on a shoestring, selling adventure tours into the Okavango wilderness. He'd put his finger on the map and say 'That looks good.' Of course it would be fantastic because everywhere in the Okavango Delta is magical and there's adventure and surprises around every bend in the rivers.

It would seem PJ approached Barney in a similar adventurous spirit. When he met her the first thing she asked him was: 'Can you ride?'

'I said "yes",' said PJ, adding another log to the fire. 'I knew if I told her the truth she wouldn't give me a second look.' Next he set about discovering that the hardest thing about learning to ride is the ground.

Across the giant sand tongue

Today there's no trace of the hope-and-a-prayer trail operations of early years. Okavango Horse Safaris operates over two adjacent concession areas (NG29 and NG30) bordering the Moremi Wildlife Reserve, which offer 2500 square kilometres of glorious free riding. PJ and Barney know every square metre of their area, probably better than we know our own back gardens.

Base camp is Kujwana (meaning baby hippo), a comfortable tented camp on the banks of the Xudum River. This is where a 10-day safari begins. After a few days, everybody rides out to Mokolwane Camp, northwest of Kujwana, on the Matsibi River. Depending on the movement of game and the water, there may also be a couple of nights at Kiri fly camp in the permanent water part of the delta.

For the most part you have your 'own' mount, though there is a fair bit of swapping and resting as no horse can endure 10 days on the trot. Similarly, guests don't have to do all 10 days – though many choose to. There's an option of joining the first or second half of a safari on a five-day plan. This is what I did, though I would have happily signed up for 10 days … or the rest of my life.

The countryside is endlessly interesting. Being at the finger tips of the giant water hand of the delta its water arrives with considerably less urgency than it does upriver, yet from one day to the next the landscape can change, either a dry area will be submersed or a floodplain will be sucked dry. It is estimated that 98 per cent of the water vanishes into thin air through evaporation.

Accumulating during summer rainfall in the Angolan highlands, the floodwater travels about 1000 kilometres before entering Botswana at Mahembo. There the inflow would sustain the water needs of both England and Wales, at around 11 thousand million cubic metres a year. By the time it reaches the riding concession it's mid autumn and the plants and animals have long forgotten summer thunder showers – and most of it has already gone.

But for the floodwaters, the delta would be endless savanna as hot and harsh as the Kalahari that surrounds it. On excursions from Mokolwane Camp, riders on safari were reminded of this by the intrusive presence of the sand tongue which licks out between the Xudum and Matsibi rivers.

'Sometimes the game disappears in there,' said PJ as we gave the tongue a wide berth on the long ride back to Kujwana base camp. 'Then we have to go in. It can be extremely hard on the horses and riders.'

The horses flicked an ear of uncertainty towards that area, where the sand is thick, and heavy on their muscles, and the cicadas shriek hysterically. On the sand tongue side, the vegetation was yellow-brown and in places still showed traces of hunting fires. The sand was parched silver-grey, a wall of heat surrounded the panting tongue. But on the water side, sometimes not more than 100 metres away, all was green, the giant fans of Mokolwane palms (*Hyphenae petersiana*) waved from their perches on small islands. The lagoons were like thoughtful eyes, fringed with long eyelashes of grass reeds.

At some point, however, we had to cross the tongue to reach Kujwana. PJ found the shortest route. About half way we stopped under the sparse shade of terminalia trees.

'Time to half-picket,' said PJ.

As I loosened Ebo's girth and tied his lead rope to a branch with a quick-release knot, I was sure Ebo was starting up a conversation with PJ's horse, Lamu. But it's hard to be certain.

Ebo: Shoo. I was getting weak at the hocks there. I'm sure my human has put on a few feed sacks worth of weight.

Lamu: Yes, that's the problem with tourists, they go on holiday, do nothing all day and expect to eat as though they had to carry us Houyhnhnms across the sand.

Ebo: Ooh, look, my human has brought me some pony nuts. She's sweet.

Mashushu (ungraciously): You think that of everyone who brings you food.

Ebo: Well, wouldn't you?

Lamu turned away to rub his nose on the broken edge of a branch of the tree to which he was tied and said, to nobody in particular: Hmm, that Ebo, he's a good fellow. Coming along nicely.

Not for the faint hearted

An average day's riding is about 30 kilometres, not lasting more than about five hours. The exceptions are moving days, which are a little longer, but still leisurely enough for a swim in one of the lagoons. Swimming is done well away from the horses – just in case there's truth in Gulliver's Travels and the Houyhnhnms tolerate us humans only because we have clothes on and don't look like naked, uncouth Yahoos*. Though I suspect they know a thing or two and are too kind to show us up.

PJ's early expedition days have taught him where crocodiles lurk. But still he had a hard time convincing me that nothing was going to lurch out the shallows and grab me by the bikini. Eventually the water was too inviting to resist.

We wallowed in the shallow water holes, squirting each other with yellow bladderwort flowers. There's a knack to it, but if you get the yellow flowers just right between your fingers, the little water pistols have a surprising firing range. All too soon it was time to mount up and complete the ride into Kujwana base camp.

The first thing Barney did when she returned was catch up on the horse news with her assistant Kate. Then each horse was inspected from head to toe.

For Barney and her husband PJ, the delta was made for horses. It is not, however, made for beginner riders. It's a serious trail requiring a competent level of horsemanship and fitness. But if you can ride well and, like PJ, Barney and all their clients, the horse madness has addled your brain, it is wild and thrilling.

I hunkered over Ebo's shoulders, my bottom in the air as if I was a jockey for the Emir. Ebo's long legs stretched in front of him, his shoulders opened up, both our eyes were blinking from the spray of water. We were up alongside the lead horse – he is too well trained and mannered to pass – but he only needed a signal, the slightest increase of pace, a squeeze from my legs, and he'd stretch further. With each stride his front feet shattered the glass surface of lagoon water sending splinters spiralling into the air.

My heart was in my mouth. It was pure joy. And it sure beat walking.

* In Gulliver's Travels Houyhnhnms are horses; the Yahoos are an uncouth species resembling humans.

Do hippotragues speak French?
David Bristow – August 2005

Hands up if you know the capital of Chad, and 10 points if you can name its world-class game reserve? David Bristow was lured there by promises of adventure travel and pictures of outstanding wildlife.

George Bush won his first presidency over Al Gore by a hanging chad. That's what they call the round bit that's removed when you punch a piece of paper – check, it's in the dictionary.

Below that entry is Chad, a country in central North Africa: formerly a French colony, independent since 1960, and beset by civil strife pretty much ever since, Collins says.

Most people will know the name, if at all, from Lake Chad, a dying wetland on the edge of the Sahara Desert. Or perhaps the Tibesti Mountains, if you're really up on your geography.

An internet search on the country revealed little besides this on the Lonely Planet website: 'With one of the most painful histories in Africa, Chad is a nation with its foundations built on the precipice of conflict. A harsh climate, geographic remoteness, poor resource endowment and lack of infrastructure have combined to create a weak economy susceptible to political turmoil.

'The country that was classified in the 1980s as the poorest nation on earth is usually generously described as "developing", and while there is a degree of modernisation occurring in Chad, "surviving" is probably a more apt term.'

The lie of the land

The capital is N'jamena, but you'd hardly call this dusty, sprawling town a city. In colonial times, pre-1960, it was known as Fort Lamy. Since the fall of colonial Algeria, N'jamena twins with Djibouti, at the tip of Africa's horn, as the main French garrison on the continent.

Around the pool deck of the hotel La Chadienne Novotel, tanned and crew-cut people wear check me-check you reflective shades: the Foreign Legion lives on, body and soul. Unless you were one of those trading/military types that

192

lurk around all of Africa's hot spots, or you were shopping for second-hand Mirages, you wouldn't want to be spending too much time there.

Early in the morning following our 02h00 arrival at La Chadienne, in the dry heat of central North Africa, our disparate group of multi-lingual travel agents and journalists taxied to the international airport-cum-French military base and set a course east-south-east in our chartered plane. A two-hour flight over flat sand revealed the thin green snake of the Salamat River winding tenuously through the barren Sahel grasslands.

We were the guests of the French–Belgian conservation and development agency, Agreco, brought there to evaluate and – hopefully – praise and publicise their work at Chad's one and only functioning national park. After the entrée to the country, we weren't expecting much from the rest.

All the same, where there's water there must be life, and soon the plane banked steeply for the landing. The entrance to Zakouma National Park looks like a set from *Beau Geste*, with its fortress-like entrance gate. It was strange and exotic, yet familiar in a surreal way; it was Africa, but the recognisable bits were chunks of conglomerate set in a mystifying Arabian matrix.

And then there was the heat. On our return drive to N'jamena someone used their cellphone to measure 45°C in the shade, and 56°C in the sun at an oasis town: and this was winter.

Tinga camp – something of a cross between a Kruger-Park-style rest camp and a private game lodge – is run by charming Spanish couple Luis Arrane and Nuria Ortega, now in their fifth year there. Actually, their fifth half-year. Pierre Poilecot was there for his third half-year studying the reserve ecology, while his partner Natalie Vanherle was studying its lion population (they had previously done similar research in Botswana).

Every year around July, the Salamat River, which flows through the park, floods an area reminiscent of Botswana's Okavango Delta. Completely, so that all the animals and all the people have to move out of the area for a few months until the waters recede.

Since 1990 the park has been funded by the European Union and for the past five years the entire Zakouma ecosystem, as well as Tinga camp, has been managed and monitored by European specialists. During this time game numbers have greatly increased and seemingly stabilised.

While the Europeans go back to Europe when the park floods, no one is quite sure where the animals go. That would include some 3000 elephants and 100 lions, numerous roan, hartebeest, gazelles and many other critters in the 3000-square-kilometre reserve.

However, Zakouma is not the braid-work of the channels and islands which characterise the Okavango Delta, it's something more like Zambia's contortionist Luangwa River. At times it was hard to believe we were in North and not Southern Africa.

Musings on relative palaeoecology

It's not only that Zakouma will remind you of places in Southern Africa; on a more micro-level there's a strange familiarity, call it déjà vu if you like (since French is what they speak here). The widespread acacias that cover most of the flat sand plains look just like the central Kalahari. But instead of the trees being *A caffra* or *tortilis* that we know from south-central Southern Africa and much of East Africa, this one is *A sayel* (from which comes that curious food additive, gum arabic).

The green-thorn here, although it produces the same oil-rich fruits, is not the *Balanites maughamii* we know in Kruger as the torch wood, but another species (*B aegytiaca*). You'll see trees that look just like Southern Africa's apple-leaf or rain tree, the silver terminalia, mopane, lead-wood or knob-thorn. But they are all different species; sometimes different genera altogether.

And the same with the animals, except here they generally are the same, or a sub-species.

The buffon, or cobe de buffon, is the kob of East Africa; redunca is the common reedbuck (*Redunca redunca*); cobe Defassa is the Defassa waterbuck (it has no rear 'toilet seat'); the bubale is Lelwel's hartebeest; damalisque is the tsessebe, or topi; and so on.

Perhaps Zakouma's greatest claim to conservation fame is its enormous population of hippotragues. While this second-largest of all antelopes is extremely scarce in all of Southern and East Africa, here you see them frequently and in large herds. While there are no official figures, you have to imagine this one park has as many as the whole of Southern Africa. That would be roan antelope, or *Hippotragus equinus*.

Birds too. And if Zakouma has anything to equal the rest of Africa, it's the birds. Being a seasonal wetland in mixed savanna, the bird life is at least as prolific and varied as in the Okavango.

Many species are the same ones as in the south – the herons and egrets are all the same species, as are most of the raptors (predominantly fish and long-crested eagles). One special is the swallow-tailed kite, a beautiful, delicate, almost all-white bird that looks more like a fairy tern than the kites we know.

Another is the crowned crane. The new name for the one you'll be familiar with is the southern (grey) crowned crane (*Balearica regulorum* – the regal one); in Zakouma you'll see northern (black) crowned cranes (*B pavonina* – the peacock-like one), lots of them, together with pelicans, storks, egrets, herons ....

194

The only time I've seen anything similar to the massing of birds at Zakouma is at the breeding islands or heronries between Xakanaxa and Xugana lagoons in the Okavango Delta.

Going back to the animals, however. In making deeper connections about the relations of species across the continent, you need look no further than the giraffe, for me the most beguiling of all large mammals. They all look much the same at first glance, and there is only one species throughout Africa – but there are eight sub-species. When you see them all together in a guide book, you realise how different they are and how odd are their distributions. What would cause those differences, while other widesread species such as the kudu, or roan, have virtually no differences?

The giraffe you see in Kruger (*Girrafa camelopardalis giraffa*) is not the same as the one in the Okavango-Chobe region (*angolensis*), or the one in Zambia (*thornicrofti*), which is confined to the Luangwa Valley. Kenya has two, the Masai variety of the Serengeti–Mara ecosystem (*tippelskirchii*) and reticulated (*reticulata*) of the arid north. Zakouma's one is *antiquorum*, which occurs only in a tiny pocket around Zakouma as well as another pocket in southern Sudan.

While in Southern Africa the dainty oribi antelope is nudging extinction, in Zakouma they're common. The cannon-fodder prey of the Serengeti is the Thompson's gazelle, which here is not rare but far from common. There are no zebras, otherwise just about the most widely distributed plains game in Africa. And so on.

The wild dogs are something of an enigma. Pierre, who is trying to follow the large elephant herds during the wet season to get some idea of how the ecosystem works, says they are not resident in the park.

Apparently they pass through, using much the same range land as the nomadic herders who use wells throughout the Sahel to sustain their herds. And when the rains and wells fail, the park allows them to decamp on the grassy floodplain within the reserve, in their tens of thousands, to use Zakouma's bountiful dry-season grazing.

Animals behaving strangely

One herder told us that the wild dogs run through a herd and strip an animal down to its bones as it stands there. 'Then the skeleton just collapses to the ground,' he said with a smile.

And the brown hyenas also act strangely. In all her time at Zakouma, Natalie says she has never seen one on a carcass. Now there's a doctoral thesis waiting.

When über-ecologist Michael Faye started his Mega Flyover project to document Africa's wild places last year, he'd never heard of Zakouma, the people there told us.

'But he was astonished, quite amazed really,' vouched Pierre in his quiet, confident way. That's hardly surprising, since Zakouma is a world-class act. If this game reserve was anywhere in East or Southern Africa, it would be world famous.

Latest news is that substantial oil deposits have been found under the sands of the Sahel in Chad. It looks certain that a lot there is going to change soon.

Arabian nights and days in Morocco
Narina Exelby – February 2006

Morocco is a country that assails your senses: the air is tainted with incense, saffron and dust; ancient cities burst with people and vibrant colours; smells of spices and incense only just mask Third World vapour; strings of shoes dangle in the markets and oases form unexpected ribbons in the desert. It's an explorer's heaven, a shopper's delight. Narina Exelby's imagination was captured by this far North African country.

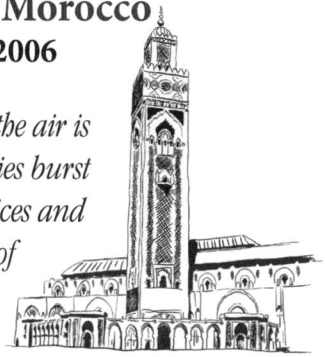

༈

'Allahu akbar, Allahu akbar … Ashhadu an la Illah ila Allah … Ashhadu an Mohammedan rasul Allah … Haya ala as-sala … Haya ala as-sala ….' (God is great, God is great … There is no god but Allah … Mohammed is His prophet … Come to prayer … Come to prayer ….)

All across Morocco the Muslim call to prayer wailed into morning. It pulled men from their beds and squashed them into mosques; it snaked between houses and down narrow alleys, was ignored by some and grunted at by jet-lagged foreigners who'd been bolted from their sleep. Even for those who didn't heed the call, it signalled the start of another day – and, like a vuvuzela at a Bafana Bafana game, Morocco just wouldn't be the same without it.

The desert awakes
There was no escaping the muezzin's wail; it even drifted into the Sahara dawn, far in the south-east of the country. As the earth tilted into morning, a very faint 'Allahu akbar' (God is great) rolled through the dunes, pulling the sun up and up with every repeated phrase.

Life at Auberge Yasmina had stirred while it was still dark; there was much to be done. The guesthouse clings to the edge of Erg Chebbi, where dunes rise from a stony desert and stretch for 30 kilometres towards Algeria; it's a popular place for tourists to get a taste of the deep Sahara.

Early every morning Youssef Kraoui would see to it that his family's kasbah-style guesthouse was clean and presentable. The fridges were stocked with bottled water; some doors were opened, some closed, to make the most of the cool, pre-

197

dawn air. It was important that the guests be comfortable: the desert days are harsh and, even within the kasbah's thick mud walls, there would be little escape from the heavy midday heat.

Just as the sun broke over the horizon, Youssef and his brothers left their busyness, gathered their prayer mats and knelt facing east. They're devout Muslim; five devotions punctuate their day.

Daybreak in a city of contrasts

The Muslim call to prayer sliced into sunrise and echoed through Morocco's economic capital. From all the minarets in Casablanca it was called out: 'Allahu akbar, Allahu akbar.' An unintended choir of muezzins spread across the city. It vibrated past Art Deco buildings, between apartment blocks with laundry hanging out the windows and through brilliant bougainvilleas that tumbled, with no sense of neatness, over their flaky balconies.

There are many mosques in Casablanca – and indeed all of Morocco – and the grandest of all is Hassan II Mosque. It was built to commemorate its namesake king's 60th birthday and comes complete with platinum-plated doors which open electronically, heated floors, painstakingly intricate mosaics and a prayer hall that holds 25 000 people. In essence it symbolises that modern Casablanca contradiction: there's a little romance of the past but flash businesses are the order of the day.

A ribbon of green in the desert

Under the dark green canopy of date-palm leaves, a soft breeze carried the scent of rich earth and running water. It was morning in the Tordra Valley and a woman worked, weeding her family's allotment while her son picked olives from their trees. She waved when three girls, baskets of carrots balanced on their heads, called to her. They were the nieces of her neighbour and, as is customary in these parts, she had given them vegetables when they had few. 'The fruits will be many this year, insha' Allah (God willing),' the girls chimed as the woman went back to work.

The Tordra Valley is – and has been for centuries – a sanctuary in the desert, a narrow, ribbon oasis that follows a stream along the valley floor. Generations ago it was divided into patches of fertile land, one to a family, and it's become a complex route of trodden pathways and water channels shaded by palm and olive trees.

The difference between the slopes, where people have built their homes, and the valley floor couldn't contrast more. The land they live off is a reassuring, tangled nest of greenery with abrupt edges defined by water supply. But the land they live on is flanked by crumbling kasbahs and thousands of rectangular houses that claw up into the hard landscape; shades of red and brown and sand that fade into desert.

The spiritual heart of Morocco

At a distance the medina of Fés el-Bali (Old Fes) is not too different from the slopes of the Tordra Valley: the monotone, rectangular boxes with black-hole windows create a wallpaper of lodgings crammed within the city's walls. It seems a quiet place but appearances, from far, can be very, very deceiving. Fes, the spiritual heart of Morocco, is the largest living medieval city in the world – and life on the streets is chaotic.

More than a million people live here, in a warren of 9000 alleys and narrow streets. The city was well established by AD809; over the centuries, buildings have been haphazardly added on and extended, each wall defining a new space and creating another passage.

Noon might have been a time when many of Medina's stalls closed for prayer, but Fes was still a frazzle of energy. Cries of 'Baja! Baja!' (Look out! Look out!) shook between walls as donkeys laden with copper kettles clunked through the alleys. Fine dust tinted an air already thick with spice, mint and urine.

Those who hadn't heeded the muezzin's call chatted outside their stalls, which bulged with wares such as leather goods, dried fruit, brass hinges and ceramic plates. In the souk, selling leather, two married women, their faces covered and black jellabas flowing, pushed past a group of tourists cluttered in an alley.

The foreigners clutched packets of shoes and desperately sniffed handfuls of mint leaves to overcome the smell of the tannery. They'd just spent half an hour at a shop that overlooks one of the potholed tanneries, where leather is treated and coloured as it has been since the Middle Ages. They'd watched men carry big buckets of dye from one vat to another, submerge hides of sheep, goats, cows and camels in mixtures containing cow urine, animal fats and fish oils.

A claustrophobic, dog-legged street led the foreigners away from the banter of the souk and on to a heavy green door. Their guide – it's necessary to have one in the confusion of streets – opened it onto a surprisingly calm, airy courtyard with leafy vines dripping down three storeys. Life in this city wasn't always as it seemed from the outside.

The magic of Essaouira

It was a tepid afternoon in Essaouira – the trade wind blowing off the Atlantic had seen to that – and 11 boys stripped off their shirts and jumped from the slipway into the harbour's fishy waters. They'd spend the afternoon there; most of their fathers were still out at sea. Next to a banter of gulls, men built or repaired wooden boats while two performed an intricate dance, balancing their way from one floating blue rowing boat to another.

The town has a history that stretches from the Phoenicians in 7BC through to Portuguese colonisation in the 15th century (when it was known as Mogador) and on to 1765, when the port at nearby Agadir was closed and a French architect was hired to create a new, fortified city. The man who commissioned Théodore Cornut, Sultan Sidi Mohammed ben Abdallah, renamed it Essaouira, meaning 'well designed' – but it's not just well designed, the old town is beautiful, too.

Every building in Essaouira is a textured shade of aged whitewash and has faded blue doors, shutters and awnings that try to withstand the insidious salt air. Hanging outside many of the shops are carpets and cotton fabric and paintings; a clutter of colour that adds to the town's character. There is a magic about this place that lures travellers back again and again.

As the afternoon sun lost its strength, some of the boys from the harbour peeled themselves off the slipway, jumbled through a stone arch and on to an informal fish market. They didn't seem to mind the stench left by rotting scales and guano, and sent gulls into a flutter as they hauled themselves onto an uneven stretch of the city's wall. They couldn't see the medina, with its wide alleys lined with strings of shoes, boxes of woodwork and towers of spices, nor could they see the cafés that tumbled French-style onto the streets. What they did have was a view over the western promenade and this, they knew, was the best place to watch the sun go down.

The night of the jugglers

Just as the sun dipped below the grand Koutoubia Mosque, Marrakech's largest square, Djemaa el-Fna, transformed itself into a frenzy of energy. There were people everywhere, music and drumbeats bouncing off their bodies, and the air became tainted with saffron and smoke. It's happened every day for hundreds of years.

Djemaa el-Fna had, by day, been a thoroughfare between the narrow alleys and souks of this fabled city. But as the evening call to prayer resonated from Koutoubia Mosque, drummers in white jellabas emerged suddenly, beating their Berber rhythm into the night.

Sweating snake charmers, hooded cobras and sluggish puff-adders looked drugged, or dulled by the heat, and swayed to a hypnotic, fluted tune. A large crowd aggregated around a troupe of young gymnasts who somersaulted and back-flipped into a human pyramid. Behind them a weather-beaten storyteller collected his own audience, his voice falling and booming as was appropriate to the tale.

Close by a woman called out a desperate, 'Henna! Henna!' from under an umbrella. She earned a living by painting henna tattoos onto foreigners' hands and feet and thrust a crumpled plastic folder of images at anyone who went too close.

As the jugglers and boxers, story-tellers and drummers joined the energy, they were held together by a humid pall that swirled from the food stalls in the middle of the square. Lanterns lit piles of red meat and peppers, rice, kebabs and chicken thighs, pigs' heads and carrots, and every chef tried to convince passers-by that his food was better than his neighbour's.

Weaving through the smoke and between all the performers, people streamed in flowing lines from the alleys and streets into the square. It was impossible not to be drawn into the spectacle that had recurred every night for more than a thousand years.

As the sky darkened and a new moon slid above the minaret, the stages intensified. The stories told had been around for centuries, though the foreigners didn't know; most of them couldn't understand, anyway. But that didn't matter. What they loved was being there, a part of the Moroccan night. And so the performances continued, on and on and on into the dark, until the people trickled away and the last drumbeat softened to an echo.

GLOSSARY

Kasbah: A fort or citadel.

Jellaba: Traditional, flowing garment with a hood and wide sleeves worn by both men and women.

Medina: The old city, a traditional Arab town enclosed by ramparts.

Muezzin: The mosque official who calls everyone to prayer.

Souk: An open-air market.

Canyon of dreams and demons
Don Pinnock – July 2006

You want to hike the Fish River Canyon? Okay, off you go.
It's an utterly beautiful place, for sure. But before
you sling your pack onto your willing shoulders,
heed some advice from Don Pinnock, who's
wandered that way before.

They're not mice. Those little paw prints you find around your sleeping bag on the beach beside the river when you wake up in the morning: no, not mice. Sorry. They're … um … let me first lure you into the story – and into the canyon – then we can talk about the paw prints.

The canyon isn't the second biggest in the world after the Grand Canyon, as some of the enthusiastic literature will tell you, but it's damn big anyway. A yawning great monster that makes your heart sink when you peer over its lip, heavy pack on your back, at the start of the trail near Hobas. In places it's more than half a kilometre deep.

So look, you don't have to go. I'm just telling you this to fill the space between some pretty pictures. Really, it's your choice.

But if you have to, make sure you've got five days of food supplies that don't weigh anything (a medal for the person who invented dehydrates), an umbrella-sized hat, a really warm sleeping bag, high boots that stop your ankles from folding over sideways and some sandals for the 20 times you're going to have to wade the river. Don't worry about water: the river's drinkable. Oh yeah, don't forget a stove and some utensils.

First off you have to get down there and, if you don't watch out, the gravelly path will deliver you to the river at speed and on your backside. There's often no wind in the canyon, it gets hotter as you descend and the cool river below will get to look like a supply of Windhoek lager from the fridges of heaven. You may find the remains of a Vespa scooter half way down. Don't ask. There are lunatics everywhere.

Okay, you're at the bottom, wet and happy, having flung yourself bodily into your drinking water. Stare up at the rock walls and down the disappearing river. Think five days and 83 kilometres. No time to lose: plod pugnaciously on.

There are two surfaces you're going to walk on, both unacceptable by normal bipedal human standards: soft, exhausting sand and water-polished boulders. I guess riverbed makes a third. Hiking over the powdery sand with a pack is like those dreams where you're running but getting nowhere. That's the easy bit. Boulder hopping seems like fun at first, but soon your calves will be on fire. You can easily twist an ankle and there are no comms to call a chopper when you come a cropper. So be careful.

A hole with soul

You can take your mind off the inevitable pains of the second day (hikes always hurt on the second day) by looking round at the unfolding geology lesson. Someone who knows about these things would rabbit on about shales, conglomerates, ice ages and a 500-million-year-old crustal fracture that invited an Eocene river to do its worst. Skip it. It's enough to say that the scenery feels as old as time itself and has presence.

Here's some travel information you may find interesting. If you have keen eyes you'll spot debris lodged in the canyon walls, maybe 20 metres above your head in places. Yes, you're right, the only way it can get there is by water. So you think the river always looks like that little trickle you keep splashing through? Listen and watch your back.

At some point, you're bound to hear the thunder of hooves. It's not the sheriff out to arrest you for not digging your toilet hole deep enough, but the clatter of feral horses that see fit to hang out down there. Also look out for the hot spring about half way to Ai Ais, a place that will become fixed in your slavering imagination as BEER AT THE END.

The spring really is hot, so rip off your kit and slide in for a cosmic massage. It's so pleasurable and erotic that when I did the hike a few years ago a guy got so excited he couldn't decently get out of the water until we'd all left.

Now here comes the lyrical bit. In the evenings, as the shadows cloak the canyon in Prussian blue, the golden canyon walls reflect in river pools and a cool breeze gently ruffles your sweaty hair and dries the fluff in your armpits. You fire up the Cadac for supper, settle your bum in the soft sand and know, beyond doubt, that the Creator was an artist and she used the Fish River to try out her abstracts.

By day four, the need for ice-cold beer at the pub at Ai Ais will reach psychotic proportions. Resist the temptation to run: you'll just twist your ankle. It has been proved, by countless hikers, that you will eventually get there.

That's all I can tell you, really. Oh yes, the little paw prints. I nearly forgot. They're made by giant scorpions which come to check you out when you sleep. Don't worry, they won't hurt you unless you roll onto them. But make sure you stuff your smelly socks into your boots when you turn in. You wouldn't want to injure the local wildlife by jamming your foot into a scorpion's overnight abode.

Spin of the wagon wheel:
Great Trek – Piet Uys
Justin Fox – July 2006

Over the coming six months Getaway journalists
will retrace some of the epic journeys of the Great Trek.
In the first instalment, Justin Fox travels in the
wagon tracks of Piet Uys's 'commission trek',
the 1834 reconnaissance for the
main event two years later.

W̲e̲ ̲s̲t̲o̲o̲d̲ ̲b̲e̲s̲i̲d̲e̲ a quiet inlet near the mouth of the Krom River at St Francis Bay. The farmer knelt down and picked up a few bricks that lay in an open field.

'My grandfather belonged to the United Party, die ou Sappe, and he didn't like the Nationalists one bit,' said Manie du Toit. 'One day, about 1948, a government car arrived here from Pretoria. Five men in suits got out and asked him where's Piet Uys's house. "What d'you want with it?" he asked. And they said, no, they wanted to turn it into a museum or a memorial or something.

'They were thrilled to finally find it, 'cause there's a lot of farms in South Africa called Brakfontein. It was a long house with stinkwood and yellowwood beams. I was eight years old and I remember how, as soon as they left, my grandfather took paraffin, soaked the thatch and put a match to it. My dad was furious, but Oupa said no, he doesn't want Nationalists on his farm. Early next morning Oupa got a bulldozer and flattened what was left of the house.'

There, on the grassy knoll, lay the remains of the foundations. In the distance were the sprawling developments of St Francis Bay. I picked up a couple of pink clay bricks – bones of the old house and talismans for my journey – trying to feel the spirit of the place, of the Uyses.

I imagined Piet and his family here on a golden summer evening like this. I could see him gazing east at those distant blue mountains and contemplating his future. The farm stretched down to the river and the sea in those days, the grass was thick: good cattle land. Why on earth did he give all this up for the tragic destiny that awaited him among the Zulus?

On trek with the Uyses

Dissatisfied with their lot in the Eastern Cape after the arrival of the 1820 settlers, and British interference from Cape Town, Boer farmers began to look beyond the colony's frontiers for alternative places to settle. To this end a number of 'commission treks' were dispatched as scouting parties into the interior to lay the groundwork for a later, greater trek.

The most successful of these was that of Piet Uys, who set off in September 1834 from the Krom River on a six-month reconnaissance expedition. He travelled through the Transkei and Natal to Zululand in order to meet chiefs such as Hintsa, Faku and Dingaan to ask for land.

It was partly as a result of Uys's reports of verdant pastures and unpeopled tracts in KwaZulu-Natal that Boer leaders decided to embark on the Great Trek in 1836. Their primary goal: Uys's Edenic Natal.

My journey in the trekker's footsteps had a personal aspect to it. My grandmother, Sannie Uys, was the first cousin twice removed of Piet Uys. During the course of my quest I felt the presence of that brave, blonde, headstrong farmer grow more palpable as the trip progressed. In my mind I was travelling with family.

My rugged wagon, the Nissan Patrol we'd be using for this entire series, left Brakfontein and headed east, following the wagon ruts of the commission trek. No first-hand account remains, but it is known that Uys travelled more or less in the footsteps of Dr Andrew Smith and Andrew Geddes Bain, both of whom had made similar journeys before him. The commission trek comprised 14 wagons, 21 burghers (including one woman) and lots of servants.

My first stop was Grahamstown, where Piet Retief lived. Here the trekkers halted to resupply before pushing deeper into contested frontier country. I was soon into the groove, the Zen of trekking, trying to feel my way into Uys's head. Was that the creak of wooden wheels, the flogging of canvas in the wind, the moan of oxen? I began looking at the land as a trekker would; judging its lie in terms of my wagon's capabilities. The Nissan oxen were producing three litres of raw power: turbo oxen. Ja neef, nou trek ons.

Then came operatic country, the world falling away into the Great Fish and Kei valleys – difficult wagon terrain with deep gorges and boulder-strewn, fast-flowing rivers. The land grew more tribal: fewer fences, more stray animals. The cattle warning signs all had good bullet-hole placings. Herd boys pretended to fire rifles at me as I passed. I waved back.

From Bain I knew that Chief Hintsa's kraal had been a few kilometres east of Butterworth. But the region Hintsa offered Uys was already occupied and he pressed on, looking for greener pastures.

Insects thwacked the windscreen, then evolved into hail so hard it forced me to a white-out standstill near Umtata. Ice balls drilled like assegais against my wagon. Then all of a sudden it was sunshine again and I dropped coastwise into a land grown forested and gorgey. Gorgeous too.

A visit to Chief Faku

Umngazi Valley was lush and green and thickly tropical, the flood plain narrow but loamy and inviting to any farmer. The road was choked with cattle and their dung caked my tyres, the smell filling the cabin. They should be towing wagons, I thought, not loafing about impeding my progress.

I outspanned at Umngazi River Bungalows, one of *Getaway's* old favourites and rated by editor David Bristow as South Africa's best family holiday destination. True to form the place was full of families: fathers teaching sons to fish, mothers and lodge staff organising boating and sandboarding expeditions, long-suffering Xhosa nannies playing with pink brats on the lawn. Meanwhile cattle sunbathed on the beach (more loafers) and herders called from the hills and kloofs. All around us was old, rural Transkei; not much had changed since Pondo Chief Faku's time.

Peaceful the scene may have looked, but that's not the way it's always been. The Umngazi River is said to have got its name from Faku, who did away with his enemies by tossing them off Mlenga (execution) Rock where their blood (igazi) flowed into the river, colouring it red.

One of my objectives at Umngazi was to find the site of Faku's kraal and Uys's crossing. Diary entries by explorers of the period put it a few kilometres upstream on the west bank.

'I think I know just the spot,' said Terry Bouwer, manager of Umngazi and fourth-generation Transkeian. 'There's a drift that all the old wagons used and I'm convinced Faku would have had his kraal there.'

Leaving Umngazi I stopped at the rocky ford and listened for my ancestral spirit, there at the talking water. On Faku's side the lantana was thick and tall as a hedge, but I heard the wagon wheels clinking across the stones and the musket shot of whips. Okay, you were here neef.

Beyond Umngazi the land grew terrible for wagonning and Uys's party probably covered only a few kilometres a day. The kloofs were heavily wooded on the descent to the wide Umzimvubu River. My 'Uys self' considered locking the wheels, or even taking them off entirely and letting the wagon slide down on felled branches – all good practise for the Drakensberg a few years hence.

Beyond, I rolled through Pondoland undulations: huts, kraals, mielie fields, hamlets with spaza shops. Then a night in a run-down stone chalet at Mkambati Nature Reserve, where I surmise Uys crossed the Msikaba River at its mouth, just as Bain and Smith before him. No laager and accordion music for me; just a cold lager and braai for one.

Behold, the promised land

From the Msikaba the Uys party wended its way north-east to Port Natal. Sometimes they crossed the many rivers far upstream at fording spots; at others the wagons breasted the sandy river mouths at low tide. Looking down on the grass-covered and rolling hills of Natal, Uys exclaimed: 'Only heaven can be more beautiful.' He was seduced by the endless green, begging to be grazed by Boer livestock, a promised land of sorts.

Teenage Zulu girls with bundles of wood on their heads trudged past Spanish-style estates ringed by high electric fences, a sugar-cane sea beyond. Scruffy boys sold baskets of golf balls by the roadside. Traffic-cop impis waited in ambush.

I stopped a night in Durban at colonial-style Somerset Guest House. Uys would have been welcomed by the British settlers at Port Natal, particularly as he came with the blessing of Sir Benjamin D'Urban, governor of the Cape.

From Durban I made a detour inland to the Voortrekker Museum in Pietermaritzburg. There I met Riana Mulder, a historian with a passion for trekker stories and memorabilia. You can easily imagine her in the back of a wagon loading muskets.

She led me into the museum's archives to show off some of the prized possessions. We talked about the only woman on the commission trek, Gertruida Uys. Why was she allowed to go along? Were she and her husband so much in love? Or was she a strong-willed Afrikaner woman who wouldn't take no for an answer?

Riana clearly liked the latter explanation. 'Gertruida would have been the first Afrikaner woman to enter Natal,' she said.

Then Riana took me into a back room hung with Voortrekker artefacts, 17th-century Huguenot garments … and Gertruida's linen frock, handed down through the family. From a side room filled with kappies (bonnets) hanging on hooks she produced the tiny khaki bonnet of a young girl. In it was a slit made by the stab of an assegai, the child's blood still staining the material.

Most pertinent were Piet Uys's blue wedding waistcoat – which would fit me perfectly – and six silver buttons found on his body where he'd fallen on his return to Natal in 1838. Cupping those precious, octagonal buttons in my hand, I felt I had my first tangible link to him.

Into Dingaan's maw

Uys pushed north from Port Natal along the coast as far as the banks of the Mvoti River. There is some dispute as to whether he actually visited Dingaan, or sent a messenger from his riverside camp. Family history is clear that Uys would have wanted to negotiate land from the great chief personally. Dingaan agreed to allow the colonists to settle, but refused to sign any agreement until they returned.

My base for visiting Dingaan's kraal and adjacent battlefields was Babanango Valley Lodge, a spectacular spot in the heart of green Zululand mountains. I joined up with two local guides who run battlefield tours. Both Rex Duke and Paul Smith are mad about the area's history and fiercely debate the finer points of military strategy as it played out in these Zulu killing fields.

The site of Mgungundhlovu was vital to my personal quest. Along with the family, I believe Uys did reach the royal kraal on the commission trek. Also, it was here that Great Trek leader Retief and his group were killed, a tragedy that sparked an attempted revenge attack (led by Uys and Potgieter) two months later on 11 April 1838. The Flight Commando, as the party came to be known, never got as far as Mgungundhlovu, but was ambushed in a valley seven kilometres to the south.

Finding Dingaan's royal kraal was easy. I stood on Execution Hill, overlooking the replica beehive huts and imagined Retief and his men being massacred – the impalings, screaming, disembowelling – their bodies left for the hyenas and vultures.

Finding the site of the fateful Battle of Italeni was much more difficult. We had maps, inaccurate diagrams, history books, manuscripts, GPS and aerial photographs. And still the spot proved elusive.

My 'trackers' – Rex with his Kruger beard and khakis, big Paul with a bloody head wound from a branch – looked the part. It felt like a scouting commando. As we hiked into the valley Paul confided, 'My great-great grandfather – Lourens Petrus Badenhorst – was in this battle too, Justin. He survived, thank God. So I'm tied to this place like you.'

We picked our way through thick vegetation along the Mkumbane Stream between the hills from which the three impis – possibly as many as 8000 warriors – swarmed down on the Uys commando. Tactically, the Zulu plan was brilliant: they chose terrain that neutralised the effectiveness of the Boer horses and, with a feigned retreat, drew them into a perfectly laid trap.

In a wood we passed eight or so graves said to be those of some of the fallen, dragged from their horses and speared to death. Above was the rocky incline that blocked their escape and the high river banks from which assegais rained down.

And it was here, or perhaps a little further upstream, that Uys fell from his horse, a spear in the small of his back. When his 15-year-old son Dirkie, who was already galloping free of danger, saw his father on the ground and Zulus running towards him, he wheeled his horse round shouting, 'I will die with my father,' and charged back. He managed to shoot three warriors, but both he and his father were quickly overwhelmed.

On an overgrown ledge, shaded by a rocky overhang, Paul led us to what looked like two graves packed with stones. 'We think these could be the bodies of Piet and Dirkie, buried here after Blood River when the Afrikaners returned victorious,' said Paul.

So it was probably here that the six buttons were plucked from the remains of a skeleton. I felt the Uyses' last moments as if it were yesterday. The wounded Piet trying to spur his horse out of the ambush, the shouts of the warriors closing in. I sensed the entrapment as a cold sweat, as nausea. Two of my family had died a terrible death here and their presence still clawed at the air. I felt the claustrophobia of a history that had suddenly come too close.

My adventure effectively ended at that spot, as had Uys's. His dreams of a promised land, the possibilities – if ever there had been – of peaceful cohabitation with its black keepers were dashed. The wheels of the Great Trek would inexorably lead to Blood River and nearly two centuries of conflict and misunderstanding.

I looked out over peaceful green hills, recently ceded by white farmers to their black labourers … and thought how, in some respects, the wheel had come full circle.

Island strife – Doing (free) time on Robben Island
Peter Frost – March 2007

It mirrors five centuries of conflict and political repression. It's also South Africa's most potent symbol of the triumph of the human spirit. Peter Frost sailed the 10 kilometres from Cape Town to Robben Island and found penguins, poignancy and a palpable sense of history.

∂

For most overseas visitors, a trip to Robben Island is one of the 'Big Six' attractions of Cape Town, along with Table Mountain, the Winelands, Kirstenbosch, the Waterfront and Cape Point. But for South Africans, it means more than that. It's a pilgrimage to a place that represents the country's journey from fledgling colony to pariah state to proud nation.

A journey to the island starts at the Nelson Mandela Gateway, from where the Robben Island ferry leaves. The docking station at the V&A Waterfront is also a museum and a destination in itself. It was opened in December 2001 and is part of the Clock Tower development on the east side of the Waterfront. The Gateway has a restaurant, an auditorium, a museum shop and a number of multi-media exhibitions that prepare visitors for what they will experience, once on the island. There's a lot of history in the exhibitions and you leave on the ferry with a more detailed understanding of how entrenched Robben Island's reputation as a 'bad place' is.

The trip across Table Bay to the island takes half an hour. The ferry passes through one of Africa's busiest working harbours, dwarfed by super-tankers and container ships from across the globe. Once out of the protection of the breakwater, the sea inevitably becomes choppy – but the ferry is built for comfort, even in the stormiest of seas. Cape fur seals, dusky and Heaviside's dolphins are often seen on the crossing and, if you're lucky, southern right or Bryde's whales.

Looking back towards Cape Town, you get a first-hand experience of what it must have been like for the Phoenicians 2000 years ago, as they sailed into Table Bay and saw the spectacle of Table Mountain – apparently. The best way to truly appreciate the majesty of the mountain is from the sea. Awe is, however, tinged with something else: this trip was anything but pleasant for countless prisoners who made the journey toward their incarceration.

From the sea the island appears flat, and it is. It's actually the summit of an ancient, mostly submerged, mountain linked by an undersea saddle to the Blouberg shore and to Cape Town itself. The highest point on Robben Island is only 30 metres, it's just two kilometres wide, three and a half kilometres long. Not much real estate for such an iconic world site.

The ferry docks and visitors are escorted onto waiting buses. It's a far cry from the chain-gang reception that greeted the first Portuguese inmates in 1525.

Today Robben Island is a place of international significance, but for the better part of 500 years it has been more infamous than famous. Its importance springs from the fact that its history mirrors that of South Africa: every controlling power that governed the Cape has had an impact – usually a negative one – on Robben Island.

The first Portuguese convicts were replaced with English ones in 1615 when the British Crown took over control of the colony. The first political prisoners were interned there in the early 1700s, followed by East Asian exiles shortly afterwards. In 1771 it became a quarantine station for 19 years before reverting to its favoured status as a prison. The first Xhosa prisoners from the frontier wars arrived in 1855, to be followed by large numbers of Zulu prisoners after the Anglo-Zulu wars of the 1870s. By the end of the 19th century it had become a hospital for lepers, the insane and the chronically ill.

Just before the Second World War it was occupied by the army and navy and used for training and coastal defence. Then, in 1961, it became a maximum security prison for political prisoners and a medium security prison for criminals. It remained a prison until two years after South Africa's first democratic elections in 1994, when finally, in late 1996, it was closed and declared a national monument.

So much misery over so many years might not, you'd think, make for an uplifting experience, but that's in fact how it turns out. The tour of the island incorporates a walk through the prison where many apartheid-era prisoners spent large parts of their lives. The ANC's Nelson Mandela and the PAC's Robert Sobukwe's years are the best documented.

The uplifting part is hearing the stories of how prisoners turned the island into an underground university. Learning was shared, teaching rarely stopped, ideas and philosophies were debated, ideologies fine-tuned and cultures revealed. Despite the harsh, hard-labour conditions, Robben Island seemed to build resolve rather than drain enthusiasm. And it could even be fun.

Ex-prisoners are employed, along with ex-guards, to conduct tours and they tell stories of the games played by master and servant to rise above the situation and reaffirm humanity, constantly trying to outwit each other. The inmates even managed to organise sporting events and political debates, despite the reluctant authorities.

One of the most sobering parts of the Robben Island tour is the walk through the stone quarry. Part of the reason the early Portuguese powers colonised Robben Island was to take advantage of the solid rock foundation of Malmesbury shale (good for building) and the deposits of limestone, built up over thousands of years of marine shell decomposition. To stand in that intense glare is to realise how much resolve it must have taken not to give in to the hopelessness of the situation. Years later, Mandela and other prisoners returned to the quarry and each put a rock on a pile to commemorate the years they spent there, breaking rocks.

But perhaps the most intense moment in the tour is Mandela's cell, which is far smaller than you'd expect. Again, the idea that one man endured such a tiny space for so long (27 years of incarceration in total) and still managed to come out of it with a forgiving, positive attitude, is difficult to grasp. Indeed, it's possibly South Africa's most cherished achievement.

It's not just about the prison

There's more to the island than the prison. The 575-hectare island plays host to a wide range of fauna and flora and visitors get a chance to see some of it, although free time to wander is frustratingly at a minimum.

There are 132 bird species known to either live on, or visit the island. Many breed there in large numbers, such as the crowned cormorant and black-crowned night heron. The African penguin, formerly known as the jackass, was re-introduced in 1983 and the colony is now a great crowd-pleaser. Mammals have also been introduced and include bontebok, springbok, steenbok and eland. Two strange bedfellows are the exotic fallow deer and the chukka partridge.

It's amusing to think that if the authorities had restocked the island along historically accurate lines, they'd have populated it with scraggly sheep: it was custom in the 1600s to leave emaciated livestock, thin from a long sea voyage, on the island and replace them with fat ones left previously by other ships. The trade was operated on an honour system, friend or foe, and prevailed for many years.

After the tour of the prison and the bus trip around the island, visitors are left for a short time to be alone. Cape Town, on a good day, looks so near, Blouberg even closer. Knowing they were so isolated despite the nearness must have been painful for the island's prisoners.

A sense of just how far South Africa has come in a short period of time is very clear as you catch the boat back to the Waterfront. It's not Alcatraz, Guantanamo Bay or Devil Island. It's a unique statement, a powerful example of how ill can be transformed by will. It represents what South Africa has achieved and what's possible for the future.

Vredefort rocks – now and then
Jazz Kuschke – March 2007

*Two billion years ago the land we call home
(it looked a lot different back then)
was ground zero for one of the biggest explosions
planet earth has ever experienced. If it had to happen today, it would
probably wipe out every living thing. Jazz Kuschke explored what's
left of this impact site after two billion years of erosion and
deposition, and found an adventure-sport paradise.*

ॐ

About two billion years ago something that could have been straight out of Armageddon – where mighty Bruce Willis saves the world from a gigantic asteroid – was hurtling towards earth. The movie was impressive, but Hollywood's version in no way resembles what happened here ....

A celestial body crashed into planet earth with an impact that can be described only as a planetary cataclysm. It left what is today the largest visible astrobleme, or star wound, on the earth's surface, and created what we call the Vredefort Dome.

Now: World-renowned impact site

Today, unless you knew, you'd hardly notice this crash site if you were on the ground. But from above, it's completely different.

'I can fly this route every day and see something new,' smiled Otto Stumke from behind the controls of his 1946 Cessna 140. 'New' is relative in geological terms. Especially if you're talking about the gnarled corner of earth 120 kilometres southwest of Jo'burg. It was rewarded Unesco World Heritage status in July 2005 because it's a veritable living star-science, geology and geomorphology laboratory.

A thousand feet below the Cessna, the Vaal River snaked round islands and boiled over rapids and shallow riffles as it traced a line south by west, through sets of concentric corduroy hills. An early-morning breeze tugged at the Cessna's wings and ruffled the river's surface.

'That's the "inland sea",' said the ex-Jumbo pilot, pointing to the left. 'It's about the centre of the collision area.' But it has nothing to do with ground zero – it just happens to be a large saltpan in the middle of the core area.

Then: Liquidised earth

The blow had a geological ripple effect best demonstrated by dropping a pebble into a basin filled with water and looking at it in slow motion: on impact, the pebble creates a concave bowl in the water. The initial Vredefort force created a 50-kilometre-deep hole in the nanosecond of impact, which was surrounded by steep and unstable walls.

In the basin, the impact is followed by a rebound action which forces a cone up in the centre, as the water returns to the point where the pebble fell. At Vredefort, the power of this rebound caused the walls to collapse and simultaneously created concentric rings of hills, leaving a shallow bowl-shaped crater. Geologists called it a dome because it was immediately filled from below by uprushing middle- and deep-earth crust. The remnant of the collar around the dome is a range of hills called the Bergland – those rumpled ones visible from Otto's plane.

If you could freeze the bowl of water at that point, you would be left with a complex crater. It's believed that the whole Vredefort drama unfolded in less than 15 minutes – probably as little as four.

The force was one of the most awesome energy releases this planet has ever experienced. As David Fleminger wrote in Vredefort Dome (which forms part of the Southbound Pocket Guides series on South Africa's World Heritage Sites): 'When it struck, the kinetic energy of the projectile released the equivalent of 100-million megatons of dynamite – that's 100-trillion tons of explosive force. By comparison, the most powerful nuclear bomb ever detonated only yielded 50 megatons.'

Now: Solidified evidence

On the eastern end of the hills lies Lion's Head Quarry. For years, export quality 'Parys granite' was mined there. But a lack of demand put an end to operations and now only square-cut trenches remain. These blemishes are cross sections of the area's underlying geological structure – proof of what happened.

There you can see pseudotachylites ('as if volcanic'). They were formed largely by frictional melting as the granite rushed upwards to fill the gigantic hole left by the blast. Some of the rocks melted because of the immediate, intense heat caused by the impact – others did not, creating molten rock rivers that probably looked a lot like crunchy peanut butter. This solidified to leave the distinctly coloured and patterned pseudotachylites.

Then: Big, bad, fast and furious

Scientists aren't entirely sure what created this 300-kilometre-diameter crater, the core area of which today encompasses the towns of Vredefort, Parys and Venter-skroon, with the outermost 'ring of gold' marked by Johannesburg, Klerksdorp and Welkom.

Was it a comet that hit the earth? One with a fragmented core of rock and ice, and trailing a gas tail? Or was it an asteroid, made of solid rock?

Although geologists aren't sure about what it was, they're fairly certain of its speed and size. 'It was about as big as Table Mountain and travelled at around 20 kilometres a second,' mused Graeme Addison, former academic and river man, now Vredefort Dome resident and author of various articles on the history and structures of the area.

They're also sure that it came from the sky – the original theory was that it was due to a huge volcanic eruption, similar to how the Pilanesberg alkaline ring-complex crater was formed. 'I prefer to call it "star science",' said Graeme. 'It's sexier than "geology", and the landscape around here is as a result of something that came out of the sky.'

He went on to explain how, when the astral projectile crashed into our planet, the earth's surface where the dome is now could've been some kilometres higher than it is today. 'Two billion years worth of geological forces have eroded, rebuilt and re-eroded this area into what it is today.'

The landforms and unique hills of the Vredefort Dome that we see originally lay well below the surface and have become visible due only to erosion. Francois de Villiers from Dome Adventures explained further: 'When you look at the satellite images, it looks like half a crater. That's because most of the southeastern ridges are buried under sediments of the Karoo Supergroup (around 150 million years old).' The dome itself is pear-shaped rather than round.

Now: Delving into the past

The tunnel was just big enough for an average person to stand in. After the searing midday heat, it was cool and damp, and quiet. Eerily so, but if you closed your eyes you could almost hear the pickaxes click-clashing against the rock, boring deeper into the hills ....

'In the late 1800s, prospectors mined horizontally into the hills around Venter-skroon,' said Francois, running his torch across the ceiling of the narrow passage. 'See the quartzite composite strata? That's the same gold-bearing ore found across most of the Witwatersrand.'

The mining tunnels are horizontal (rather than vertical as in the Witwatersrand) because the explosion caused the deeply buried strata to be turned through 90 degrees. And so miners have picked their way across the land rather than vertically into it.

Then: A life-changing event

Of course, the effects of this impact reached far further than the original shallow bowl – 70 cubic kilometres of earth had been flung into the sky. Debris was deposited over a wide area, and dust filled the atmosphere and blocked the light from the sun – just as in those B-grade movies about how the dinosaurs died.

So was it the Vredefort explosion that killed them? No, this happened some two billion years ago. It's believed that the Chicxulub impact in the Gulf of Mexico was responsible for the extinction of the dinosaurs a mere 65-million years ago. Although primitive one-celled life in the form of blue-green algae had already existed for a billion years or more, there is no evidence of extinction – what is possible is that the DNA of life might have been changed, altering the course of evolution.

Now: An adventure playground

Instead of wiping out anything, the Vredefort incident, combined with another two billion years of erosion and deposition, created an adventure destination conveniently close to Gauteng. Most of these centre around the Vaal River, which runs through the Vredefort Dome, and is arguably one of the world's oldest watercourses. The area is certainly the heir of a long ancestry of rivers which have built and re-eroded the landscape to reveal the deep structure of the dome as we know it today.

The Vaal's riffles are home to wily yellowfish to target with fly-fishing gear and lively rapids to tackle in rafts and kayaks. There are unique mountains for hiking and climbing and spectacular 4x4 and mountain-bike trails.

The biggest problem for visitors is being able to see the geomorphology of the Vredefort Dome (which can be viewed as a whole only from space) and understand its scientific interest and importance: some reading and expert guiding are recommended. Geology, history or adventure sport – whatever your interest, Vredefort rocks. Now and then.

Blown out of the water –
The Orange River with the family
David Bristow – November 2007

On a river, the current determines time and there's nothing to do but get carried along. It's a great place to contemplate the meaning of things and to reconnect with your mojo and your loved ones, says David Bristow.

෴

The word sjambok is derived from the Malay samboq and to be sjambokked means to be given a heavy whipping. When a rapid on a big river is given this name, you can expect a wake-up klap. Sjambok is the fifth and most challenging rapid on the prime white-water canoeing section of the Orange River between Vioolsdrif and Grootpens: the main Richtersveld gorge.

The Khoi people of ages past told how Kouteign Koorou, the serpent master of the river, created both this and the Fish River Canyon nearby in a terrible rage while fleeing hunters. The gnarled Richtersveld landscape and the fury of the water still express the water monster's anger.

Our lead guide, Max, alone in his Indian-style canoe, made it through Sjambok okay and, from a rock below the big standing wave, directed us through one by one – and one by one, we foundered. Next to dare the beating was Martin, another guide from Wildthing Adventures, but the standing wave klapped him hard and his boat went over and down, losing some of its bits and pieces (mostly our camping equipment).

Then it was our turn. The thing is, my son Ben had only recently learned to swim. I'd paddled the river twice before, but in inflatable boats. These canoes were different; they didn't float as well when inundated with water. Still, we had our helmets and life jackets, and had been working well as a team so far. But ultimately, I was responsible for my seven-year-old's well-being.

I had to use all my resources to keep our line right through the long, curving rapid, judging the down-river 'arrows' that marked the best line through the lurking dangers. The river took a sharp turn to the left and was funnelled between sheer-sided grey granite banks, where they were cut through by a smooth, black dolorite dyke. Because of the river's extremely low level, there was a hole right where there oughtn't to be – just where we had to turn our nose sharply left … too late.

First our nose dipped into the hole, then we hit the metre-high standing wave that was the crux of this liquid, but very real, obstacle. It completely swamped our boat, then the rolling motion of the water inside simply flipped it over. I could see the panic in Ben's eyes as he tried to hold on, calling for me to help him. Suddenly the power and the speed of the Orange River became life threatening. All the 'what ifs' flashed through my mind and my stomach knotted. 'Don't panic, hold on!' You're not sure if you are shouting aloud or to yourself.

An inconvenient wake-up call

The water was tugging my feet, sucking off my aqua shoes, pushing my chest hard against the overturned boat and making it almost impossible to get to my frightened son. The whole scenario lasted only seconds before both I, and one of the forward guides, got to Ben and swam him and the canoe to the shore. But in that time, I knew how easily and how quickly – and irrevocably – an accident can happen on this river. I'd heard stories about the power of rivers and knew experienced paddlers who'd been drowned by flowing water. And where did Dead Man's Rapid, the first on our route, get its name?

I remembered the tale of Graeme Addison, known as 'the old man of the Orange', who came within seconds of drowning when his kayak was tipped over by an unseen rock just below the surface. While he was going through his death throes, the rest of the party were relaxing on the bank, unaware of his situation.

There is no way to fight the water when this happens. All river paddlers know what to do, but sometimes the river has other ideas. It's one of the first safety lessons you learn: never get trapped between your boat and a rock. If your boat is pushed against a boulder, lean as hard as you can into the rock, or you'll flip and get trapped against it. Luckily for Addison, one of his party went to check on him and casually flipped Graeme's kayak over when all had seemed lost.

Sjambok Rapid took its toll and Max and Martin were kept busy diving into the Orange to help more capsized canoeists to the bank.

When it was Frik and his Aussie mate Mark's turn, everyone readied themselves – for photos or rescue dives – as the pair had tipped over in most of the rapids so far. With taut faces, the two out-of-sync paddlers steered (badly) through the whip's S-bend, lined up skew to the hole, dipped into it and then – somehow – punched right through the standing wave and paddled triumphant to the bank.

Last came Francois, a first-time river guide carrying the rest of our equipment. It was inevitable that, with his top-heavy canoe that had already cracked its hull, Max and Martin would swim yet again. And so they did. While clothes and kit dried on the rocks, glass fibre and resin were used to patch up the boats that had been worst hit by the power of this aquatic lashing.

A river is an eternally mysterious and seductive thing. It represents the demon serpent that can take away a life as easily as diving into a clear pool. It's the flow of time, forever moving towards, and being absorbed by, the timeless ocean. It is both a metaphor for life's journey and the best place to make a life-defining journey: to choose darkness, or light.

The Orange is a special river. It's the only permanently flowing course for hundreds of kilometres to the south and for a much greater distance to the north. It's a big river by any measure, running 2340 kilometres from its source in northeast Lesotho to its mouth at wave-pounded Oranjemund.

Yet at all times, except in the highest floods, it is navigable for most of its length by even novice paddlers, making it a wonderful escape from the urban jungle.

Our days were spent in an easy combination of floating, muscle-hardening paddling when the water was flat and the wind up, and whiplash runs through rapids. In the Richtersveld, the days are warm even in mid-winter and the invigorating water was the perfect counter-balance to the desert sun. In the mornings and afternoons, there was ample time for lazing, reading, photographing and exploring the intriguing river banks. Wildthing Adventures' website says you'll 'overnight under the star-filled African sky with raging campfires and good company' – and that sums it up as well as anyone could.

When the rapids come, you take them. There is no option. Sometimes you tip, sometimes you don't and you feel rewarded. Unless you are a seasoned kayaker, there will also be occasions when you experience all-focusing fear. The river takes you there and it carries you beyond. There is no other way.

The speed of the flow of the river and the arcing of the sun are the only markers of direction or progression. You are abandoned to the river's rhythm and you lose your own sense of time. It's great for friends and family to enjoy the experience together, without any outside distractions and nothing to do but go with the current.

The river carries you and you exist only in the present. You get up, have breakfast, paddle, float, swim, have lunch, paddle, float, walk, paddle, snooze, have supper, watch the stars. If you're lucky, someone in your party will know more than the Southern Cross and Orion. If you're clever, you'll take a star guide and small torch to plot the currents of the sky, because you're not likely to get a better view.

Who knows what young Ben made of it all. His older siblings had twice before been taken down the river. It must have seemed like an eternity to him till he was deemed ready for his Orange baptism, which has become a family tradition.

But photos from the trip are now gummed to his bedroom door, alongside his poster of the Bok team, some noxious rapper and Harry Potter.

Following the heart's path
Don Pinnock – June 2008

Every journey has its reason and its road. For Belinda Kruiper,
it may have been the push of an authoritarian father or
the pull of ancient genetic memory, but at a certain point
in her life, she bounced off the road of Western
civilisation down a dusty track that led to a grass hut
in the burning sands of the Kalahari.

❧

The pretty, honey-skinned girl from Calvinia tried to fit in. Coming from a family of teachers and preachers, she attempted to do what was expected – began studying social work, joined the United Building Society and became a hostess on a Translux bus.

There was, however, a strange restlessness in Belinda Kruiper's blood, a searching for something she couldn't name. She married a Mauritian, incurring family disapproval, and travelled up through Africa to Europe with him. But she found that he was no less violent than her preacher father and the relationship fell apart. Conventional society just wasn't working for her – she needed to get away.

It was impossible, when I met her, to guess her age. She's small, with the quick movements of a teenager, an impression reinforced by a colourful shirt, tight jeans and a jaunty cap. Her face is elf-like with an easy grin, but her eyes have a depth and wisdom that could have come only from pain and long experience.

'After the breakup, I wanted to get to some remote place,' she said, 'as far away as I could. I needed a place to lick my wounds.' She applied for, and got, a job at the Kgalagadi Transfrontier Park, cut her long hair to a spiky topknot, bought tough Cat boots and headed for the wilds.

The Kalahari proved to be balm for her soul, but in the park's reception office, her confidence and complete disregard for entrenched racial prejudices immediately raised eyebrows. But it wasn't long before Belinda's competence and sunny nature won over most of the white staff.

'I loved being at the park,' she remembered. 'I loved the desert surroundings, the bigness of the sky, the startling red dunes, the distinctive camel thorn trees. And they gave me a nice house with a cactus tree in the garden.'

One cold day, Belinda looked out and saw a little old man with Rasta dreadlocks wearing nothing but a goatskin loincloth and a threadbare jersey. He was shivering. 'I went outside and introduced myself. He said he was Dawid Kruiper. I invited him into reception to have some coffee and warm up.'

After he'd gone, a staff member said to her: 'You're going to get into trouble. You can't invite Bushmen in here. It's the land claim thing.' Dawid was a member of the #Khomani Bushmen who'd been forced out when the park was proclaimed and were claiming it back.

Unlike most of the staff, who felt this was a threat to their jobs, Belinda became intrigued. Who were these little people who drifted in over the dunes in rags? She began inviting them to her house and visiting their village, Welkom, outside the park. There she met the Riverbed Kids, as she called them. They weren't kids but young men who sat along the road to the park making beads and trinkets for sale to tourists.

They were often painfully thin, often unwell and drank too much, but they were free people, rebels who answered to nobody and still lived in the old ways, coming and going as they pleased without regard for fences and often causing havoc.

Belinda looked beyond this and saw people of the spirit, strong in sacred knowledge, gifted in healing, able to call rain and access the potency of trance. She was enthralled. 'They opened up to me as if I was one of them,' she said, 'accepting me without reservation, giving me their unconditional love.' Also in the village was the wise old shaman, Dawid Kruiper.

Belinda enjoyed her work with the park, but her relationship with the Bushmen was causing tensions. A senior ranger warned her that her visits to the Bushmen were 'like dancing round the fires of Satan'. She was thought to be siding with them in their land claim – and their presence around Twee Rivieren reception 'bothering' tourists didn't help.

What shocked her was the often vicious discrimination against them. 'The #Khomani had this incredible wealth of knowledge which could have been so valuable to tourism and park management, but the official attitude was that they were not worthy enough and just dronklappe (drunkards). Vetpiet, who was probably Africa's best tracker, was never given promotion because he couldn't write. He once said to me: 'I can read the book of the world but here I get treated as nothing.'

In March 1999, the contradictions became untenable and Belinda resigned from the park. 'It was becoming increasingly clear to me that I couldn't continue to live such a divided life, torn between the Bushmen and my job,' she said. 'Management couldn't believe that my involvement with the Bushmen was based on friendship and love, and this put me under a permanent cloud of suspicion.'

She moved to the village and joined the South African San Institute (SASI) as a field worker. Under the wise, although incidental, tutoring of Dawid Kruiper, her life seemed to somersault. Strange things began chipping away at her Western logic.

One morning she stopped her vehicle to watch a herd of wildebeests, sitting with her chin resting on her arms. The antelope stopped milling around and formed a V behind a large black bull, which stepped forward straight to the open window and pushed his nose against hers. Then it wheeled and walked away.

On another occasion, when she was walking over the dunes, a pale chanting goshawk flew from behind, touching her shoulder with its wing, and snatched a snake from under her feet, moments before she would have stood on it. For her, at first, these were coincidences. For the Bushmen, they were signs, omens and indicators.

One night she dreamed of a herder named Vetkat. 'I was standing on the banks of a dark river in which a figure was lying. A second figure stepped over him, the water rippled and there was blood. I said: "People are trying to kill Vetkat. Why him, who comes and goes like the wind?" I awoke with a pain in my heart. I hardly knew him at the time.'

When she told someone about the dream, they said Vetkat had also dreamed about her and saw her crying. They said in this way the two had been united in marriage by the ancestors. She dismissed it as rubbish, but their hearts defied her logic and they were drawn together into a beautiful harmony. Shortly afterwards, they married.

Vetkat's daily life may have been herding, but he was both a shaman and an artist. Although untutored, he produced strange, beautiful paintings, reclaiming the lost traditions of Bushman rock art. 'The drawings that poured out of him was the ancient art of his forefathers,' said Belinda, 'the sacred gift of spirit.'

The marriage, however, caused unexpected problems. There was jealousy among the #Khomani about an 'outsider' marrying into the Kruiper clan and her job with the San Institute was mysteriously terminated. She and Vetkat went to live in a grass hut on a farm named Blinkwater.

'It was a time of wonder and learning,' Belinda recalled, 'but also of great hardship. There was a drought and we had no money and no means of earning. I was sitting with Vetkat's sister and we were down to a bit of sugar and coffee. I was freaked out and began bitching about the Bushmen and their fatalism. She just told me to tighten the belt around my stomach and wait, because something would turn up just as long as we kept the fire going. And it did. A friend drove up with a carload of food.'

Belinda began to understand that the Kalahari had to remake her and, in the process, deprive her of resources, status and ego. 'I had to take on the pain of the Kalahari people,' she said. 'Now I understand what it's like to live with nothing, to become a person with no capacity and no resources, broken down to the shell of myself and feel hunger clawing at my insides. I've looked over the edge of the abyss and learned that my will to survive is the strongest force there is.'

Vetkat kept painting and people began to notice. One interviewer described him as 'one of those who walks between the worlds – his art is sacred because it's the spirit of the ancient ones and of the desert itself.' Belinda and Vetkat were given flights to travel to the United States and share experiences with indigenous people there. Tourists visited them and film crews followed.

Belinda, meanwhile, was struggling with the deteriorating situation among the #Khomani in the village. They won their land claim in March 1999, but it was tied up in bureaucracy and managed by outsiders. On the ground nothing was happening. The Riverbed Kids were drinking and fighting. Arguments were breaking out about leadership and property rights.

'I drink because I feel like a caged animal,' a Bushman named Sillikat told a researcher at the time. 'In the old days, when we disagreed, we'd split up. But we can't move, can't go anywhere except the road. So we drink and when we drink, the anger comes and we fight.' And without the possibility of hunting, they were starving.

'It was heartbreaking,' said Belinda. 'There were all these meetings and paperwork, but the Bushmen's souls were withering. Their dignity was being missed.' One of the Riverbed men told her: 'We are lost, beyond help. Please look after our children.'

'The Bushmen just needed space, to be left alone,' she said. 'But they've never been allowed to be just people like everyone else. They're always a symbol, an exhibit, a display item on somebody's agenda. That's where their spirit stays trapped, between the truth and the lie, the myth and the reality. Frozen in the amber of the past.'

Belinda dreamed of a school to reintroduce the children to their ancestral art and teach them bush lore and tracking. She travelled to Botswana and spent time with a shaman named Besa who, in a trance dance, took her to spiritual heights she'd never imagined possible. She learned to stop demanding logical explanations and trust the Bushman way.

'The desert teaches you to think differently, ' she said, 'to be more open to what is less tangible, to the world of spirit. Things happen here that have no logical explanation. A different energy holds.'

Then, unexpectedly, in April last year, Vetkat died of lung complications. While he was being buried, a huge male lion appeared on a dune and watched – accepting his spirit, Belinda believes. 'One day,' she said, 'I'll walk up to a lion. It has become my totem.'

She refused to give up, working tirelessly to set up centres for art in the Kalahari and Botswana. 'I'm going to be here until the Bushmen are wandering in the park again like they used to,' she said. 'Who knows how long it's going to take? But when it happens, I'll be there.'

'Sometimes I look back along the road I have travelled and I wonder: why that way? And why me? What was the role I was chosen for? The end of the story hasn't been written yet. What was foretold has not yet come to pass.'

The indri and me – Madagascar
Alison Westwood – September 2008

*When Madagascar parted company from the rest of
Gondwanaland 100 million years ago, it went its
own evolutionary way. About 40 million years
later, refugees from mainland Africa washed up on its shores
and found a new world to colonise. Alison Westwood
went looking for long-lost lemur cousins.*

A raindrop plops from leaf to leaf, somersaults through layers of forest canopy and lands with a splash on my nose. I wrap a soggy hat more tightly around my camera and follow Zaka up the steep path. Watch the ground for slippery roots, duck to avoid a slap from a liana. Stop! There it is, the sound we've been waiting for. Either the largest balloon in the world is being deflated, or the indris are singing in Andasibe this morning.

I scramble to keep up with Zaka as he disappears in the direction of the cries, then almost bowl him over when he pauses, pointing. 'Where? Where?' We edge forward. Between dripping foliage, on long grey limbs bearded with lichen, two black-and-white teddy bears are regarding us sternly. One opens her mouth with a great roar. Her mate joins in. The howl-wail song starts again and the forest dissolves in a downpour of noise.

The indri is the largest lemur alive today (there used to be one the size of a gorilla). Some people think it looks like a humanoid panda and say its call resembles that of the humpback whale. Indris belt out their duets loud enough to be heard several kilometres away and neighbouring groups keep in touch by singing about territory, mating, weather conditions and warnings. Sure enough, a distant answer floats back over the hills.

Zaka and I are in Andasibe-Mantadia National Park, a primary rainforest where the trees are older than memory and taller than stories. Next door is the Analamazaotra special reserve, a secondary rain forest set aside specifically for the protection of the indri. It had to be, because the indri is also the most obstinate lemur alive. Unlike other lemurs, it refuses to live or breed in captivity and doesn't do well outside its natural habitat.

At the turn of the 20th century you could have heard indris sing every morning anywhere from Tamatave on the east coast to Antananarivo in the central highlands. But their song has been fading with the rainforests. The Malagasy believe the indri is closely connected to humans and it is fady – taboo – to harm them. But while the indri is protected from man by fady, most of its habitat isn't.

Sacred forest of the place of mud
Since humans arrived on the island a few centuries ago, the virgin forests of Madagascar have been eaten away by tavy – slash and burn agriculture. In recent decades, as population and poverty have proliferated, it raged out of control. Trees were turned into charcoal, hills into rice paddies. The great green seas of forest shrank into isolated puddles, then disappeared completely. It's not only the indri's eastern rainforests that are vanishing, either. The spiny forests of the dry south are critically endangered too. It's incredibly sad. Because if there's anything as thrilling to see as an indri is to hear, it must be a dancing lemur in an octopus tree.

I went to look for one in the Alafada of Ifotaka – the sacred forest of the place of mud – a bumpy three-hour drive from the town of Tolagnaro. Beyond a village full of children clamouring for photographs, we waded across a river towards a bristling forest full of the tombs of their forefathers. Like most things in Madagascar, the spiny forest confuses scientists, who aren't sure whether it's a forest or a desert, so they call it a thicket. Normal people don't worry about what to call it. They're too busy thinking 'woah, man'.

Scientists describe the spiny thicket as one of Madagascar's seven ecoregions and list endemic species like red-flowering dwarf baobab, 20 species of *pachypodium* or elephant foot, and the dominant *Dideraceaea* family, or octopus trees. Non-scientists gesticulate as if they could wave the long legs of an octopus tree into the air above them, 50 feet tall, like fronds of some giant terrestrial seaweed. Both scientists and tourists are fascinated by the dancing lemur's ability to jump around on octopus trees, which are covered in long, sharp thorns.

The dancing lemur is more correctly called the Verreaux's sifaka. It's a member of the same family as the indri and is almost as large. Unlike the indri, which many believe never descends from the trees, the dancing lemur will occasionally walk on the ground. It does this by sashaying along sideways on two legs, arms waving wildly to keep its balance – an unforgettable spectacle which explains its common name. Its local name, sifaka-bilany, needs no explanation. It means 'sifaka of the cooking pot'.

Fortunately, this forest is fady because of the tombs inside it. The Malagasy have a special relationship with death and the dead. Rich or important people have tombs many times the size of the homes they once lived in, and much better built (they have to last longer, after all). As many zebu cattle as possible are slaughtered at funerals, and their horns decorate the tombs. Scenes from a person's life, and occasionally the manner of their leaving it, may also be painted on the tomb, and their descendants will visit frequently for a chat. The dead of Ifotaka are neither gone nor forgotten and their ghosts protect the forest.

It's quiet in the sacred forest. Too quiet. If there were sifaka around, we'd probably hear them. Although they don't sing, they do bark, kiss, grunt, grumble and growl. We find flat brown scorpions under rocks and sparkling crystals inside rocks. A tomb the size of a tennis court bakes in the sun. Couas rustle in trees, feathery false alarms. The atmosphere is stifling and I don't argue when we wade back across the river without seeing a sifaka.

Just as I've brushed sticky river mud from my feet and put my shoes and socks back on, our local guide, Popo, jumps up and starts pointing at trees, the universal expression for 'I see lemurs'. Off with our shoes, and back across the river. Popo dives into the thicket, Gino hangs a right. I run after him. No, we're lost. A cry over there. That way, quick! We find Popo sitting quietly near a clump of octopus trees in which a furry bundle is perched. I stalk the sifaka with my camera while it growls at me like a cat. Then, in a flash of white fur, it's gone. I wade back across the river without worrying about mud in my socks.

Islands within an island

These river crossings are significant, because lemurs can't abide water. At Ifotaka, the river protects sifaka who'd probably be potted if they got across to the village. Along the east coast, rivers create boundaries that cut lemur populations off from one another. Similar species have evolved separately between rivers in a kind of microcosm of Madagascar itself. One of the most striking examples of this is found on the Masoala peninsula.

Masoala is one of the Rainforests of the Atsinanana, a natural world heritage site inscribed in 2007. The peninsula is covered with the largest continuous rainforest left on the island and is one of the few places a rain forest meets the sea. The forest is protected as Madagascar's largest national park and its coral reefs are preserved by three marine parks. Masoala comprises less than two per cent of Madagascar's landmass, but contains 50 per cent of its plant and animal species. It's also the sole home of the red-ruffed lemur.

Separated from its closest relative, the black-and-white ruffed lemur, by only a river, the red-ruffed lemur was once classified as the same species. Red-ruffed and black-and-white lemurs can understand one another's calls, but they haven't met in millennia. Their long separation has resulted in completely different colouration and quite possibly some unique adaptations to their environment.

Farmers of the forest

Finding the red-ruffed lemur involves taking a stroll along an impossibly perfect beach. Flamboyants festooned with orchids and panther chameleons lean lazily over soft golden beaches sheltered by melted chocolate boulders. Behind them rise dense ranks of mist-puffing trees. In front, warm turquoise water laps against coral reefs. Hundreds of humpback whales will arrive any day now to start breeding in Antongil Bay. A rainbow shimmers on the horizon. The two British honeymoon couples I'm sharing this long stretch of beach with keep looking around and grinning.

We cross a stream by bucket-ferry and step into the Masoala rain forest. It's altogether different from the highland forests of Andasibe. Here are mangroves with a thousand roots surging into the ground, tripod trees balanced on finger-thin legs ten feet tall, and cathedral-high trees whose trunks flare out into mighty flying buttresses.

Half an hour later, our guide Fred finds a family of six red-ruffed lemurs, high in the forest canopy, catching the sun so their fur blazes. I move directly underneath one to get a better view, but have to look down for a moment to relieve symptoms of lemur-neck. Whap! Something lands in my hand. Something yellow, squishy and stinky. Lemur poo. Fred almost splits his sides. 'It's the first time that ever happened,' he says, between hoots. 'Ho ho ho! Your face!'

But as we walk back along the beach, Fred provides a new perspective on this gift from the forest. 'When I see fresh lemur droppings, I always look inside and find they are full of seeds, and these seeds have already started to grow.' He looks at me to make sure I understand. 'The only way the seeds can grow is if they have first been inside a lemur's stomach. Lemurs are much better farmers than people. They can plant a thousand trees a month this way. But no lemurs, no forests. And no forests, no lemurs.'

The aye-aye and I

I thought about that on the boat to Nosy Mangabe, an island reserve and sanctuary for the aye-aye, a ludicrous-looking lemur so well-adapted to stand in for Madagascar's missing woodpeckers that its bony middle finger is elongated to dig grubs and insects out of holes in trees. Yet lemurs were late arrivals on Madagascar. Nobody's sure how they managed to cross the Indian Ocean after the island broke away from the mainland. One theory is that they floated here on huge rafts of vegetation. It was a lucky escape.

While their prosimian ancestors in the rest of the world lost the race against other primates and became extinct, the lemurs who stowed away to Madagascar had no competition. They multiplied into a hundred different species. They grew

228

long fingers, learned to sing and dance and helped to plant the rain forests. In evolutionary terms, lemurs inhabited a parallel universe to our own where primates became monkeys and apes and, eventually, humans.

Lemurs are long lost relatives who took a totally different course. In them, we can see a shadow of our early counterparts who were wiped out long ago. Indeed, the word lemur comes from the Latin for 'ghost', although that may also be because of their wailing cries. Which brings me back to the indri.

The indri's local name, babakoto, can be translated as 'ancestor' or 'father' and the Malagasy have a myth about it. Long ago, there were two brothers who lived in a forest. One brother decided to leave the forest and raise crops. He became the first human. The other brother stayed behind and became the first indri. He still cries in mourning for the brother who went astray.

The Ngorongoro Dusty Boots Society
Alison Westwood – May 2009

Ngorongoro Conservation Area is of one Africa's most spectacular tourist destinations. A walking safari through its highlands will take you to boundless plains, fairytale lakes and terrifying peaks.

M y delight turned to dread as dawn broke and we could see where we were. A full moon had clothed the volcano's slopes in glamour, but sunrise slid across an immense landscape to expose us as specks clinging to a monster's furrowed hide.

Gullies yawned on either side. Stones dislodged by our boots tumbled and bounced, gaining momentum as they disappeared. A twisted branch stuck out of the ash like a dead hand waving for help. Swollen pinnacles of lava loomed above. My footsteps faltered; my smile shrivelled. I sat down, suddenly.

We'd started climbing Oldoinyo Lengai, the Masai's Mountain of God, at midnight. Eight of us with three guides picked out a path with headlamps and trekking poles. We plodded along, pacing ourselves for a 1600 metre gain in altitude, our march slowed further by slippery ash and a 40 degree incline.

The plan was to summit at dawn, but our guides were no longer familiar with the route since massive eruptions – the last only days previously – had obliterated paths, landmarks and vegetation. As the sun peeped over the horizon, we were well behind schedule. Three of the group of 8 turned back exhausted.

Fellow walkers Marc Reading and John Berry chivvied me up and we clambered on, ducking rocks sent flying by another climber and hauling each other over near-vertical sections. Denise and Jean-Paul Lechanteur, our group's grey-haired comedians and veteran adventurers, were some distance behind as we picked our way along a vertiginous ridge and crawled to the crater's rim.

I lay on my stomach and peered in. Precisely the colour and texture of an elephant's skin, the crater appeared to have no floor. It was a perfect cone, sucking what should have been the summit down to invisible depths. I thought of gravity wells, wormholes and an Old Testament Hell. 'I want to get out of here,' I thought. Without looking back, I started slithering down the Mountain of God on my backside.

The Bulati Lapdancing Association

Six days earlier, I'd gazed into another crater with a very different view. Ngorongoro's golden floor was encircled with forested walls turned blue by distance. Lake Magadi gave off clouds of white salt and pink flamingos. Flecks of black leapt into focus through binoculars to become wildebeest.

This huge caldera is sometimes described as a zoo because it's so easy to see the animals, most of which don't (or can't) ever leave. Sure enough, we watched lions spooking zebra, cheetahs lounging under trees, big tuskers striding solemnly through Lerai forest, hippos rolling in mud like rotisserie chickens, a thousand crowned cranes on the plains and black kites dive-bombing tourists for their sandwiches at Ngoitokitok picnic site.

Our camp was right on the crater's edge, so we could stare at the magical moonlit cauldron while we sat around a fire sipping hot chocolate. Despite this, I was happy to move on. Nainokanoka, just outside another smaller crater called Olmoti, heralded the start of our walking safari: a four-day journey through the Ngorongoro Highlands to Lake Natron, which would (eruptions permitting) culminate in a climb up Oldoinyo Lengai, the volcano the Masai call the Mountain of God.

Smoke still drifted from the ashes of our campfire as we set off, leaving tents pitched and piles of luggage on the grass. The crew would whisk away the camp to have it ready and waiting when we arrived at our next destination 18 kilometres away. Our only duty was to walk. And walk. And walk.

Leading us up a long hill was a Masai guide, clad in traditional shukas (blankets), army boots and, regardless of the heat, a thick woollen blazer. At the crest, he paused dramatically to allow us to take in the view. Even after Ngorongoro, Olmoti Crater drew several appreciative gasps – and one or two wheezes. The altitude at the rim is more than 3000 metres.

As we climbed out again, a tinkling stream of Masai cattle flowed in from the other side, coming to drink from the water that collects inside the crater and cascades through its broken lip as a 100-metre waterfall. After the Serengeti National Park was created, 1000 Masai were relocated to the Ngorongoro Conservation Area (NCA) with all their cattle, sheep and goats. Today, more than 40 000 Maasai live inside the NCA, their herds mingling amicably with wildlife, their huts tracing fairy rings on the hillsides.

We passed several villages as we started across the Embulbul Depression. In the rainy season, this is a vast expanse of muddy emerald grass, but now the savanna was brown and dusty, sewn with hundreds of tiny mole skulls. It stretched before us like a giant treadmill and no matter how long we walked, nothing seemed to come any closer.

At last we reached Bulati, where our tents glowed purple in the setting sun and donkey trains kicked up luminous dust. Worn out by the day's walk, we collapsed onto camping stools, complaining of aching legs. Then someone proposed a remedy.

Children gathered, keeping a cautious distance from the crazy foreigners. Sheep looked askance. Our crew pretended not to notice. All eight of us lay supine on the grass, knees propped high on stools, ankles in the air, staring at the sky. The Bulati Lapdancing Association was born.

The Flamingo Photographic Club

The association's members were relieved to discover that the first day's walk was the longest, especially Natalie Tonking and Susan Mynhardt, who had been dubbed the blister sisters because of the trouble their new boots were giving them. The second stage was an easy 10 kilometres, with an unforgettable surprise at its end.

Our path led to a thick forest growing down a steep slope, where we stopped to peek through a gap in the trees. Far below was an iridescent aquamarine lake, bordered with snowy soda and candyfloss flamingos. It sparkled with sunlight and pink dots of flying and floating birds. Clouds sent snaggled emerald shadows scudding over Lake Empakaai, which appeared to cover the entire crater floor.

It took almost an hour to descend the steep shady steps, pausing to marvel at (and swing from) giant *Ficus natalensis* trees with streaming aerial roots. Then we stepped out into the dazzling spectacle, tumultuous racket – and almost overpowering reek – of thousands of lesser flamingos. Empakaai, we were told, is the local word for 'stinky'.

Eight adults immediately forgot blisters, thirst, sunburn and sweat, and became children again, lost in wonder. While some drifted around in dazed enchantment, the photographers launched a series of flamingo-shooting forays involving equal measures of clumsy leopard crawling, frantic sign language and muttered swearing when our memory cards ran out. By the time we returned to the top, a thick mantle of mist had rolled over the crater, hiding its fabulous treasure from view.

The mist started to lift the next morning, but we turned our faces away from the lake, towards a conical mountain visible on the skyline. Almost immediately, it too was obscured. The road from Empakaai to Nayobi contains a lifetime's supply of powdery red dust. Each step sunk our boots in over the ankle and sent great puffs over our heads.

To make matters worse, all the Masai men from the villages in the area were working on the road. This seemed to involve marching up and down in large groups, kicking up as much dust as possible. All we would see of an approaching work party was a red cloud filled with flashing teeth and spears sticking out of the top. Then it would engulf us.

When we emerged, an interesting shade of orange, Oldoinyo Lengai dominated the landscape. Near Nayobi village, the volcano's effects became frighteningly apparent. Eruptions starting in June 2007 had choked the land in grey ash, killing 1000 cattle, countless wildlife and destroying crops. More than 10 000 people, mostly from Nayobi, were forced to flee their homes.

At Acacia Camp, only the fever trees had survived Lengai's suffocating embrace. Our tents were pitched on a desiccated ridge with a view that resembled the end of the world. Water was scarce so, for the third day in a row, we each bathed in a small basin of water. No matter: Debbie Addison who, as one of Wild Frontiers' directors, knew about such matters, assured us that the campsite at Lake Natron had running water, flush toilets, hot showers and – incredibly – a swimming pool.

The Lake Natron Pool Party

The trail to Lake Natron was jaw-dropping. The last vestige of road petered out and died at Acacia Camp, so all our gear was loaded onto donkeys. We walked down the ashen slopes of the Great Rift Valley Ridge towards the wide soda lake, which lay 1000 metres below, shimmering like heat haze on the horizon. Trudging up the other way were donkey trains loaded with salt blocks cut from the lakeshore. On the lower slopes of Oldoinyo Lengai, three 4x4s were waiting to take us to camp.

The water wasn't running when we arrived (although the camp manager soon was), but after four days heavy on exertion and light on ablutions, I wasn't prepared to wait. I found the swimming pool and, after a moment's careful consideration, stepped into it fully clothed. Encouraged by the heat and the fact that the pool was next to the bar – which served cold beer in quarts – the others soon joined me.

The barman told us that the ascent of Lengai was open, so we could climb it that night if we chose. On the bar counter was a papier mâché model of the volcano with a strongly worded notice warning prospective climbers of its difficulty. Obviously, this didn't apply to veteran hikers like us. Celebrations in the swimming pool continued all afternoon until the beer ran out.

It was perhaps not the best preparation, but I was happy I'd carbo-loaded when John Berry and I paused a little way from the summit the next morning and shakily took stock of our supplies. Gulping down vertigo, we shared a semi-liquid banana, one small ginger biscuit and a stale carrot sandwich I found squashed at the bottom of my pack.

From our vantage point, more than 2000 metres above the camp, we gaped at a world that seemed somehow tilted over. The mountain slid away under us in a preposterous slant and the valley floor keeled over at a rakish angle. We could see right over the wall of the Rift Valley ridge and all the way to the Serengeti. From this height, we could even see the earth's curvature. John and I both decided we liked it better when it was flat.

West Coast – A bitter-sweet symphony
Alison Westwood – August 2009

*The stretch of coast between Cape Town
and Lambert's Bay is heart-breakingly beautiful,
but it's also suffering from a severe case of progress.
Alison Westwood went to see if there's still any soul left.*

T o say the West Coast can be moody is like saying there's a pinch or two of salt
in the sea. One day it's all smiles and sunshine, the next it's spitting in your
eyes and chucking sand in your teeth. Japie Greeff, Cape Columbine's lighthouse-
keeper, prefers it that way.

It was a disgusting night and Japie had been out in it since 03h00 while clouds
flashed like rabid paparazzi, the sky rumbled as if a doomsday meteor was on its
way, and the wind grappled like a sumo wrestler with anything stubborn enough
to stand. He strode up the next morning as I picked a path through puddles. 'Did
you hear the storm?' he asked. 'It was a big one, hey!' A grin lit up his flinty face
like a – well, a lighthouse.

Cape Columbine is at the westernmost point of this part of Africa's west coast.
On a map, the chunk of land between Langebaan and Velddrif resembles a great
hook hanging in the Atlantic Ocean, waiting to snag passing ships. In fact, it did
so with alarming regularity until the lighthouse was put up, only 30 years after the
1906 lighthouse commission had agreed it would be a good spot for one.

Irresistible temptation for urbanites

The previous day, Japie had ushered us to the top of its rather squat, blocky tower
where the lens – the first in South Africa to be designed for an electric light –
threw fractured reflections of scrub, sea and sky. A barn owl and a kestrel were
sharing digs in a disused fog-horn (decent nesting sites are rare in these parts) and,
as I watched, the kestrel launched itself towards Paternoster, where we could see
crowds of white cottages gleaming smartly in the sun.

Hidden from view by a reef was the beach where we'd spent all afternoon
messing about with boats. Paternoster's painted wooden fishing boats are so
perfectly pretty and so essentially seaside that visitors, feeling arty, will spend
hours photographing or painting them.

234

As with the whitewashed fishermen's cottages, they wield a charm beyond practicality. To see these boats, or those cottages, is to want one. So the original fishermen's village is being smothered in imitation fishermen's holiday homes. They're all tasteful, adorable, desirable – and about as genuinely West Coast as frozen fish fingers.

At least Paternoster is only in danger of being gentrified. It's a process that has advantages for the visitor: plenty of attractive houses for hire, shops that sell fancy jam and a handful of first-class places to eat. Other parts haven't fared as well.

Yzerfontein had me burying my head in a well-trimmed verge between estate agents' signs groaning, 'Why? Why?' The bay's haunting natural beauty has been shoved aside by a ghost town of face-brick-and-aluminium mansions. When we found somewhere to have dinner that evening, I was relieved it didn't have a view.

One farm labourer we spoke to in Jacob's Bay, formerly a fishing village near Vredenburg, described the bewildering symptoms of holiday-house disease: 'The people come here, build a big house and then they go away.' Roberto Marrero, who manages the crayfish factory there, told us it was pretty much all that was left of the original settlement. 'Everything else you can see was put up in the last six or seven years,' he said.

It got worse. A golf estate we bumbled into near St Helena Bay was so enormous, and its deserted streets and houses so indistinguishable, that we drove round the same roundabout for 13 hours. It was more terrifying than the time I got lost in a desert. Later, we had lunch at a hotel where the view was a procession of construction trucks roaring off to another development.

Getting away from it all

Fortunately, the malady seems to be confined to the coast. Although Darling is slightly closer to Cape Town than Yzerfontein and has – in my eyes at least – the far greater attractions of five wine farms and Tannie Evita, people are actually living there – and in houses that weren't built last week. One family hasn't moved far in almost two centuries.

William Duckitt was brought out to South Africa in 1800 to help the Boers update their old-fashioned agriculture. His first experimental farm was near Paarl, but he didn't make much progress with the land or the Boers there. Duckitt finally settled at Klaver Valley near Darling and explorer Dr Heinrich Lichtenstein noted he'd picked one of the best and most fertile spots of the whole colony.

John and Jeanette are seventh generation Duckitts in the area. They've set aside a large portion of their farm, Waylands, for the region's famous wild flowers and they cultivate guests in the old homestead. I had to wonder if William would be as puzzled as the Boers by these new-fangled farming techniques.

Much as I liked Darling, I couldn't justify staying 200 years, so once we'd pottered into town and tottered out of tasting rooms, I took the map and pointed my Grand Vitara firmly at the coastline north of the Berg River. 'It's a big blank space,' I reasoned. 'It must be good.'

We crossed a bridge at the drift where, not so long ago, school buses had to be ferried across on a pontoon for rugby matches. At the river mouth, fishing trawlers bobbed like big brothers of the boats at Paternoster. At the petrol station, five attendants fought to wash our windscreen. Velddrif may look as unappetising as the bokkoms (dried fish) we bought there, but it is at least as salty and authentic.

A little way on, I started to feel hopeful as I stood in the drizzle on a shell-speckled shore in front of Dwarskersbos. The houses were mostly unoccupied but they were smallish, only one block deep and hadn't been made in the same factory. But then I saw the hideous complexes squatting across the road.

Silver linings, black cloud

By now, if you're an estate agent on the West Coast, you've crossed me off your Christmas list and, if you're planning a holiday, you've probably crossed the West Coast off your list. That would be a mistake. For one thing, its allure rises above the spreading rooftops like an elegant gull above fish-guts. For another, there are still several good spots that haven't gone to rot.

The West Coast National Park, on a slice of salt marshes between lagoon and sea, is a treat for birders and hikers. It also hides the keenly secretive fishing village of Churchhaven, perhaps the last corner on this part of coast that's still got more than a splash of the old Cape spirit. Knowing what they have to protect, locals kick visitors in the shins unless they have an invitation or reservation.

The warm welcome travellers get at Paternoster can make it difficult to leave, unless you're going camping at Tietiesbaai next door. Then there are the roads criss-crossing the countryside, criss-crossed in turn by determined tortoises. In autumn, brown fields roll in clouds of blue smoke as farmers ready the land for winter wheat. In spring, you never know where you'll strike it rich with a pot of golden wildflowers. Windmills sing and tar unfurls across the plains towards a blue promise that perhaps there you'll find what you're looking for.

At Elands Bay, after a lovely, lonely drive past coastal reserves, I finally did. Mist swathed the shore, and waves shushed around our feet, as we walked past surfers on a smooth left break. Then the veil lifted to reveal Baboon Point's rocky face and a broad smile of shining beach. Mountains to the left, strandveld to the right, white sand in front and, out back, the Verlorenvlei – a Ramsar site of international importance for birds.

There's a cloud on the horizon, however. A proposed open-cast mine in the

Moutonshoek Valley would poison water that flows into the Verlorenvlei and turn the wetland into a wasteland. Elands Bay's little community seems to stand as much chance as a bull terrier in front of a bulldozer. Yup, there's a storm coming alright, but it's not the kind Japie Greeff would enjoy.

Riding the Dragon's tail
Alison Westwood – January 2010

A long way south of where most people think the Drakensberg ends, its basalt tail lies twitching in the sky. Wilder and less developed than the KwaZulu-Natal mountains, the far southern Berg offers untamed adventures that are the stuff of fantasy and legend.

ॐ

I t was a sunny Tuesday morning in late spring and the verges in the village of Rhodes needed trimming. The 30 or so mowers who'd been brought in to do the job paid no attention to the grass. They sat under shady willows or stood gormlessly in the middle of the street, which might have obstructed traffic, had there been any. Village custodian Susan Koelz shot them a disapproving glance. 'They're obviously not hungry,' she remarked. 'We're going to have to bring in another herd.'

While the cows neglected their civic duty, Susan took me and my friend, Dirk Odendal, on a walking tour of the few dozen clay and corrugated iron cottages that constitute the community, which is a national monument. Established in 1893 as a church centre for mountain farmers, Rhodes hasn't changed much since, except that visitors now come for fly-fishing and snow skiing instead of nagmaal and race meetings.

Today's visitors are better behaved, if TV Bulpin's descriptions of fights, dice and big card games are anything to go by. The bookies, wool buyers and cowboys are gone, as is Thys Volstruis, the man employed to sweep up the droppings from their horses, which they rode straight into the Rhodes Hotel. The action has moved up the hillside to Walkerbouts Inn, where a man who could be Father Christmas's witty twin presides.

The bar at the centre of the universe

Dave Walker has a firm grasp on geography or, you might say, a stranglehold. Chat to him at the bar and he'll tell you everyone else is completely mistaken about the location of the southern Drakensberg. It's not, as they claim, anywhere near Himeville or Underberg in KwaZulu-Natal. The last references to the mountain range on official 1:50 000 survey maps are found between Elliot and

Barkly East in the Eastern Cape. And, since the surveyor general is the final arbiter of location in South Africa, Rhodes is undeniably at the southernmost end of the Drakensberg.

It's also the centre of the known universe. Dave doesn't quote any evidence for this, but after a few beers or a not-so-wee dram of whisky, it seems a reasonable enough claim. Admittedly, it takes a while to get there, but although there are plans for an airstrip in the offing, it would be a shame to forego driving over the spectacular mountain passes that circle the area like citadels.

We hopped into a 4x4 with local fishing-and-flower guide Tony Keitzman for a ride to the top of Naudé's Nek. At 2500 metres, it's the highest pass open to traffic in South Africa. The gravel road winds up steep, lonely pastures and across wind-blasted moors of broom-grass that mistily echo the Scottish highlands – complete with a public phone that's never been connected.

Tony took us to weeping rock shelves where creeping euphorbias and crassulas clung to tiny pockets of erosion and to a glen where scores of malachite sunbirds quarrelled over a cavalcade of red-hot pokers. He pointed wistfully at long, crystalline stretches of streams – his favourite beats for trout – and stood with us at the summit watching as a black-and-blue thunderstorm bruised the dale below.

Back beside the Bell River, we passed a peculiar monument: a series of stone walls that spelt the name Naudé. It was built to commemorate brothers Stephanus and Gabriel who blazed this route over the Drakensberg on horseback. Just how daring a feat this must have been, Dirk and I were about to find out.

Amphitheatres without audiences

'We're complete beginners,' I told Kathy Mitchell of Skyriders on the phone. 'So perhaps we could just ride for an hour or two?' But Kathy said we'd need more time for a worthwhile horse trail and when we arrived in Wartrail, she'd put together a full-day expedition.

'Normally we do this over two days,' said Kathy as we crested Lundin's Nek and turned off the road onto sweeping, scrubby slopes, 'so we'd best get a move on.' It was an injunction she had to repeat several times: Dirk and I were too busy admiring the scenery to spur on our horses.

Fold upon fold of green hills bared smooth, sandstone shoulders. Deep in their drapery glinted the beadwork of boulders and sequins of a stream. Across the Telle River loomed Lesotho's pointy blue mountains, the Malotis.

'What waterfall is that?' Dirk asked, as we approached a high white thread tumbling down basalt cliffs at the apex of a vast amphitheatre.

Kathy consulted with local guide Ntate Moshesh. 'It doesn't have a name.'

Dirk was indignant. 'A waterfall like that deserves a name,' he muttered. But it seemed there was no one there to give it one. In the six hours it took to ride to Dangers Hoek, we saw only one other person.

We traversed more breathtaking amphitheatres and several hair-raising gullies, but our sturdy horses managed to hang onto their goggle-eyed riders. It was with regret, as well as relief, that we dismounted at last and were driven out of the Telle Valley into the sunset. Our consolation was that the next valley we'd visit was said to be even more bewitching.

Valley of giants

Arriving at Balloch Cottages in the dark was like being led blindfolded by a conjuror. We followed Graham and Margy Frost's bakkie between black and dripping trees, across a gushing brook and up a bumpy mud track. Inside our stone cottage, we piled wood onto the hearth and Margy's lasagne onto our plates. Rain pattered a lullaby as we fell asleep, floating in an unseen landscape.

When dawn drew away the mask, we found ourselves in a valley of giants. A huge woman wearing a Xhosa headdress sat on a cliff top blocking out the sun; a 50-metre high cobra reared up beside a Brobdingnagian hut. Knobbly orbs, sceptres, towers and thrones lined the lush gorge. Clarens sandstone glowed red, yellow and orange.

Margy took us to see some of her treasures. We climbed past a cave that shelters campers and the oxwagon that arrived with the farm's first owners to a ridge where two conical boulders perched precariously on their sharp ends. Dirk tried, tentatively at first and then with all his might, to push them over.

Beneath another rock, a great black and tan lioness with whip-like tail chased little red men across a wall. Legs kicked up like ballet dancers', they transformed into antelopes, then birds and flew through the roof, insouciantly eluding death. Bright colours and exquisite outlines defied the decay of years.

Beside the road out of the valley, Balloch's most remarkable stone sculpture, the giant's thumb, stuck out in a shaft of sunlight. The sight hitched a ride with us all the way over the Barkly Pass, beyond Maclear to the Tsitsa Falls.

The river rat and his goat

The first thing we noticed at The Falls backpackers was a large, brown goat. 'Hang onto your valuables,' said Adriaan Badenhorst when we shook hands, 'or Billy will eat them.' Billy was already nibbling Dirk's shorts. We followed Adi up a hill for a tour of the farm. Billy leapt up and butted me to the back of the line. Adi handed me a small stick to fend him off. 'Billy has a thing about women,' he said.

Occupied in this way, it took me a while to notice the waterfall. Below us, the

Tsitsa River, curving across a wide green plain, reached a crescent-shaped ledge and plunged 26 metres before swooshing around a horseshoe gorge. Rainbows shimmered in the spray. Billy barged me from behind.

Adi told us how he found his piece of paradise. A former river guide in the Kalahari, he came to the Eastern Cape several years ago on a kayaking trip, rounded a bend in the river and fell headfirst in love. Something prompted him to ask if the farm was for sale. So, for a price that sounds silly to city-dwellers but was nonetheless hefty for a river rat, Adi acquired 80 hectares of wattle-choked land, a tumbledown farmhouse and his own waterfall.

Since then, he and his wife, Angela, have built up the backpackers and cleared away the wattles. They've also helped formulate a plan to transform part of the overgrazed Tsitsa Valley into a wildlife reserve, replacing cows with eland and hartebeest. It was tough going with scant resources in this remote area, but things are looking up. The main road to Maclear was recently tarred and European Union funding through Thina Sinaku, a provincial support programme, has been approved for their project.

Shimmying down a rock chimney where Billy couldn't follow, we peered at a Bushman painting that the farm's previous owner never found and waded through long grass to the top of the falls. Adi carved up a watermelon for tea, then buckled us into harnesses. An invisible wire stretched across the roaring face of water. Adi clipped us on. Then, with a whoop, he leapt off the edge. A tiny figure, waving exuberantly, in his element.

A painted procession
Not far off, the elements had conspired to reveal records of a race who'd lost their corner of Earth. Storm Shelter was found at the dawn of the new millennium by hikers driven under a sandstone ledge by malevolent weather. Hailed as South Africa's most significant rock art find in the last century, it's a palimpsest of manifold figures – hunters, shamen, animals, gods and ghosts – parading across a large slab.

To see it, we headed back to Maclear and out towards the Pot River Pass where the gravel roads were flanked with far-flung cattle farms and pine plantations. At Woodcliffe Farm, Phyll Sephton packed us into her 4x4 with a picnic lunch and drove until the road became a donga. Vultures wheeled in morning thermals as we trekked into a twist of slopes burrowed by a stony creek.

The shelter is so well disguised that Phyll walked right past it. Seclusion has saved the paintings; they are still remarkably fresh and clear – down to the pupil in the eye of an eland. The rock opposite is polished with animal fat worn by Bushmen who must have sat as we did, poring over the army of images. For them, its meaning must have been clear as a story told many times. For us, the message was garbled, perhaps entirely misunderstood. Baffled, I turned to leave at last.

Phyll stood silhouetted by the overhang, her outline quite different from those shaped by the long ago artists. Rock framed a landscape brightly daubed in blue and green, a counterpoint to the tawny, white and burnt umber that flickered in the shadows. The people who'd made this magic were gone, as were the elands and lions, the rhebok and hyenas. There was nobody left to witness the mystery of these mountains but us, the vultures and a herd of cows cropping the long grass.